PRAISE FOR
YOU DON'T HAVE TO BE A DOCTOR

Life is about making choices. This book provides practical advice and a road-map for you to use today and every day in choosing and working in careers that will improve health and healthcare for all. Over the past 16 years, students and graduates of the UC Berkeley School of Public Health have benefited from following Jeff Oxendine's 9-step framework and you will too. It is more important than ever that we make wise choices that align our talents, goals, and interests to meet the needs of the emerging challenges that face health and social care systems locally and throughout the world.

Stephen M. Shortell, PhD, MPH, MBA
Professor of the Graduate School
Distinguished Professor Emeritus and Dean Emeritus
School of Public Health, UC Berkeley

Jeff's passion for decades has been to nurture, mentor, and inspire the next generation of health professionals, particularly those from under-resourced backgrounds. This book is full of the wisdom he has gained and imparted from those experiences. It's an invaluable resource for students, and those of us who work with them. I look forward to sharing it with my colleagues, as we work to achieve a robust health workforce that reflects the diversity of our communities and country.

Nancy Turnbull, MBA
Senior Associate Dean for Educational Programs,
Harvard T.H. Chan School of Public Health

A powerful book and tool that parallels my career journey. By working with Jeff at UC Berkeley and Health Career Connection, I experienced firsthand many of the book's concepts: exposure; aligning my education and career with my passions, values, and purpose; the power professional relationships; and risk taking. Thank you, Jeff, for developing this in a way that people of all career stages can benefit from.

Ikenna "Ike" Mmeje, MHSA, FACHE
Chief Operating Officer
Memorial Care
Long Beach Medical Center
Miller Children's and Women's Hospital

In a world where public health and healthcare are such important parts of our lives and the economy in the U.S and globally, Jeff Oxendine's book aimed at helping people find their *authentic health careers* could not come at a better moment. Like Jeff, having long been connected to public health training for students and helping them find diverse careers in the healthcare and public health sectors, I can affirm that the framework, tools, and stories contained here will help people at all stages of their career journey to more effectively explore their inner self and the broad range of emerging health career options as a means to find the authentic career path that is right for them.

I often meet with students who only have known about clinical career paths in healthcare, and this book will help them to explore other non-clinical health career alternatives, as well as think critically as to which among clinical or these other paths are their more authentic paths. I have found that applicants who can genuinely articulate their authentic path and have effectively prepared for it strengthen their chances of acceptance to medical, public health, or other health professions programs.

Faculty members like myself and others who advise students in their career path development in the healthcare arena, will also find this book to be an incredible resource that can be utilized to offer more robust advice and support to students as they make choices about educational paths and job decisions.

Paul A. Hattis, MD, JD, MPH
Senior Associate Director, MPH Program
Associate Professor, Tufts University Medical School

There are hundreds of jobs in health from directly caring for patients, families, and communities to technical and professional roles. All roles are important. We are living in an exciting time because the healthcare system is transforming and creating new ways to deliver care in a team-based model. *HealthImpact* is the California nursing workforce and health policy center and is shaping the future by leading transformations through nursing innovation. With the nearly 3 million nurses in the United States who represent the largest healthcare workforce, nurses are on the forefront of change and innovation. In *You Don't Have to Be a Doctor*, Jeff Oxendine provides an easy and practical method to help readers discover their passions and strengths. It is a must read for anyone looking for guidance in creating an action plan for a career in health.

Garrett Chan, PhD, RN, FAAN
CEO, HealthImpact

There are people in life who you meet who stand out as being really sincere about wanting to help others; this is our author, Jeff Oxendine. Mr. Oxendine has dedicated his career to supporting all students, but particularly first-generation college students from disadvantaged backgrounds, in their quest to identify and pursue the health career of their dreams; helping them navigate the educational journey into and through the health professions. He has served as a mentor, an advocate, and a guide, advising students to explore their options and select the path that resonates best within themselves. In his book, he shares a well-thought-out strategy for students to thoughtfully and realistically assess the what, the why, and the how of their career selection to assure that at the end of their academic journey, they remain happy and fulfilled in their health professional choice. I think that it is an excellent resource for all who are contemplating their future career, as well as for their teachers and counsellors.

Katherine Flores, MD
Director, UCSF Fresno,
Latino Center for Medical Education and Research

Health Career Connection, which the author leads, continues to change the career trajectories of students by broadening their exposure to a variety of experiences and overall thought processes. This book acts a guide-post, especially sharing wisdom and pearls. Through vignettes along with exercises, one is guided on ways to foster their professional and leadership development. He challenges one to be strategically reflective in their journey and of their values. In this ever-changing world and healthcare field, we all need to be flexible, collaborative, and continually practice ingenuity. Through organizations such as HCC, Jeff demonstrates the importance of cross-collaboration, working toward strengthening and creating pipeline programs to increase diversity within higher education, the sciences, medicine, and ultimately healthcare. Through this book, Jeff continues to serve as a mentor to students of all levels, to foster needed transformational leaders!

Evita Limon-Rocha, MD, MPH
Child and Adolescent Psychiatrist
Kaiser Permanente

My story is like Sam's story, which opens the book. After telling my mother that I wanted to be a doctor at age 4 and then at age 12 telling her exactly what medical school I wanted to attend, I marched steadfastly toward that goal and achieved it at age 22, but like Sam, I realized that it was nothing like what I thought it would be. All along my journey, my family, friends, and professors just blindly cheered me on. No one ever pulled me aside to offer me the kind of sage insight and perspective that Jeff Oxendine's book provides. Our only guide back then was the cynical, and arguably racist, *The House of God* by Samuel Shem. Had I had *You Don't Have to Be A Doctor* early on when I was considering a medical career, I would have entered into it with a much more critical eye. Thankfully, while in medical school, I was afforded opportunities to explore other domains of health, law, and policy, which whet my appetite for a broader health career. I know so many young doctors who yearn for exposure to other aspects of a health career but feel constrained by narrow conventional career guidance. Oxendine's book radically changes that. Now students intrigued by the potential of a health career have a versatile 9-step tool that allows them to gain a window into the diversity of opportunities within the health sector, and a better sense of how their passions align with the varied career options. Jeff Oxendine's decades of insight, experience, and passionate stewardship of hundreds of young and talented students is distilled into a rich and comprehensive guide to the wide constellation of opportunities in the growing health sector.

Over the past three decades as a physician, public health official, university faculty member, and health foundation executive, I have had the pleasure of working with medical students, residents, public health students, and researchers. Virtually all of them received, at some point in their career, the uncritical family or peer advice to become a doctor. So many of them seek me out for informational interviews and career guidance. I now have a powerful and sophisticated tool to share with them, allowing them to imagine and explore a vastly wider array of stimulating opportunities within health and to forge a fulfilling career based on meaningful insights into their unique talents. This book is the long-awaited ethical and compassionate replacement for *The House of God*.

Anthony Iton, MD, MPH, JD

Senior Vice President
Healthy Communities
The California Endowment

From vision to practice, how to align your life and career choices—great advice from someone who has devoted his own career to guiding successful and happy healthcare professionals. This book inspires while being refreshingly practical with hands-on tools and exercises. All of my pre-health students need a copy so that they can consider or re-consider their authentic health career.

Alice Ho, PhD
Director, Academic and Research Programs
UCLA Academic Advancement Program

You Don't have to be a Doctor can help you develop practical insights and action steps to make well-informed choices, secure jobs, and advance in your public health career. My colleagues and I benefited from the framework and tools in this book and Jeff's guidance early in our careers as undergraduate Health Career Connection Interns and MPH students at UC Berkeley, and as we have navigated our paths as health system executives and public health leaders. I am confident you will also benefit as you pursue your life and career goals.

Denise Fair, MPH
Chief Public Health Officer,
City of Detroit

YOU DON'T HAVE TO BE A DOCTOR

YOU DON'T HAVE TO BE A DOCTOR

Discover, Achieve, and Enjoy
Your Authentic Health Career

JEFFREY S. OXENDINE, MBA, MPH

PUBLISH
YOUR
PURPOSE
PRESS

Publish Your Purpose Press
141 Weston Street, #155
Hartford, CT, 06141

PUBLISH YOUR PURPOSE PRESS

The opinions expressed by the Author are not necessarily those held by Publish Your Purpose Press.

Ordering Information: Quantity sales and special discounts are available on quantity purchases by corporations, associations, and others. For details, contact the publisher at orders@publishyourpurposepress.com.

Edited by: Heather B. Habelka
Cover design by: Nelly Murariu
Typeset by: Medlar Publishing Solutions Pvt Ltd., India

Printed in the United States of America.
ISBN: 978-1-951591-19-9 (print)
ISBN: 978-1-951591-21-2 (ebook)

Library of Congress Control Number: 2020901052

First edition, May 2020

Publish Your Purpose Press works with authors, and aspiring authors, who have a story to tell and a brand to build. Do you have a book idea you would like us to consider publishing? Please visit PublishYourPurposePress.com for more information.

To my parents, Carl and Jeanne, who gave me love, support, education, and opportunity.

To my wife, Lydia, for her unconditional love and faith in me, and to my wonderful children—Jake, Elizabeth, and Ben—who bring me great pride and joy.

To my many mentors, teachers, and friends who saw potential in me and provided me with invaluable guidance, inspiration, and opportunity.

To friends I grew up with and members of similar communities who inspire me to expose people to what is possible and empower them to discover and realize their full potential.

To each reader in hopes that this book will help you live the life and career you really want and find happiness and fulfillment.

CONTENTS

CHAPTER 5
FRAMEWORK STEP 3: PRACTICAL EXPERIENCE

FOREWORD

I have been doing research and teaching in the health field for over 60 years. I have been a professor in the School of Public Health at Berkeley for over 50 of those years. During that time, I have trained doctors, nurses, physical therapists, social workers, health policy scholars, epidemiologists, behavioral scientists, and many other young people working in the health field. I have seen these people happy in their work, frustrated, hopeful, disappointed, still exploring, ready to quit, or ready for the next joyous step. Wouldn't it be great if we could help people early on to find a life position that more perfectly fit their dreams and goals? This book will go a long way to helping people better find their niche in life. That is, of course, important.

It has come to light that there is another important reason for doing the kind of work you would like to do. In our health research, it is now turning out that one of the most important determinants of good health is our ability to control our destiny—to behave in ways that allow us to accomplish the things we cherish. I remember learning about something related to this in an introductory psychology class I took many, many years ago concerning mice in cages. We watched a movie showing that mice that could push a button to escape their cage were in much better condition than those that couldn't figure a way out. Research evidence is now clear that we are better off when we learn to control the events that impinge on our lives. We have a better chance to develop a richer and more fulfilling life. This is one of the most important lessons that can be learned from this book.

There are many other powerful forces that affect our health and well-being. If you want a career that helps people to be happy and healthy, it is important to know about these issues. We used to think that the most important matters affecting health were having good medical care, eating well, getting enough exercise, and having good genes. These things are, of course, important. But the research I started here at Berkeley many years ago clearly has shown the influence of many social determinants in affecting health. Being poor is a major risk factor for health. So is having a poor education. But surprisingly, the most important of all these problems is having good social relationships! We are not clear on how this affects our body, but it turns out to be a major determinant of health. So, while health is affected by personal medical factors, the world in which we live also has a major impact on our well-being. Population health matters, too. This is especially true if one is concerned about the prevention of disease rather than just the treatment of disease once it has occurred. If one of your goals in life is to help others, it is important to recognize that medical care is only one of a wide variety of important predictors of health.

I remember several years ago when I came across a book that changed my thinking about these matters. The book was called *Changed Lives*, and it reported the results of an early education project in Ypsilanti, Michigan, for three- and four-year-old children. This program recruited children from very poor, high-risk families and offered them a two-year early education program (before the much larger, and less effective, national Head Start program). They then followed up with these kids at 18 years of age and found higher rates of high school graduation with better grades, fewer police contacts, and higher rates of college enrollment. They also did other follow-ups on 97% of these children at ages 27 and 37 and found more homeownership, more employment, higher rates of marriage and children in intact families, and so on. What was the magical educational ingredient in those early years at ages three and four that brought about these wonderful results? Not what you would think. Not formal lessons and "repeat after me" exercises. It was asking every child what they would like to do each day and then helping them to do just that. If they failed, they were encouraged to try again. And again. In the end, these children learned that there are ways to succeed in doing what you want to do and that any obstacles can be overcome if you work at it. They learned to control their own destiny, and that changed their lives forever.

Having a solid understanding of the things you really care about in life is also of crucial importance in applying for admission to health profession education programs. For example, I serve on the selection committee for the Joint Medical Program at Berkeley. This is a very competitive training program that involves three years of study at the School of Public Health followed by two additional years of clinical training at the University of California, San Francisco. When interviewing applicants, it becomes very clear early on which applicants really want to become medical doctors and who are really interested in another career. Authenticity comes through clearly and quickly. Knowing what students really care about is obvious to all of us on the committee.

There are few things more important for all of us to learn. Think about things that really matter to you, explore ways to learn about these things, and pursue your dreams. Not the dreams that others have for you, but your own desires. This is crucial for your own health and welfare and it is crucial for those you would like to help in your career.

S. Leonard Syme, PhD
Professor of Epidemiology and Community Health (Emeritus)
University of California, Berkeley

INTRODUCTION

SAM'S STORY

Sam had been a great student. He graduated from UC Berkeley with excellent grades and a strong determination to pursue the plan he had worked toward since freshman year in high school: going to medical school and becoming a doctor. Sam loved science, was fascinated by the human body, and wanted to immerse himself in learning more. He was also motivated by the status, income, and autonomy he associated with being a doctor. Sam's plan pleased his parents and extended family. They had always wanted and expected him to become a doctor. The day he graduated from medical school was the proudest day of their lives. Sam subsequently completed his residency, joined a successful medical practice, and started living his dream. At least, that was the plan.

Sam soon found that the practice of medicine wasn't what he expected. Treating more patients in shorter appointments was much less satisfying, he spent an increasing amount of his time on bureaucratic responsibilities, he didn't have much autonomy, and the long hours consumed his life. He had gotten married, had young children, and found he wasn't getting to spend time with them. It was expensive to raise a family where they lived and the more money he made, the more they spent. He also had the burden of paying off over $300,000 in debt from college and medical school. The longer Sam practiced, the more his disenchantment with medicine grew. He eventually began to realize something he could barely stomach to admit: after devoting his twenties, early thirties, and far more money than he had to becoming a doctor, he didn't really want to be one. Though it wasn't the right fit for him, he felt trapped by his identity, financial obligations, and family expectations. So, he continued to practice. His unhappiness significantly undermined his work, family life, and health—he simply wasn't living the life he wanted. Like many doctors he knew and went to school with, he was also experiencing burnout.

Sam dreamed of discovering what he was really meant to do and having the courage to pursue it. Maybe he could pursue work related to the love for science that he still had. He wondered how life could have been different had he explored or pursued other science- or health-related career paths. He was scared to change his path now, after all it took to get where he was and his family's high cost of living, but he was in such pain that he had to do something. Sam was now determined to forge a new path that was more authentically aligned with who he was and would enable him to be happy and fulfilled. He just wished it had not taken so long and cost so much to get to this point. He approached me about how to discover and achieve his authentic health career.

In my more than 30 years in the health field, I have encountered countless stories like Sam's. I also have firsthand experience with the pain and consequences of being in a career path and jobs that were not aligned with the life and career I really wanted. My primary motivation to write this book is to inspire and empower you to choose and succeed in the health career path—or a path in another field—through which you can be your authentic self, live the life you want, and make the impact you are meant to have. I want to prevent you and the growing number of people throughout the world interested in health careers from experiencing the suffering and consequences of choosing and being trapped in a career path or job that doesn't suit your true talents, passions, and goals. I call this common problem: *costly misaligned career choices.*

Sam's story is a classic example of a costly misaligned career choice and, unfortunately, he is not alone. Countless people in health and other fields—including me—have devoted some of what could have been their most productive and enjoyable years, lost time away from families, negatively impacted their health, and invested tens of thousands of dollars in pursuing educational and career paths that ended up not being aligned with who they are, what they want, and the impact they were meant to have.

> *You don't want to climb the ladder of success only*
> *to find it is leaning against the wrong wall.*
> —Stephen Covey

Instead of these costly consequences of misaligned choices, I want you to experience the joy, power, and success that comes from living your authentic life and career. Many of my colleagues, students, and I have experienced this, and you can too! My initial motivation to pursue a career in public health was to help people make better life choices to prevent illness. I was inspired to write this book to help *you* make better life and career choices to prevent costly misaligned career choices and their consequences. More importantly, I want you to have the experience of living *your authentic health career.*

MARIA'S STORY

One of my former students, Maria, used the frameworks, tools, and resources I am sharing in this book to make well-informed choices along her journey to living her authentic health career and very fulfilling life. Maria, like Sam, ended up becoming a doctor. However, unlike Sam, she loved it, and every day she was grateful that she got to use her talents and passions to do the work she was "meant" to do. Also, unlike Sam, she had really questioned and doubted whether she should become a doctor. She spent years—while often very anxious and confused—trying to decide on the career path that best suited her. Because she wanted to be completely sure before she made the commitment, Maria devoted herself to utilizing the Life and Career Planning Framework—which serves as the basis for this book and is detailed in Chapter 2—to gain the exposure, experience, and mentorship she needed in order to make well-informed career decisions. The insights she gained from this approach, during and immediately after college, led her to put her initial goals of going to medical school on hold. Instead, she followed her passion for the prevention of infant mortality among low-income and minority populations by obtaining a Master's degree in Public Health (MPH) and working in a local health department. She loved her job and felt that she was utilizing her talents to have a positive impact on the health of communities she cared deeply about.

Though she was thriving, she discovered that her calling to pursue medicine and help reduce individual patient suffering never went away. In addition to her job, Maria volunteered part-time at a local community health center so she could continue to be involved with patient care. Her experience assisting doctors and nurses to provide patient care to low-income patients affirmed that she had true passion and an aptitude to do that work. She decided in her mid-twenties to devote herself to becoming a doctor who treated low-income women and who also utilized her public health passion and training to work tirelessly on reducing infant mortality for underserved populations.

Getting into medical school and becoming a doctor did not come easy; science and math were very challenging for Maria. She flunked organic chemistry the first time, didn't get the Medical College Admissions Test (MCAT) scores she needed, and was told by premed advisors that her chances of getting in were slim. After she got rejected the first time, she completed a post-baccalaureate program that helped her become a more competitive applicant and build the skills, confidence, and knowledge she needed. Throughout the process, she persevered through each barrier because she knew that she was pursuing her authentic career path. Now, looking back on the struggle and reflecting on her long hours on the job, she says—with a huge smile—that it was all worth it. Maria's family (as well as the patients and communities whose health she has improved) agrees. When we live our authentic lives and careers, we find fulfillment and make the contribution we are supposed to make to the world. We also inspire others to do the same.

While Maria had a happy ending, and we do need more people to become doctors, **you don't have to be a doctor.** COVID-19 has reminded us of how invaluable doctors and all health workers are and the heroic work they do. If, like Maria, after in-depth consideration, becoming a doctor fits who you truly are and what you want to do, then—by all means—pursue it. If not or if, like me, you were drawn to impact health in other ways, there are hundreds of other rewarding health career paths that could lead to a fulfilling life and career. This book will provide you with insights to explore and assess your options and make a well-informed choice.

You Don't Have to be a Doctor is designed to inspire and empower you to discover, create, and live your own authentic life and career. I define your *authentic health career* as the one that best fits your unique talents, passions, goals, and lived experience. I want your life story to turn out as authentic and fulfilling as Maria's. I want to prevent you from having a story like Sam's. It all comes down to the choices you make and the actions you take toward living the life and career aligned with who you really are and what you really want.

HOW THIS BOOK CAN GUIDE YOU

This book provides insights, tools, and stories to help you make well-informed choices as you discover and live your authentic health career—starting now and throughout your journey. This applies whether you are early or more advanced in your career. It does so in the spirit of these Oprah Winfrey quotes:

> "As you become more clear about who you really are, you'll be better able to decide what is best for you— the first time around."

> "Understand that the right to choose your own path is a sacred privilege. Use it. Dwell in possibility."

There are many paths to the discovery and achievement of your authentic health career. They can come through an intentional process—as Maria chose through the Life and Career Planning Framework, which you will learn and apply throughout this book— or it can come by making the best of an unexpected opportunity that presents itself along your journey to end up in a path you never intended but that works out well for you. It can also come through learning from costly misaligned career choices or a welcome epiphany after a long period of confusion. I have met several colleagues who didn't take a conscious approach to planning their career plan and never dreamed they would be in the roles they are today but are very happy. They stumbled into their career path and happiness. I know more colleagues and former students who took a similar route but are not happy in their lives and careers. Regardless of which path they have taken and how successful and happy they are now, when I describe my approach to discovering and achieving your authentic health career, almost all of them say, "I wish I had that when I was in college or choosing my career," or "I could really use this now." As you use the Life and Career Planning Framework to refine your career plans, you will become empowered to proactively create your future and be better able to recognize and seize opportunities that will serve you well.

WHO IS THIS BOOK INTENDED FOR?

Whether you are a student, recent graduate, graduate student, early careerist, or mid- to late-career health professional, this book can help you discover, refine, and achieve your authentic health career path. Given all the opportunities in the health field, it is also a great resource for career-changers from other industries and people who are unemployed who are considering a career in health. It is also designed to be a practical resource for faculty, advisors, career counselors, coaches, parents, and mentors to better assist the colleagues they work with and students they care about to make better-informed career and educational choices.

Whether you already know exactly who you are and where you want be, are lost or struggling with choosing among options, or have already made costly misaligned career choices (as many of us have as part of discovering who we are) it's okay! As one of my mentors, Jack Kornfield, says, "You are exactly where you are supposed to be." The key is to commit to the mindset and set the intention that you can achieve your authentic health career and the life you want and begin taking action now. The world is an abundant place and rewarding health careers are projected to grow significantly in the decades ahead. Set the intention and begin acting now on the health career path that best suits you and you will discover and lead a rewarding life and impactful health career.

Our intention creates our reality.
—Wayne Dyer

With the intention that you can discover and achieve your authentic health career, this book will help you develop the insights, skills, confidence, and action plan you need to navigate your journey and succeed. Each chapter provides you with practical tools and exercises to develop a road map and begin taking action to advance from where you are to where you want to be. Now is the time for you to start creating the life and career you really want! No matter where you are on your journey, it is not too late or too early to discover and make meaningful progress toward the achievement of your authentic health career.

This book will empower you to do the following:

1. Increase your awareness and knowledge of potential health career options
2. Discover or refine your authentic life and career path.
3. Make well-informed choices about your next steps in alignment with your longer-term life and career direction.
4. Strengthen your confidence and ability to successfully obtain the education/training, experience, and networking you need to enter and advance in your chosen profession.
5. Secure rewarding jobs and be on a path to achieve your life's purpose and goals.
6. Adjust and successfully navigate your career path as the industry and jobs change and as your own passions, values, and goals evolve

> *Give a man a fish and you feed him for a day. Teach a man to fish and you feed him for a lifetime.*
> —Chinese proverb

This book **will not** tell you which health career is the best fit for you, nor should anyone else—including parents, professors, advisors, significant others, and friends. You are the only one who can discover and decide, based on who you are, what you are good at, and what you want. Therefore, this book will provide you with a framework and processes you can use to choose your own authentic health career path and then navigate it as your circumstances, preferences, and options change over your lifetime. It offers steps, success stories, and practical exercises for you to develop and succeed at your plan for the next chapter of your health career and throughout every stage of your life and career journey.

HOW TO USE THE BOOK

The book is organized around/according to elements of the Life and Career Planning Framework (the Framework) in sequential order. The Framework and two other practical models that go hand in hand with it are described in Chapter 2.

The remaining chapters address each of the Framework elements in more detail with practical strategies, stories, tools, and resources that will help you strengthen your clarity, progress, and positioning. Each chapter also includes a list of resources that you can use for additional or more in-depth exploration of topics that you find most useful and practical, including many that are available on my website (Jeffoxendine.com). The Framework elements and exercises are meant to build upon each other, so many of you will find it useful to go through the chapters in sequential order. However, many of you will already be strong in one or more of the elements or may have a specific pressing need, such as improving your packaging and self-belief for an immediate job opportunity As such, each chapter is also designed to be utilized on its own in whichever order works best for you. Utilize the table of contents to pick and choose which chapters or topics and which order works best for you. Each chapter begins with a brief summary of what is included in the chapter and how it can assist you. You can take what you need and leave the rest. You may find some insights will benefit you as you get further in your journey or that you can use to help struggling colleagues in their search for their authentic careers.

The final chapter, "Developing Your Action Plan," helps you bring together all you learn from the book with your aspirations and experiences to chart your actions steps for moving forward and committing to a timeline and accountability for achieving your goals.

WHAT IF YOU FIND OUT YOUR CURRENT PATH OR THE HEALTH FIELD ISN'T RIGHT FOR YOU?

By using the tools in this book to actively pursue a health career, some of you may discover that the health field is not for you. That's okay, too, and can be a great outcome, especially if it prevents costly misaligned career choices and their consequences. It is much better to find out now and discover a rewarding alternative path that is most aligned with who you are. The framework and tools will then help you choose and succeed in that path.

For the readers who will pursue a health career, even if it is not the one you are currently pursuing, this book will help you choose and navigate among the hundreds of growing, dynamic, and rewarding paths and jobs to achieve your authentic health career. Chapter 1, "Health Careers are Growing and Changing," and Chapter 3 on exposure provide more details and resources on many of the exciting available paths to help you make informed choices. The key is finding your authentic path, knowing how to best pursue it, and taking necessary action steps so that you can have the life and career you want.

THE MORE YOU PUT INTO IT, THE MORE YOU WILL GET OUT OF IT

Given that the focus of this book is on empowering you to discover and achieve your own personal authentic path and goals, the more effort, reflection, and honesty you invest in the content and exercises, the more you will get out of them. Some of them may initially seem challenging and make you uncomfortable. I encourage you to use the ones that seem most relevant to you and to at least give some of the others a try. You never know what you will discover. Being outside your comfort zone may be just what you need to make breakthrough progress.

When you are uncomfortable, think of it
as a sign that you are about to grow.
—Jack Kornfield

I am confident this book will help you grow and make mean-ingful progress on the journey toward your authentic life and health career. I am excited for the fulfillment and rewards you will experi-ence as you create your own story and the impact you will have on your family, community, and our world. As more of us pursue our authentic careers, together we can transform the world and inspire many who follow in our footsteps.

HEALTH CAREERS ARE GROWING AND CHANGING

Our world has never witnessed a time of greater promise
for improving human health.
—Dr. Francis S. Collins, Director, National Institutes of Health

IMPACT OF COVID-19

As I release this book in May 2020, our world and the health field have been dramatically changed by the devastating COVID-19 pandemic. Billions of people around the world are sheltering in place to protect themselves and mitigate the spread of COVID-19. It breaks my heart that, despite the heroic efforts of healthcare and public health workers, more than sixty thousand people have died (to date) from the disease in the United States and millions around the world are suffering. More than 30 million people in America are unemployed and hundreds of thousands of health workers are furloughed, redeployed, or are struggling with reductions in hours and pay. We are all dealing with the financial fallout and an unprecedented economic crisis. Everyone is wondering when the spread will stop, restrictions will be lifted, and we will transition to the "new normal." Scientists and health professionals are racing to find successful treatments, ramp up testing, implement contact tracing, and find a vaccine.

Prior to the pandemic, the title of this chapter was "Now is the Best Time to Pursue Health Careers." This phrase was also the first line of the book description. While the harsh realities of the current crisis make the near-term "now" not the best time to pursue health careers, I believe it soon will be again. Regardless, people working in or considering health careers will have to carefully navigate and adapt to changing paths and job requirements in rapidly evolving, financially challenged employer settings and economic conditions.

Hundreds of thousands of new jobs are being created to battle the pandemic and assist with the recovery, which will likely take years. Thousands more roles yet to be determined will be created as part of the recovery and as innovations are advanced in science, healthcare, public health, treatments, and technology. Health providers will ramp up their operations to provide care for all conditions, which will allow many workers to return and for the improvement of the financial states of most health organizations. Hopefully, there will be greater investment and jobs in public health infrastructure, prevention, and preparedness for future disasters.

The global pandemic has shown that everyone's health and economic well-being depend on a strong and effective health workforce. Based on our COVID-19 experience, we clearly need a robust, well-trained health workforce capable of not only meeting immediate health needs, but one that's also able to respond to crisis situations and prepare for future disasters. The pandemic exposed critical workforce vulnerabilities and gaps, exacerbated shortages and inequities, and underscored the importance of a health workforce with the knowledge, skills, and experience to care for all residents—particularly the most vulnerable. Having currently experienced the painful consequences of health workforce challenges and inequities, we must address them now and as we move forward, in order to ensure our health and well-being.

Federal, state, and local governments and health systems quickly implemented innovative strategies to increase workforce capacity, care for patients, protect workers, and leverage limited resources. Telehealth and other remote means of patient care, public health, and administrative work became the new norm overnight. Thousands of contact tracers, testers, case managers, and data analyst were hired.

At this point, much remains unclear: the rate that people will return to work, what roles they will play, and what this means for future jobs. But I am optimistic that many of the health workforce challenges and opportunities that existed before the pandemic will still be relevant and that major new needs will develop. The only things that are certain is that there will be growth in some areas, declines in others, changes in all roles, and that the health industry will continue to transform in unprecedented ways. Going forward, all people pursuing health careers will need to become more comfortable with an ambiguous future health landscape and be willing to be more flexible, adaptable, and resilient.

PRIOR TO THE PANDEMIC

Health was one of the largest and most rapidly growing industries— both in America and globally. There was and will continue to be a critical and growing need for the right health workers in the right places with the right skills. Workers are needed to promote health, build healthy communities, develop new technology solutions, and deliver high-quality, accessible, affordable, and equitable health services. Workers will also be needed for years to come, to assist with COVID-19 mitigation and recovery. A major unknown factor will be how many health workers will choose to continue in their current roles or will shift to different roles or industries as a result of their COVID-19 experiences.

All these factors will likely offer tremendous career and employment opportunities. Previous projections are likely to be less accurate as the industry continues to change, but prior to COVID-19, the US Bureau of Labor Statistics projected that employment in healthcare occupations would grow 14% from 2018 to 2028—much faster than the average for all occupations, adding about 1.9 million new jobs.[1] Of the 30 fastest-growing occupations, 18 were in healthcare and related occupations.[2]

The demand for health workers globally was also projected to grow dramatically.[3] One article predicted that, by 2030, global demand for health workers will rise to 80 million workers, doubling 2013 levels, while the supply of health workers is expected to reach 65 million over the same period, resulting in a worldwide net shortage of 15 million health workers. More skilled health workers will be needed to implement and scale essential health interventions and meet health goals in upper-middle, middle-, and low-income countries. A key lesson learned from previous disaster recovery efforts is the importance of providing people from the communities most impacted—particularly low to middle income and communities of color—with opportunities to be part of the recovery and to develop skills for higher skilled jobs in the new economy.

In addition to COVID-19, the demands for health professionals and health job growth were fueled by the aging of baby boomers, population and economic growth, technological advances, and growing rates of chronic and infectious diseases. Waves of aging baby boomers had already begun retiring from the health industry, contributing to the demand for new health professionals. Given health needs and economic realities, it is unclear if COVID-19 will slow, reverse, or accelerate this trend.

Governments will grapple with how to balance the need to invest in crisis mitigation, enabling reopening of businesses, providing

---

[1] U.S. Bureau of Labor Statistics, "Healthcare."
[2] U.S. Bureau of Labor Statistics, "Employment."
[3] Liu et al. "Projections."

relief to health employers, protecting us from further outbreaks, and investing in treatment and vaccines. Continued implementation of health and payment reforms at the national and state levels, local community health improvement efforts, transformations in the delivery of health services, and technology advances will dramatically increase, eliminate, and change health jobs and career opportunities. The global COVID-19 pandemic has shown the critical need for investment and changes that result in a stronger public health workforce capable of advancing population health and health equity, responding to crisis situations, and preparing for future disasters. It has underscored the need for a stronger, more accessible mental health workforce.

The health industry is large, diverse, and dynamic enough for EVERYONE to find a rewarding career path. There are hundreds of professions and roles (more than 260 in hospitals alone) in a range of growing private and public health sectors. And as mentioned above, the global pandemic could create thousands of new jobs that don't currently exist. Current opportunities include administrative, clinical, research, education, community, and business roles. Data science, health information technology, genetics, robotics, and artificial intelligence will play increasingly important roles in health and create thousands of new jobs. The growth of health career and job opportunities is projected for a wide range of professions and sectors. There are growing needs in numerous critical professions, including primary care, nursing, allied health, care for older adults, mental health, and public health, but there will ultimately be shortages of health workers and leaders in almost all health sectors. Across all health sectors and professions, there is a growing need for a health workforce that reflects the demographics, cultures, and languages of our increasingly diverse population—a workforce that will serve all communities, including under-resourced, rural, and urban communities, locally and globally.

Chapter 3 on exposure provides a description of the dynamic health careers, jobs, and employers, as well as detailed, proven strategies for you to successfully choose and succeed in the one best suited for you. You can experience rewards in so many areas; from doing community-level work with underserved communities or developing countries to treating patients, doing research, working in a start-up, or cashing out stock options and high compensation in profitable public companies, the options are growing and almost endless. As my professor and mentor David Starkweather used to emphasize, "The health field provides the powerful opportunity for you to do well, by doing good."

HEALTH PROFESSIONS ARE GROWING AND CHANGING

In the wake of COVID-19, transformation in healthcare and public health will accelerate, so health careers and jobs will change accordingly. The industry is shifting from a primary focus on diagnosing and treating illness in individuals to prevention of disease and injury and promotion of wellness, health improvement, and equity for populations. Technological advances are also disrupting and enhancing how we all engage in health and wellness and are changing jobs and spawning new companies. The response to COVID-19 has forced transformations in disease monitoring and intervention, patient care delivery, health worker utilization, and remote work. These transformations will result in significant changes to many professions and jobs, and the emergence of many new roles. The job that best suits you now may change dramatically in the coming years or not even yet exist. Therefore, it is important for you not only to identify paths that suit you now, but to also know how to navigate changing roles to stay aligned with your talents, passions, and goals.

THE PERFECT OPPORTUNITY FOR YOU?

This is where you come in. Though how the industry and jobs will evolve is unclear, I believe the need and opportunities for health professionals will continue to grow. You can—and please do if it is your authentic career—but don't have to be a doctor. There are hundreds of other rewarding health careers. Is this a perfect opportunity for you? If so, which among the vast variety of health career options is most authentically aligned with your passions, talents, and goals? Which will allow you to live the life you want and make the most impact? How will you know? Once you know, how can you increase your chances of sustained success and impact? How will you prevent costly misaligned career choices?

Your life and professional experience and chances of success will vary significantly depending upon which health career option you choose. Given differences among factors such as day-to-day work, professional and lifestyle demands, educational and training requirements, and financial costs and rewards, it is critical that you find the health career that best suits you. It is important that you explore and make well-informed decisions on this BEFORE you commit to or invest in a specific path in order to enhance your chances of success. And, since dramatic change and innovation will be continuous in the health field and over time your life preferences will also change, you will need to make well-informed adjustments in your path to stay aligned with what is needed and what you want (See Chapter 11 on Adjustment).

Each of us has unique talents, passions, and goals. As Oscar Wilde said, "Be yourself, everyone else is taken." *You Don't Have to Be a Doctor* will assist you in being yourself and choosing which among the numerous health career opportunities is the best fit for you and enables you to make the most significant impact. It will help you do well by doing good. Collectively, the more of us who succeed at our authentic health careers, the more likely we will effectively address the complex, emerging health challenges in our local communities, nationally, and globally and, in turn, enhance overall health, equity, and economic well-being.

LIFE AND CAREER PLANNING FRAMEWORK AND THE ORGANIZATION OF THE BOOK

The biggest adventure you can ever take
is to live the life of your dreams.
—Oprah Winfrey

The privilege of a lifetime is to become
who you really are.
—Carl Jung

This chapter describes the Life and Career Planning Framework and its elements, which you can use to discover or refine your authentic health career path, strengthen your preparation for success, and develop clear next steps. It starts with an important mindset shift and approach for you to design the life you want and the career and educational paths that will enable you to achieve it. You will then learn how to use a tool called the Life and Career Alignment Triangle to help you discover your authentic health career by finding alignment between key life and career elements. The remainder of the chapter will help you understand the stages involved in your career journey and how the Life and Career Planning Framework provides a path and practical steps to advance through the stages to your authentic health career.

START WITH A PARADIGM SHIFT

In my experience working with thousands of students and professionals over the past 30 years, I have found that most people approach deciding what they want to be when they grow up by first trying to decide which career path they want to pursue ("I want to be a doctor.") or which educational path motivates them ("I want to get my master's in public health or go to law school."). While this is natural and, for many people, results in great success, I believe there is a better approach. I encourage you to approach discovery and pursuit of who you are and what you really want to do in the following order:

Life → Career → Education → Action

1. **Life:** First, clarify who you are and your unique life values, goals, passions, purpose, and lifestyle preferences. I know this isn't always easy to do at earlier stages and transition points in your life, but knowing what you want from life can be a powerful guide and filter for your career choices. Chapter 4, "Assessment," is all about discovering and clarifying your values, goals, passions, purpose, and lifestyle preferences.
2. **Career:** Find or create a vocation or career direction that will be rewarding and is aligned with and will enable you to attain what you want from your life.
3. **Education:** Choose and secure educational knowledge, skills, and credentials that are aligned with your life and career directions.
4. **Action:** Begin acting today to move from where you are to where you want to be in your life, career, and education. While knowing what you want is critical, you cannot get there without the necessary and persistent will and action.

Approaching discovery or refinement of your life path and authentic career path in this order is important because you want to be sure that the career and educational choices you make will enable you to have the lifestyle, fulfillment, success, and impact you want to have throughout your life.

Tell me, what is it you plan to do with your
one wild and precious life?
—Mary Oliver, "Summer Day"

Developing clarity and deciding about the life you want—over time—and using this as a key filter for deciding on your authentic career and educational path can increase the likelihood that you can avoid significant investments of time, dreams, money, and educational preparation for a path that ends as a costly misaligned career choice. Many of us end up seeking major career and/or lifestyle changes that better suit us after having made significant personal and financial sacrifices.

There is also an opportunity cost[4] to the choices we make (aligned or not) such as giving up your twenties for medical school, residency, and fellowship, and entering practice with $300,000 in debt or paying $150,000 or more to get your MBA. You want to be sure the long road, sacrifice, and return on investment results in the life and career that you want. Given the high and rapidly rising cost of undergraduate education and health professions training, the opportunity and financial costs of career and educational choices will only continue to increase. While significant, these may not be anywhere near the life costs. Job dissatisfaction, burnout, stress-related illness, substance abuse, family challenges, or divorce are common consequences that come from not having a career aligned with your authentic values,

---

[4] An opportunity cost is "the loss of potential gain from other alternatives when one alternative is chosen." (New Oxford Dictionary)

goals, and life preferences. Plus, if your vocation and actions are not aligned with your most authentic values and goals, you may not realize your full potential or have the impact that you are capable of on others and the world. Therefore, it is important that you **first** carefully clarify what you value and what you want to get out of **life** and your associated lifestyle preferences, **then** choose and actively pursue an aligned career direction, and **then** ensure that your education will enable you to achieve your life and career goals.

As a public health professional who came into the field motivated by prevention, I want to prevent you from making choices that won't allow you to have the life and career you really want and that are possible. I want to help prevent unnecessary life and career suffering or crises by sharing and helping you apply valuable insights and lessons learned from experts and that I and others discovered through successes and failures. The framework, tools, and strategies provided in this book will not guarantee that you will choose the perfect path for you and that it will sustain you throughout your life and career. However, they are designed to empower you to make more well-informed, conscious choices based on extensive exploration, reflection, experience, and trial and error. Hopefully, the end result will be more clarity and commitment to what you want and can do. It is also designed to enable you to adjust your goals and consciously navigate your life and career as you and your priorities change (which they will) and in response to changing developments in the industry and world.

FINDING ALIGNMENT TO ACHIEVE THE LIFE AND CAREER YOU WANT

It can be challenging to know or project what you want from life and which, among the vast growing and changing health career options, are possible for and best suit you.

Over the past 30 years, I have developed and utilized two interrelated tools with practical considerations to help you get from where you are to where you want to be. You will learn and apply the elements of these tools throughout the remainder of this book. I will introduce them and describe how you can use them in this chapter. The remaining chapters include more in-depth content, stories, practical tips, and exercises to help you focus your mindset, energy, and actions on discovering and advancing your authentic health career path and living the life you want. The first tool is the Life and Career Alignment Triangle.

THE LIFE AND CAREER ALIGNMENT TRIANGLE

This provides a practical way to understand and visualize the elements that, when aligned, will indicate that you have reached your authentic health career. It also depicts the powerful rewards that come when your life and career are aligned. The Triangle also helps you determine where you can seek greater clarity and progress to move from where you are toward greater alignment and authenticity of your path.

The diagram below depicts the Life and Career Alignment Triangle. I adapted it from the organizational Strategy Alignment Triangle developed by my colleague Professor and Dean Emeritus Stephen Shortell of the UC Berkeley School of Public Health.

The three elements of my adaptation of the Triangle include the following:

◆ Health industry and organization trends and needs (**what is possible and needed and what employers will hire and pay you for**)
◆ Your personal passions, values, and life goals (**what you want**)
◆ Your capabilities (**what you are good at, what you enjoy**)

Finding alignment among these elements helps you be more focused, authentic, and powerful. You will be highly motivated by the work you do, be more effective, and devote the time and energy needed

Health and Employer Needs and Opportunities

Being

Searching

Surviving

Purpose

Fulfilling Work

Impact

Financial Rewards

Satisfaction and Happiness

Health and Wellness

Passion, Values, Goals   **Good at/Enjoy**

Authentic Alignment

to succeed. When your life, career path, and job are in alignment with these three elements, I believe you are more likely to enjoy the personal and professional rewards in the center of the triangle and have a greater impact on health. You will also be more likely to have a greater impact on the health of individuals and communities and the health field.

Finding authentic **alignment** among all three Triangle elements is essential because any misalignment can lead to career challenges. For example,

◆ You can have goals and passion aligned with your talents, but if they are not aligned with employers' needs, you may struggle to find a career path and job that matches your skills and interests. You might also have the nature of your profession or job change to no longer match your skills and values and goals, which can mean it is time to adjust your path.

- You can have goals and passion aligned with employer needs, but not having the right skills/talents can lead to frustration and a profession or job that isn't a good fit.
- You can have your skills/talents aligned with employer needs, but if your passion/goals are not aligned, it can also lead to frustration, dissatisfaction, and unfulfillment.

> *To build the life you want, create the work you love.*
> *Do what you love, the money will follow.*
> —Marsha Sinetar

FINDING ALIGNMENT IS A PROCESS/JOURNEY

The goal of the Life and Career Alignment Triangle is to help you create the life you want by creating the work you love and are good at. For most, this is a journey that takes time and struggle. It's okay and normal if you don't yet know who you are and what you want, what the health industry needs, or the work you love. Don't feel defeated or too much pressure to have it all figured out. Realize that discovery and achievement of the alignment depicted in the Triangle is a process and journey. Your level of clarity and progress may depend on your stage of life and circumstances. The key is to believe you can find alignment and begin taking action now to make it happen. Doing the work in this book will help you focus your actions.

STAGES IN THE PROCESS

Marsha Sinetar describes the journey to finding the work you love as having three stages: Surviving, Searching, and Being.[5] I have applied these to the process of discovering your authentic health career.

---

[5] Sinetar, *To Build the Life You Want.*

When you are in the **Surviving** stage, you are simply doing what it takes to survive and make ends meet. You might be working just to pay rent; you might be dealing with family or personal issues or trying to survive organic chemistry. In short, you are doing all you can just to make things work, just to survive. It can be more difficult to discover and advance toward the life and career you want at this stage because your attention is required for other purposes. The good news is that while this phase can be really challenging and painful, is usually temporary. You will get beyond it, grow as a person, and be able to devote more energy to searching for who you are and what you want.

When you are in the **Searching** stage, you are trying to figure out what you really want. You are willing to make a change, willing to try new things, and you are in a place to take the risks you need to get where you want to be. Many people reading this book are probably in the Searching stage. It can be a long and challenging stage to go through, and you will certainly enter it more times in your life because of changing personal and industry circumstances. Please know that the Searching phase can also end quickly with a moment of inspiration or knowing as a clear direction and path forward emerge (I have experienced this multiple times). This is not meant to be a linear or one-time process. The Searching stage is a good one to be in, because it means you are ready and able to do the work it takes to create the life and career you want. However, I know from experience it can also be a very anxious, uncertain, and even painful stage. It is often made more challenging by the pressure that we and others apply to have certainty and make the right choices and plans.

Finally, when you get to a place where all the elements are in alignment, you reach the **Being** stage. When you are in this stage, your focus and hard work can enable you to *live and enjoy* the benefits that the alignment brings you. In my experience this is an incredibly powerful and rewarding stage. This tool somewhat corresponds with Maslow's hierarchy of needs, with "self-actualization" similar to the Being stage.

It is important to remember that getting to alignment may not be a linear process and it may not happen on your desired timeline. Life can be messy and challenging. Things will happen. But don't give up hope! We also learn from our trials and tribulations and successes and failures. Even when you do all the right things and find your perfect job, life and industry circumstances are changing and unpredictable. Another reality is that you will not always make the right choices. Mistakes in life and in your career journey are inevitable. But remember that mistakes and changes aren't final or fatal. Oftentimes, in fact, they result in important growth and will lead you to new and possibly better opportunities. Mistakes and changes are part of figuring out your own personal path. This book is intended to help you minimize the number and costliness of your mistakes and the lag time of getting to alignment.

Being adaptable in the world of health is more important than ever. Health careers are constantly changing, given the natural progression and twists and turns of life and the health industry, all of us will go through these stages at various times throughout our lives and careers. The reality is that many of you are just trying to survive. Others are searching and others are fortunate to be at the Being stage. Whichever stage you are in is okay. It's where you are supposed to be. The key is to work through whatever you are encountering, and—with intention and hope—take steps to pursue your authentic health career path.

THE LIFE AND CAREER PLANNING FRAMEWORK

I developed the Life and Career Planning Framework (the Framework) to provide you with a practical path and steps to decide on and find the alignment between the life and the career you want and the educational preparation and actions that will enable you to achieve your goals. It provides the path to discover and achieve your authentic health career, including defining and finding alignment between the elements of the Life and Career Alignment Triangle. It provides practical steps you can take to make adjustments when needed to get back in alignment.

The Framework is based on my own health career journey and experience with more than 30 years of assisting thousands of students and health professionals to discover and achieve their authentic lives and health careers. I have also used the Framework elements to go from being a totally lost college physical education major to deciding to become a hospital administrator, obtaining my graduate degrees at UC Berkeley, and having a successful 20-year senior health executive career. I also used it to successfully navigate three subsequent major adjustments to my health career path as the industry, my personal preferences, and my life circumstances changed.

The comprehensive Framework consists of nine interrelated elements that you can work through in sequential order to discover and achieve your authentic health career. Each chapter of this book covers a Framework element. The work you do on each element builds on the ones before and readiness you for the next ones. Each one gets you closer to your authentic health career. However, I designed the Framework and this book so you don't have to go through them in sequential order. You can go directly to the chapter and Framework element that you believe will help you the most based on where you are in your journey.

The overall Framework is not based on empirical research but many of the concepts, strategies, and exercise in each chapter are, and I have firsthand experience with thousands of people who have used it for their benefit. It is based on my work with thousands of students and health professionals at UC Berkeley and Harvard and from hundreds of colleges and universities through my work in Health Career Connection and MyHealthCareerNavigator. People who have used the Framework have successfully pursued careers in a broad range of health professions schools and health professions, including medicine, public health, health policy and management, behavioral health, nursing, pharmacy, physician assistant, digital health, health IT, biotech, and many more. I know it works and have seen the powerful results.

The nine elements of the Framework are:

1. **Exposure** to current and future health industry trends, employer workforce needs, career options, and dynamic professionals in a broad range of health career paths (the top of the Life and Career Alignment Triangle on page 14). Exposure activities enable you to discover, explore, and refine possible career options and help you make more well-informed choices.
2. **Assessment** of who you are, what you want, and what various career options of interest offer and require relative to your unique talents, passions, values, and goals (the bottom of the Life and Career Alignment Triangle)
3. **Experience** to affirm or refine your career options and build your track record for further advancement, employment, and health professions training
4. **Career Direction(s)** you choose and actively pursue that are aligned with your talents and goals and provide focus for your plans and actions
5. **Educational preparation (degrees, certificates, training, licensure)** aligned with your life and authentic health career direction and goals
6. **Personal Branding, Packaging, and Promotion (online profiles, resumes, profiles, interview skills, statements of purpose)** that convey your unique direction and qualifications to employers and health professions schools
7. **Belief** that you can achieve your life and career goals and **Courage** to fully go for your dreams, take action, stay the course, and overcome challenges encountered along the journey. Belief and courage to make authentic choices and act, even if others don't understand or agree with your plans and strategies to gain needed support.

8. **Networking**, both professional and personal, through which you gain valuable insights, opportunities, and support
9. Lifelong **Learning, Adjustment, and Flow** to navigate your career as priorities and circumstances change for you and in the health industry

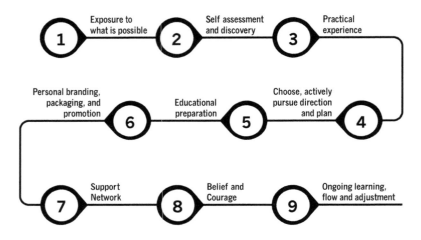

HOW YOU CAN USE THE FRAMEWORK

There are many ways you can use the Framework to discover and advance toward your authentic health career. You can:

◆ Assess your strengths and areas you need to strengthen for each and all components (i.e., I am clear about my career direction but need to strengthen my educational preparation and personal brand packaging, or I have completed my education but need to strengthen my network, belief, and courage).

◆ Identify strategies you can use and take action to build on your strengths and address Framework elements that need to be addressed (i.e., I am going to conduct informational interviews to strengthen my: exposure to career paths, dynamic individuals, job opportunities, and build my network).

◆ Prioritize strategies and action steps that will help the most to advance toward your authentic health career and develop a road map with goals, action steps, and timelines.

◆ By taking action to strengthen your preparation for each element of the Framework (or those that are most relevant to where you are in your career development journey), you will increase your ability to choose and achieve your authentic path. The components are interrelated and overlap to some degree. What is most important is that you utilize the components, particularly those most relevant to you now, to discover and advance in the direction you really want to pursue.

YOUR PERSONALITY TYPE, THINKING STYLE, AND EXPERIENCES

Depending on how you think and process information and your personality type, different elements or a different sequence of pursuing them may be more beneficial for you. For some people, using the Framework approach may seem too structured or linear. Some of us believe in serendipity, fate, or spontaneity or believe that we will stumble into in an amazing career rather than an intentional planning approach (this happens to many of us). However, there is an old saying that "luck is where preparation and opportunity meet." My experience is that using the Framework is even helpful for those who want things to happen more spontaneously or naturally, as it is the *preparation* component that puts you in a position and creates *opportunity* for the *luck* to occur and for you to recognize it and seize it when it does.

Here's an example, as a junior in college, my focused pursuit of public health and hospital administration as my career direction, utilizing many of the Framework elements, led me to luckily "stumble upon" a summer internship opportunity that ended up changing my life and launching my health career. Since I happened upon the application the night before it was due, I was fortunate that I had the preparation and packaging to submit a strong application on time and be selected for an interview. I was extremely nervous during the interview—my first ever—but I was able to speak about how my relevant exposure, experience, and education made me a solid candidate for the internship and how my authentic goals, values, and passions were aligned with the program's goals. Though I walked out concerned that I had blown the interview, I received a letter a few days later welcoming me to the program.

The internship provided me with additional exposure and experience and taught me how to network. I got a job, mentors, and a connection to UC Berkeley where I ended up going for graduate school and where I now teach. Most importantly, I gained the belief and courage that I could achieve my authentic dreams of becoming a hospital administrator and that my dream of going to UC Berkeley for graduate school was a stretch but possible if I applied myself. A few years later, the program ran out of funding, and because of the position my preparation put me in, I was able to resurrect it and have run it for more than 29 years. It is now a national nonprofit called Health Career Connection (https://www.healthcareers.org) that has inspired and empowered thousands of students to pursue their authentic health careers. My *preparation* helped me seize the *opportunity* that was *luckily* available to me and led me to the life, career, and impact I dreamed of having—and more! Doing the work on the Framework elements in this book will help you be ready when opportunity knocks, and/or it will also help you create your own opportunity.

YOU ARE EXACTLY WHERE YOU ARE SUPPOSED TO BE!

Whether you know exactly what you want to do and are motivated to move forward, or you are stuck, confused, or discouraged, you are exactly where you are supposed to be. Choosing and pursuing a health career and finding your authentic path isn't supposed to be easy (and is truly a journey).

It's supposed to be hard! If it wasn't hard, everyone would do it.
The hard ... is what makes it great!
—Jimmy Duggan (portrayed by Tom Hanks)
talking about baseball in the movie *A League of their Own*

There is much at stake in the journey to your authentic life and career, and it involves life experience, personal discovery, and opportunities that aren't always on the time schedule we would like. Many health careers, like public health, are not well publicized and have complex and ambiguous educational and career paths. There are often significant barriers to entry and advancement. On a personal level, simply trying to succeed in school along with work, financial, family, and social obligations often doesn't allow much time for career exploration or make it easy to try new things. Often, we approach critical life choice points, such as graduation or being laid off, without sufficient knowledge or experience to make well-informed career choices. Some of you have found and even had the job that you wanted only to have an organizational or life change that made it no longer possible. Others of you are doing better than ever in your career or educational pursuit and now want to make a good choice for your next step and long-term plans. The key is to start from where you are right now and have an intentional commitment and action plan for moving forward in your journey.

*If one advances **confidently** in the direction of his dreams,*
and endeavors to live the life which he has imagined,
he will meet with a success unexpected in common hours.
—Henry David Thoreau

Applying the Framework to Your Journey

Now, on to working on elements of the Framework to help you define and advance confidently in the direction of your dreams and achieve a level of success and impact beyond even what you can imagine.

3

EXPOSURE

GAIN EXPOSURE TO HEALTH CAREER OPTIONS AND WHAT IS POSSIBLE FOR YOU

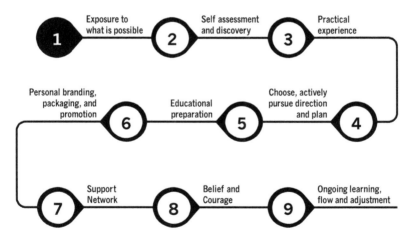

Increasing your exposure to health industry trends, career options, and professionals is essential to knowing what is possible for you and making well informed choices about your authentic health career path.

—Jeff Oxendine

Exposure is the first step in the Life and Career Planning Framework. In this chapter, you will learn the importance of gaining as much exposure as possible to the vast and growing range of health career options and the major industry trends and changes that will shape them in the future environment you will be pursing and working in. You will gain insights into some of the health career paths that are projected to be in the highest demand and resources to find out more. You will increase your knowledge or an ability to pursue practical strategies to increase your exposure to what is possible and strengthen your ability to discern which career paths might be the best fit for you.

MUCH MORE THAN DOCTORS AND NURSES

Everyone knows about the important roles that doctors and nurses play in bringing us into the world and taking care of us throughout our lives. Many people are inspired as children by their pediatrician or nurses. Others are exposed to and become motivated to become a clinician as a result of a personal or family health issue. In addition to personal and family experiences, there are numerous television shows and movies that give us a glimpse (though highly sensationalized and often inaccurate) into their work and lives. Television also brings us sensationalized views of other health-related professionals on shows such as *Grey's Anatomy* or *CSI*. While these depictions of health professionals are entertaining, stimulate interest, and often raise important issues, anyone interested in health careers would be best served by gaining real-world exposure to those careers they are interested in and to the multitude of other health career options.

There are literally hundreds of health career options beyond medicine and nursing in healthcare and other dynamic sectors such as public health, elder care, biotechnology, health information technology, behavioral health, and global health. Many people are unaware of some of the health careers that are the fastest-growing, that are in the highest demand, and that could be the most rewarding. Each one of us has unique passions, talents, goals, and backgrounds. COVID-19 has dramatically increased the need for workers in public health, telehealth, artificial intelligence, surveillance technology, and mental health. Many new roles will be developed as mitigation, recovery, treatment, and vaccines advance. The key—and the challenge—is to discover and consciously choose the options and authentic path that best suit you and enable you to make the most significant difference. We also need to believe that the careers we seek are possible for us. Therefore, the vital first step in pursuit of any health career is **meaningful exposure** that provides tangible options, direction, motivation, and belief.

> *You need to be able to see it in order to be it.*
> —Jeff Oxendine

WHAT IS EXPOSURE?

For purposes of health career discovery, I define *exposure* as becoming aware of, informed about, and engaged in industry trends, emerging issues, and **career options** to gain insights into what they offer and their alignment with who you are and what you want to do. Exposure strategies create opportunities through which a spark can be ignited within you about a particular issue, person, or career option. The spark, vision, and hope gained through exposure can also help you gain important sustaining energy that you need to embark upon and succeed in a compelling career direction.

> *Inspiration means to breathe life into.*
> —Dr. Marshall Kaufman

Exposure is often a powerful source of inspiration that breathes life into a health career direction. Exposure activities can also lead you to develop contacts and opportunities for progressing in your career direction and gaining support.

Exposure can provide an invaluable reality check before your pursuit of a profession goes too far. Every year during the graduation celebration of the Health Career Connection Summer Internship Program I run, I ask how many interns—by virtue of the exposure during their internships—discovered a career path or work they love and how many found that they really don't want to do something they went into the program wanting to pursue. The show of hands for the people who found out what they didn't want to do is almost as large as those who found or affirmed something they loved. This is a positive outcome because students were able to make a more well-informed choice to not pursue a path that wouldn't suit them BEFORE they invested considerable time, energy and money.

As I mentioned in the Introduction, I know many students who have pursued a profession they thought they wanted (sometimes because it was the only thing they knew), and by the time they realized that it did not align with their goals, passions, and purpose, they had already invested a lot of time and money into the career. Finally, exposure (along with practical experience, pursuing a direction, and networking, all of which will be discussed in subsequent chapters) provides the opportunity for what one of my students called the *snowball effect*. This is when your interests or passions are sparked by a health issue or career option through exposure, and the more that you pursue it, the more people, insights, and opportunities arise that help fuel and advance your progress.

WHY EXPOSURE?

In my work with thousands of students and people of all ages to pursue health careers, I have found that gaining as much exposure as possible is absolutely essential. Without it, people are only able to consider options that they are aware of, and I have found that most people are seriously underexposed to most health career options. They also typically only have a limited conceptual perception of those careers that they are aware of and often lack an accurate understanding of what the careers actually involve and how to pursue them. This is true of the general public but is particularly true for people who come from backgrounds in which they do not have professional role models or much interaction with the health professions. It is also true for many cultures in which becoming a doctor, lawyer, or engineer is considered the only professions for which you are judged a success and held in esteem. I have worked with hundreds of people who are struggling because they are expected to be a doctor, but they are not convinced they want to or they don't have the grades. They still have a passion for health but aren't aware of or open to other options. With greater exposure, they may find other avenues for pursuing their passions and end up making better choices, being happier, and having a greater impact.

Still others are exposed to a variety of health careers and are motivated to pursue one of them but have doubts about their ability to succeed and/or how to proceed. Exposure to role models, peers, mentors, and others with similar passions and interests along the way as well as to empowering resources can be life-changing. I know firsthand as this has happened to many of my colleagues, students, and to me.

Exposure can inspire people to discover and pursue something we didn't even know existed that aligns with our talents, passions, and goals and/or otherwise thought they couldn't do.

> *If you can dream it, you can do it!*
> —Walt Disney

It's Not Your Fault—Why Are We Underexposed?

A lack of sufficient exposure is very common due to many systemic and individual factors. People in high school, community college, and four-year universities are often primarily focused on academics and may be aware of or have access to health professionals in their lives or communities. Teachers and counselors are busier than ever and can't possibly keep up on all the information about health profession opportunities. People already working in health organizations often barely have the time to do their own jobs and keep up with their other obligations.

Health employers are typically focused on recruitment for immediate positions and, with some exceptions, often don't place much
emphasis on exposing students to the range of available health career
options. They also often don't come to college or high school campuses
to recruit or participate in career fairs, and if they do, they promote
a limited set of current job openings. Many health careers require
multiple steps and advanced degrees, while others have multiple entry
points and numerous paths with ambiguous educational and career
paths. Many health professions have not done a good job promoting
their profession and career opportunities nor have they invested in
activities to provide exposure. Some important, growing careers, such
as behavioral health, may have stigma associated with them or may
be perceived as not being financially rewarding, such as public health.
There are numerous health professions that are in high demand that
large numbers of potentially interested people don't know about.

HIGH-DEMAND HEALTH CAREERS THAT PEOPLE ARE LESS AWARE OF

◆ **Public Health**—During the 20th century, life expectancy in
the US increased by 30 years—25 of this gain is attributable to
advances in public health.[6] However, until a major disease out-
break or disaster, the work of public health professionals to keep
us healthy is often invisible or taken for granted. The COVID-19
pandemic has highlighted the wisdom of this quote from former
Surgeon General C. Everett Koop, "Healthcare is vital to all of
us some of the time, but public health is vital to all of us all of the
time." It made very visible the importance of having a strong public health workforce and the critical roles a wide range of public
health professionals play. A 2008 article estimated that 250,000
additional public health professionals were needed to meet the

---

[6] CDC, "Achievements."

demand in 2020.[7] Instead, governmental public health departments lost over a quarter of their workforce during that period.[8]
COVID-19 and many other factors will fuel a compelling continued growth in the need for public health professionals. Factors
include a population growing and aging, an increased emphasis
on improving health outcomes and health equity, and emerging
infections. Climate change, environmental hazards, and increasing natural disasters are other contributing factors. These developments will occur simultaneously with a huge wave of current
workforce retirements and retention challenges (nearly half of
local and state governmental health department employees plan
to leave their organization by 2022)[9] and advances in technology
and data analytics that will transform future public health roles.
It is urgent and important that more investment is made in the
public health workforce and more talented, diverse people pursue careers in public health.

◆ **Health IT, Telehealth, and Digital Health**—Former Secretary
of Health and Human Services Kathleen Sebelius said, "Health
IT is the foundation for a truly 21st century health system, where
we pay for the right care, not more care." As health information
technology plays an increasingly important role in health promotion, prevention, and delivery, jobs in health IT and digital
health will continue to grow and have greater impact. Health IT
jobs include securing, organizing, planning, and overseeing the
proper application of technology in administering and exchanging of health information to improve outcomes and workflows.
Telehealth and telementalhealth have already become the primary way that services are being delivered. More people will
be needed to support the technology, workflow redesign, and

---

[7] Rosenstock et al. "Workforce Crisis."
[8] Casalotti and Mullen, "ASTHO."
[9] Castrucci and Valdes-Lupi, "Coronavirus."

impact evaluation. Professionals will also be needed to advance AI, technology, and advanced data analytics to map the spread of COVID-19 and other infectious diseases and inform mitigation strategies. The Healthcare Information Management and Medical Systems Society (HIMMS) identified five growing health IT jobs people should be aware of and explore (https://www.himss. org/resources/five-growing-health-information-and-technology-jobs). With the growing role that tech companies—ranging from start-ups to Apple, Google, and Amazon—are playing in health, careers and jobs in digital health will continue to grow and offer innovative opportunities to transform health.[10]

◆ **Radiologic and Magnetic Resonance Imaging (MRI) Technologists**—Rapid advances in technology to use less invasive diagnostic imaging tests and estimated retirements will lead to continued growth in the need for radiologic and MRI technologists. These technologist jobs are projected to grow by 9% between 2018 and 2028, faster than the growth rate for other occupations. You can enter these professions with an associate's degree.[11]

◆ **Primary Care**—The United States and most states are facing a severe shortage of primary care clinicians at a time when the demand for and importance of primary care is rising. The American Association of Medical Colleges predicts a shortage of between 21,000 and 55,200 primary care physicians by 2032.[12] Primary care is also provided by nurse practitioners and physicians assistants, which are also high-growth professions on this list. Telehealth will transform how and where primary care will be provided, but there will continue to be a huge need for primary care providers.

◆ **Behavioral Health**—There is no health without mental health. There is a growing recognition of the importance of addressing

---

[10] HIMSS, "Jobs."
[11] U.S. Bureau of Labor and Statistics, "Technologists."
[12] AAMC, "Shortage."

mental health and substance use disorders and issues for individuals and communities. Unfortunately, stigma surrounding these common and significant issues has been a barrier for people seeking support and treatment and for people to seek behavioral health careers. There is a rapidly growing need and huge shortages of mental health professionals, including psychologists, psychiatrists, licensed clinical social workers, marriage and family therapists, and psych nurses and nurse practitioners. There are also growing needs for psych techs, peer support specialists, and substance use disorder and addiction counselors. For example, demand for substance use and addiction counselors is projected to increase between 21% and 38% by 2030, and the demand for marriage and family therapists is expected to increase by 14%.[13]

◆ **Nurse Practitioners (NPs)**—The rising need for NPs will be so great that the US Bureau for Labor Statistics (BLS) predicts that openings for nurse practitioners in the United States will increase 36% between 2016 and 2026, substantially faster than the average 7% growth anticipated across all occupations during that time.[14]

◆ **Physicians Assistants (PAs)**—Demand for PAs is expected to grow by 31% between 2018 and 2028.[15]

◆ **Care for Older Adults**—By 2050, there will be an estimated 27 million individuals in the United States in need of long-term care services. California alone has a need for up to 200,000 additional home care workers by 2024 and as many as 600,000 by 2030.[16]

◆ **Health Executives**—The need for health services managers, people to manage hospitals, health centers, health plans, digital start-ups, and medical groups, among others, is projected to grow 18% between 2018 and 2028.[17]

---

[13] Pellitt, "Analysis."
[14] U.S. Bureau of Labor Statistics, "Nurse."
[15] U.S Bureau of Labor Statistics, "Physician Assistants."
[16] Thomason and Bernhardt, "Crisis."
[17] U.S. Bureau of Labor Statistics, "Managers."

◆   **Health Data Analysts**—Electronic health records, mobile apps, sensors, social media, and online purchasing generate a huge amount of data about our behaviors, habits, health status and preferences. There is a growing need for professionals to analyze and transform this data into actionable information that health organizations, businesses, researchers, and government agencies can use to promote health, prevent disease, transform care delivery, and improve health outcomes. Analysts also monitor disease outbreaks, project impacts, and inform interventions. Demand for health data analysts is expected to grow by 15% by 2024.[18] Ninety percent of health executives rate data analytics as extremely or very important to their organizations.[19]

THE BENEFITS OF EXPOSURE—MARTA'S STORY

Marta was a junior at a university in Boston. She was the child of Puerto Rican immigrants who came to New York in search of better opportunities. In high school, she pursued her passion for dancing by attending a performing arts high school. While she loved it, her exposure to and experience in the dancing world made her realize that she didn't have the talent or the body type to make it as a professional dancer. In college, she was pursuing a combination of biological and social sciences with a passion for health, but she wasn't sure what she wanted to do. Like many undergraduate students I meet, she had an interest in becoming a physician, but she wasn't sure if it was right for her. She also had an interest in policy, working with youth, and domestic violence as a public health issue.

The summer between her junior and senior year, Marta choose to pursue an internship with Health Career Connection, a nonprofit I run, to gain more exposure and experience to help her discover what

---

[18] USF Health, "Data."
[19] Health Catalyst, "Healthcare."

she wanted to do. She interned in a public health department—a type of health organization that she knew nothing about prior to the internship. During her internship she was exposed to many diverse people, roles, and issues. She had the opportunity to work on a project related to domestic violence, and she also got to work with teens on sexual health education issues. She discovered that she wanted to work "upstream" on domestic violence and date-related violence prevention, as well as on education and policy-related interventions. She was so thrilled to discover her passions that once the spark was ignited, she seemed to meet person after person—including in places like on the "T" (the Boston transit system)—who shared her passion, offered key insights, and had opportunities she could pursue. She called this the snowball effect. She decided to write her senior thesis on domestic violence prevention and to continue her pursuit of creative ways to engage and educate youth regarding date-related violence prevention. She decided to pursue a Master's in Public Health to do more upstream prevention and policy work, and it all started with the **exposure** she gained through her internship.

SO HOW DO YOU INCREASE YOUR EXPOSURE TO HEALTH CAREER OPTIONS?

There are many proven strategies for increasing health career exposure. This is the best time ever to gain exposure as health workforce shortages, health academies and pathway programs, the internet, and other sources have made information and opportunities about health careers widely available. COVID-19 conditions will require some new and creative ways of securing exposure, particularly given remote work and social distancing. However, the strategies in the chapter can be done online and remotely. The desire to provide exposure and needs will not go away so new options will be created. The strategies that will work best for you depend on your background, learning styles, what you have access to, and where you are on your health career exploration journey. The key is to make it a priority, build in enough time for it in your schedule (treat it like a meeting or class), and get started. I am confident that once you do so, you will be inspired, and the snowball will keep rolling.

A solid place to start is to get more firsthand exposure to the health careers you already have an interest in or at least know exist. This will help you be sure that, if you end up choosing one of those careers, you are going into it with your eyes open about what they are like now and could be like in the future. It can also provide you with insights and contacts that will assist you with the next steps. If exposure confirms your career interest is a good fit for you, it will typically provide additional motivation, clarity, and resolve. If it is not a good fit, exposure helps you find out sooner rather than later, it enables you to have tangible reasons (for you and others) why you don't want to pursue a particular career path, and it gives you a chance to move on to another option (see Elliot's' story on page 106). Sometimes discovering what you **don't want** can be as valuable as discovering what you do want.

As you gain more exposure to the health careers you already know about, I encourage you to also actively pursue exposure to the broad range of other health careers that you don't know about. There are many that might interest you if you knew they existed or knew more about them. For example, at the beginning of my career I was focused on being a hospital administrator, a path I was laser-focused on for seven years, and had no idea there was an entire profession of medical group executives. Medical group executives run the strategy and business aspects of physician groups. After I resisted an executive job offer from a medical group that approached me, because of my inaccurate perception of it, I discovered many medical group executives were in high demand and had very interesting jobs and rewarding careers. They often had more autonomy, ran smaller more nimble health businesses, and could be more entrepreneurial than many hospital administrators. In some cases, they also made more money and had more lifestyle flexibility, vacation, and retirement funding than hospital administrators. The second time the same medical group offered me their executive job, I decided to give it a try, figuring the worst case was that I could do it for a couple of years, learn from it, and then return to being a hospital administrator. I ended up being a medical group executive and consultant for more than 13 years and enjoying many life and career experiences and benefits I would not have had as a hospital administrator.

Another example of the power of health career exposure is my experience developing and leading a program in Boston that exposed and supported hundreds of high school and community college students, career-changers, and incumbent workers to radiologic technology careers. The Partners Medical Imaging Scholarship Program provided outreach, loan forgiveness, and case management support to people throughout Boston to increase the supply of radiologic technologists and to provide employment opportunities to local residents and incumbent workers. We systematically exposed hundreds of people to a career option that most had never known existed. Many had no idea what they wanted to do or were in jobs that were not utilizing their full capabilities and potential. When they found out that with two years of community college training they could have a rewarding job as a radiologic technologist in a growing profession that combined providing patient care with the use of the advanced technology and paid a $50,000 plus starting salary with the potential for $100,000 with overtime and more advanced training many asked, "Where do I sign up?" Hundreds signed up to pursue training and participate in our loan forgiveness program. Within four years, more than 125 had graduated and secured radiologic technologist jobs in our health system. Hundreds more were in the process of securing training. Seeing people go from not having a direction or having low-wage jobs to having rewarding jobs and career paths with advancement potential was very inspiring. It all started with simple exposure to what existed and what was possible.

Where Do You Start? How to Gain More Exposure

There are many key actions you can take to gain the exposure you need to explore health career options as part of discovering your authentic career path. First, identify the trends.

Trends

A key place to start regardless of your interest is to get exposure to major health industry and organizational **trends and needs**. This is the peak corner of the Life and Career Alignment Triangle. As my friend Chris Hessler—Executive Chairman of Linkwell Health and a very successful entrepreneur—says, it is important to be "on trend" or be aware of the trends so you can create your own innovative business or role to disrupt or transform the industry. Gaining greater exposure to emerging trends will show you where there is a need for jobs, how the field is growing, and where your interests intersect with the trends. Start with learning the major health industry drivers and macro trends that are important now and are projected to be over the next 10 to 20 years. For example, between 2017 and February 2019, I served as Co-Director of the California Future Health Workforce Commission (https://future healthworkforce.org/). The Commission's charge was to develop a strategy and recommendations to build California's future health workforce based on expected supply and demand needs for health workers. We started by making assumptions about the most significant trends that would determine the type, number, and distribution of health workers that would be needed in 2030. The following are trends identified by the commission as having a significant impact on health workforce between now and 2030. These assumptions were developed prior to COVID-19 and may now land differently, but will still likely have a major influence on your health career options, so I encourage you to learn more about them. I also encourage you to closely monitor additional developments related to COVID-19 and recovery through the exposure strategies detailed later in this chapter.

1. Population Demographics
California's population will become significantly larger, older, more diverse.

- California will grow to 44.1 million people (an increase of almost 6 million).
- The Inland Empire, Sacramento region, and San Joaquin Valley are projected to grow faster than other regions of the state.
- Latinos will make up 43% of the population, whereas whites will make up 34%.
- The number of adults over the age of 65 will grow from 5 million in 2014 to 8.6 million in 2030.

2. Payment Method and Incentives
A shift to value-based payment will reach a tipping point, a true financial incentive to focus on population health management and outcomes.

3. Payment Levels
MediCal and Medicare reimbursement levels to providers will remain relatively at the same level of net payment. Commercial levels will likely be reduced. The total cost of care will be static or lower.

4. Focus on Social Determinants of Health
Focusing on social determinants of health and cross-sector collaboration to tackle community health issues will become a statewide and regional priority.

5. Team-Based Model
The standard of care is team-based, integrated, whole-person, and coordinated across the health continuum.

6. Technology Integration

Widespread technology integration supports a shift to self-management; redistribution of expertise will increase access to behavioral healthcare, rural healthcare, and home care across geographies; and technology integration will transform care delivery as well as workforce training and education.

7. Culture, Institutional, and Systems Change

Culture, practice, and systems change within health and educational institutions may not fully support full adoption of assumed payment, technology and team and other transitions, but we should plan as if the direction of change will be supported.

8. Federal Policy and Budget

Federal government policy and budgetary changes will, at best, be benign neglect and, at worst, result in significant reductions in subsidies to California.

9. Health Coverage

At least 90% of Californians will have some form of health coverage for essential healthcare, preventative, mental health, and oral health services.

10. Immigration Policy

Immigration policies will support access to a labor pool to help meet the demand for key health workers, especially in underserved areas. However, plans should include both ways to support foreign-trained workers and immigrants to pursue health careers and an increased use of workers of all ages from California and other states.

11. Mass Incarceration

Mass incarceration has decreased, and a large incarcerated and reentry population will need health and social services support.

12. Increased Emphasis On the Need to Reduce Health Costs

Health costs already make up close to 20% of the US gross domestic product. Our rapidly aging population, technology advances, drug prices, and other factors will increase cost to unsustainable levels if major changes are not made.

Other future assumptions to consider:

◆ Demand for noninstitutional care to support aging in place
◆ Who will be cared for in the future will look different—groups of consumers who will prioritize things differently
◆ Employers will exert more of a voice and demand more accountability and value
◆ New corporations moving into healthcare space (e.g., Walmart, Amazon) will influence demand for and new model of providing care
◆ Public higher education will have limited capacity to meet future demand
◆ Impact of the opioid crisis and prescription drug addiction

I encourage you to check out these additional sources of trends related to the future of the health industry and health career opportunities:

◆ The Future of Nursing 2020–2030
  https://nam.edu/publications/the-future-of-nursing-2020-2030/
◆ Public Health 2030: A Scenario Exploration
  https://kresge.org/sites/default/files/Institute-for-Alternative-Futures-Public-Health-2030.pdf
◆ Healthcare 2030
  https://institutes.kpmg.us/content/dam/institutes/en/healthcare-life-sciences/pdfs/2019/kpmg-healthcare-2030.pdf

- What Will Healthcare Look Like in 2030
  https://www.weforum.org/agenda/2017/04/what-will-healthcare-look-like-in-2030/
- Impact of Digital Technology on Healthcare
  https://www.aimseducation.edu/blog/the-impact-of-technology-on-healthcare/

All these trends are opening up new jobs in new places and are reshaping current jobs, so once you identify the trends, you can identify the jobs that go along with them. Trends have strong implications on how health will be provided in the future and, therefore, what kinds of jobs will be needed.

Once you expose yourself to the industry trends, you can determine which of the trends align with your passions, interests, and talents. You can narrow it down even further from there by identifying specific organizations, professions, and jobs that fall into the trend you have aligned yourself with and discover what roles they are looking for, the training you will need, and so forth. You can even take it a step further and identify leading organizations and health profession training programs that are on the cutting edge of the trends and exploring the types of jobs they have available now and project to have in the future.

Abundance of Opportunities

One of the strengths of the health field *right now* is that there is something in it for everyone. The field is dynamic, diverse, and expanding to cross over into other fields that you may have never dreamed of combining with health. For example, would you ever have thought that you could have a health career in online gaming? Check out bluegoji.com to see creative ways that interactive fitness games made to play while working out on cardio equipment can make exercise, fun, easy, and rewarding. There are so many changing and growing opportunities in the health field right now that nobody should feel limited. In most states as well as in local areas, health is usually one of the fastest-growing sectors that has high-wage, high-growth jobs, and long-term career stability. Not only do you get to have a positive impact on your community, but you also get to make a good living out of it. Because it's an ever-changing field, with tech and policy playing a big role and medical advances all the time, there is an enormous abundance of opportunity in the health field that you just have to delve into to understand what's out there.

HOT AND EMERGING HEALTH CAREERS

I encourage you to increase your exposure to the hot and emerging health careers nationally, globally, and in the areas where you may want to work. You want to learn about which are in high demand now and will be when you finish your education and training (this could be many years away) and beyond. You want to understand how experts, educators, and people working in the field believe that the professions and jobs may change with health industry changes and advances in health and technology. Armed with this information, you will be in a better position to assess if a health career path will be a good fit for you and if there will an abundance of job opportunities over the course of your career. For example, when I was a sophomore in college, my mother sent me an article about the fastest-growing careers in America. Hospital administration was the third-fastest growing career—after computer science and engineering—had the potential to make an important difference in community health, and had a good level of compensation. This influenced me to get further exposure to the field by taking courses, talking with administrators, and pursuing internships. I ultimately discovered it was a great fit for me.

As you explore your options, keep in mind that supply and demand for health professions vary by geographic area, health sector, and type of health organization. There will be some health career paths, like primary care and behavioral health, that may be in growing need nationally or even globally, but the need for others, such as nurses and medical assistants, may depend on where you want to work. The need for and job growth in specific health professions will change over time, so be sure you continue to monitor the latest projections and talk with people in the profession about future needs. You want to have your eyes open about the future of the paths you are interested in and make a well-informed choice before investing your time, energy, and money in training programs. You shouldn't choose a health career path just because it is projected to be a hot career of the future—you also need to be sure it aligns with your passions, values, and goals and what you are good at and enjoy (remember the Triangle)—but it is a very important consideration.

At the time this book was published the following were some of the highest-in-demand health careers in the United States:

Clinical

◆ Primary care clinicians: family practice physicians (MDs and DOs), nurse practitioners, physician assistants

◆ Advanced practice nurses: nurse practitioners and clinical nurse specialists

◆ Registered nurses: nurses make up by far the largest number of health workers. There are more than 3.8 million nurses in the United States.[20] (Although, in some states, associate-degree nurses make up the majority of nurses, having a baccalaureate (BSN) has become preferred by many health systems.

◆ Physician assistants

◆ General surgeons

◆ Direct/home care workers: home health aides, certified nurse assistants

◆ Pharmacists

◆ Psychologists

◆ Radiologic technologists

---

[20] American Association of Colleges of Nursing, "Fact Sheet."

- Social workers
- Substance use disorder counselors
- Care coordinators
- Occupational therapists
- Physical therapists
- Peer support specialists

Non-clinical

- Health administrators
- Public health professionals
- Health IT
- Big data
- Community health worker
- Health coach
- Health navigator
- Scribe

Specific Roles and Organizations

To find out what specific roles and organizations are out there that align with your passions as well as the current trends, you simply have to look. Look online for large health organizations ranging from health systems and health plans to start-up companies. Look at what kinds of positions they have available. Spend time looking at job descriptions and finding out what's required and whether you might like that type of job. There are other strategies listed below for exposing yourself to specific organizations and roles, but for an online search, here are some good places to start:

Association and Health Career Related Websites:
California Primary Care Association Job Center: http://www.cpca
   .org/index.cfm/health-center-resources/clinic-careers-
   online-job-center/

Public Health Career Mart: https://www.apha.org/professional-development/public-health-careermart

Explore Health Careers: https://explorehealthcareers.org/

23 Mental Health Professionals Interviewed About Their Jobs: https://www.psychologytoday.com/us/blog/design-your-path/201506/23-mental-health-professionals-interviewed-about-their-jobs

PA Job Source: https://jobs.aapa.org/

Nurse.org: https://nurse.org/jobs/

Healthecareers: healthecareers.com

Major Job Sites with Many Health Job Listings

Idealist: http://www.idealist.org/

First Job: https://www.firstjob.com/

LinkedIn: https://www.linkedin.com/

Glassdoor: https://www.glassdoor.com/index.htm

TWELVE STRATEGIES TO GAIN EXPOSURE

In addition to staying abreast of major trends and considering how they shape your options, here are 12 other valuable exposure strategies you can use to gain more exposure to health career options:

1. Informational Interviews

I have found informational interviews to be ***the number one exposure and networking strategy.*** An informational interview involves you reaching out to someone in a career or educational path or organization that you want to explore and setting up a time to meet with them to get information about what they do, what they like and don't like, how they got there, the future of the field, and advice they have for you. Informational interviews with alumni from your school, people who come to speak to your class or student club, or someone an instructor refers you to are good places to start.

Informational interviews are best done in person so that you make a great impression and personal connection. You can use social distancing if needed. However, they can also be done by phone or remote technology. Many health career seekers hesitate to do informational interviews. They ask, "Can't I just send an email?" The answer is a resounding no. This is a great, nonthreatening way to put yourself into the flow of opportunities and people. It's going into an interview without any pressure on yourself at all; you are simply looking for information about the person (as described earlier) and an organization, its roles, and what the organization might be looking for in the future. As a bonus, you could end up establishing a good rapport with the person you are interviewing and making a valuable new professional connection. The people you interview get the benefit of finding out about you and your talents and goals. They may keep you in mind for a future job opening within their organization or network. So not only do informational interviews give you exposure to a profession, role, and organization that may interest you, but they also help you build your network. This is why I always tell my students to do as many informational interviews as they possibly can.

One student of mine, Susan, was always intimidated by the idea of informational interviews and no matter how much I told her to at least give them a try, she couldn't get over the fear of awkwardness and putting herself out there. In her last year of college, she was applying to jobs every day and simply couldn't get any responses. I urged her once again to set up informational interviews, and feeling desperate, she finally did. Three weeks later, Susan had a job—not from one of the online applications she sent in but from the contact she made in her informational interview. Now, informational interviews don't always (often don't, in fact) end in jobs, and you shouldn't view them that way. Susan was very lucky and had an informational interview that went fabulously well, and she was in the right place at the right time. She told me (even before she got the job) that it was a great experience and she wished she had been doing them all throughout college, making contacts and simply seeing what was out there. So, don't wait until you graduate! Don't wait until you're desperate to get a job. Do some informational interviews **now**, and get valuable **exposure** to jobs, people, and key career insights.

It is natural to be nervous about your informational interviews; particularly when you are just beginning to do them. However, have the mindset and confidence that he will go well and just be yourself. Oftentimes, you will ask one question and then the person will talk for the entire 30 minutes or longer and leave feeling good about you; regardless of what you said or did (though appearance, eye contact, active listening, and note-taking do make a difference). When asked how many informational interviews one should do, I tell peoples: As a rule, do one a week. If you could spend one to two hours per week on one informational interview, by the end of the year you would have 50 people whom you've learned from and added to your network. However, I know for busy students and health professionals that once per week is a lot (though it would pay off). So even once every couple weeks or once per month would still be of great benefit. However, the closer you are to wanting to secure a job or get into health professions schools, the more info interviews you should do.

Speaking of health professions school, doing informational interviews with faculty, students, alumni, and program staff are also a great way to get exposure and make connections to different health professions training programs and schools. You can do this before applying, after and after you have been accepted.

For more insights to help you develop your informational interview strategy and questions, please see Exercise 3 at the end of the chapter.

2. Internships

Internships are extremely valuable ways to get experience, so we will revisit and expand on them in Chapter 5. But note that they are also excellent exposure tools. I have placed more than 8,000 undergraduate and graduate health professions students in internships and am amazed at the valuable exposure, experience, and relationships that people gain. Interns are exposed to specific jobs and different types of professionals and health organizations, and often are able to do many informational interviews. I encourage you to pursue practical, research, and clinically related health internships, perhaps pursuing a different type or setting each summer of college for maximum exposure. Remote internships may become more common given COVID-19 work conditions and the likelihood that many people in the health field will continue to work remotely. Structured correctly and with your best efforts, they will be provide valuable exposure.

3. Attend Conferences

Conferences provide excellent opportunities for exposure to emerging topics, the latest developments, and key leaders in the health field. Conferences are also incredible places to network and meet people you can follow up with for informational interviews, shadowing, mentorship, or job and internship opportunities. Conferences are offered throughout the year by national, state, and local health associations, coalitions, health professions schools, and student groups. If you are a student, there are many pre-health career or prospective student conferences that you can attend to gain exposure, get valuable preparatory information, and make key contacts. Many conferences have discounted student rates, scholarships, or volunteer opportunities. Due to COVID-19 many conferences may be offered remotely, which will still provide great exposure and networking through interactive tools. Remote conferences may provide even greater access to top speakers and content.

4. Read Online Blogs and Newsletters

Where do you get your health industry news? You should have a consistent way you keep up with news about the industry. You can get updates on the latest industry trends, developments, and key players. Fortunately, there are more useful sources than ever. Examples include California HealthCare Foundation, Kaiser Family Foundation

Health News, Health Leaders Media, and the Robert Wood Johnson Foundation. Both have regular newsletters with information on the latest trends in health and various industries. Some others include the American Public Health Association, National Institute of Health, Prevention Institute, and more. Visit Jeffoxendine.com for more sources and to find the one that best suits your interests. Check out and sign up for my blog on health workforce and career developments and links to other useful resources.

5. Read Academic and Trade Journal Articles

Modern Health Care and *Health Affairs* are examples of leading trade and academic journals. *Modern Health Care* is a journal that people in the healthcare industry read. You will learn a lot about the leading organizations, players, and transactions in the health field and the latest industry trends. *Health Affairs* is the leading academic journal for health management and policy. *Health Affairs* includes scholarly articles on timely and relevant industry topics. Both, and others like them, are valuable resources to gain exposure to and stay current with the latest industry developments.

6. Follow Influencers and Thought Leaders on Social Media

Finding out what these people are saying and writing about is a great way to stay on the forefront of the health industry. LinkedIn is set up to help you find these people by suggesting them to you based on your experience and interests, so once you find them and follow them, be sure to read as much as you can of their posts. Twitter, FaceBook, Instagram, and other social medial platforms also have health leaders that you can follow.

7. Do a Project with a Health Organization in the "Real World"

Use your class projects strategically. Often, with the internet, class projects are seen as at-home assignments, something you can research and complete from behind your computer. If you do this, you're missing out on an important exposure and networking experience.

I was once given a class project on finding a new trend in hospital services with the option to research from the library or to go out and do field research. I chose field research and went to a local hospital that had an urgent care center. Not only did I get exposure to jobs in a hospital and learn a lot about urgent care centers, but I also made some good contacts at the hospital. A few months later, this hospital had an internship opportunity so when I applied, I was selected because I had already met and made an impression on some of the people hiring. That internship led me to a job at that hospital after I graduated, and I subsequently worked in that community for 14 years. So one class project ended up launching my career. As I'm sure you've noticed by now, there is a lot of overlap of elements in the Life and Career Planning Framework. In this case, getting exposure can also strengthen both your networking and experience.

8. Take Courses that Widen Your Perspective on Health

Take college, graduate school, continuing education, or online courses that broaden your exposure to different aspects of health or related fields. Be open to areas that may be very different from your primary course of study. Learn about the social determinants of health and environmental health. There is always something to learn and you never know what you will discover and who you might meet. For example, many premed majors discover they like public health or nurses find they like health management or quality improvement. At a minimum, you will gain valuable perspectives and knowledge that will help you be effective as health improvement becomes more interdisciplinary and integrates medical, social, behavioral, environmental, and political factors.

9. Join and Actively Participate in a Professional Association

Almost every major category of health professionals has a professional association and/or trade association. There are professional associations for nurses, public health, community health workers, social workers, doctors, Health IT, and pharmacists. There are also associations of students in each of these areas and more. You can participate in national, state, local, or school-specific chapters. Examples of professional associations include the American Public Health Association, American College of Health Executives, and American Association of Nurse Practitioners and National Association of Community Health Workers. Look for associations that have student board members or volunteers to be part of a symposium committee. This can also be a fantastic networking opportunity. When I was a grad student, I was a student board member for a local professional association called Health Executives of Northern California. I did that for a year and when I graduated, I became Membership Chairperson. This allowed me to meet everyone coming to the organization that led me to other roles within the association, and within three years, I was president of the association. By virtue of that, I started Health Career Connection and have run it ever since. A big part of networking and exposure is making sure to put yourself into the flow of people and opportunities. That's how you get exposure, build your network, and meet people that will lead you to the next step. For a list of healthcare professional associations, please see my website, Jeffoxendine.com

10. Job Shadow

Reach out to health professionals who work in the kinds of roles and organizations you are interested in pursuing and ask if you can shadow them. Ideally you could shadow people for a day or a half-day to learn about what a day in their life is like. If you are a student, you might pursue shadowing with someone who is an alumnus of your school or is affiliated in some way. When I was at UC Berkeley

School of Public Health, our alumni association had a shadowing day once or twice per year during which alumni allowed current students to shadow them.

For people out of school, it could be someone doing a clinical role you want to explore or something you can organize through your professional association.

11. Volunteer

Volunteering in the type of organizations or community where you might want to someday work is an excellent way to get more exposure. For example, many students at UC Berkeley get great exposure to patient care, public health and meeting client social needs when they volunteer at the student led Suitcase Clinic for homeless residents. You can also volunteer in organizations that you are curious about just to get more exposure. You might discover something you love that you never knew existed! Volunteering is also an excellent source of gaining experience so more details are provided in Chapter 4.

12. Research

Paid or unpaid research experience with faculty members or people doing community based or clinical research is also an excellent way to gain exposure. These opportunities may be available on your campus or with public health and healthcare organizations or research institutes in your community. There are also numerous national and health professions school summer research programs for undergraduate and graduate students. Research experience is particularly valuable for students who want to pursue academic, research or clinical careers to help you decide if you want to do it before making a commitment, build your track record and position yourself for success. Many people start researching an interest based on faculty research exposure and encouragement. I encourage you to get solid research exposure and experience and explore some practical health experience for comparison.

HEALTH CAREERS EXPOSURE WEBSITES

In addition to the websites listed earlier, here are some additional resources through which you can gain exposure to hot and emerging health careers and strategies for pursuing them:

- **Explore Health Careers:** https://explorehealthcareers.org/
- **The Student Doctor Network:** https://www.studentdoctor.net/
- **Mi Mentor:** https://www.mimentor.org/
- **Exploring Health Careers:** https://ca-hwi.org/career-pathways/exploring-health-careers/
- **Explore Public Health Careers:** https://www.publichealthonline.org/careers/
- **My Health Career Navigator:** http://myhealthcareernavigator.com/

END OF CHAPTER EXERCISES

Steps to Take to Get More Exposure *NOW*

Develop Your Exposure Strategy or Action Plan

Now that you have read about different ways you can increase your exposure, it is time for you to start *implementing* the strategies that will get you the exposure you need. Here are three exercises to get you started and on the right track.

Exercise 1: How will I get more exposure over the next six months?

From the following list of strategies, identify three exposure strategies that you will pursue over the next six months. Be specific about how and when you will pursue them.

- Keep up with relevant health industry news. Which sources of regular news will you read, watch, or listen to?
- Join and participate in a professional association (as a student or regular member).
- Participate in a conference or on-campus presentation aligned with your interests.
- Actively engage in a student health club or event.
- Attend workshops or career fairs on health career options.
- Participate in professional development or networking events.
- Shadow health professionals in your areas of interest and one path you know little about.
- Conduct informational interviews.
- Work on a class or thesis project in an area of interest.
- Participate in an internship.
- Volunteer.
- Secure a full- or part-time job in areas relevant to your interests.

◆   Review job postings for roles and in organizations aligned with my interests.
◆   Other?

Strategies I will pursue:

Strategy 1:
Key next actions:
Timeline for completion:
How will I benefit and grow?

Strategy 2:
Key next actions:
Timeline for completion:
How will I benefit and grow?

Strategy 3:
Key next actions:
Timeline for completion:
How will I benefit and grow from pursuing these strategies?

Exercise 2: Exploring Emerging Trends and Possibilities

First, identify five major health trends:

1)

2)

3)

4)

5)

Of those five, pick three that are the most compelling and interesting to you relative to your authentic health career path options.

1)

2)

3)

Now, identify three ways that you will get exposure to career paths and jobs aligned with those trends:

1)

2)

3)

Exercise 3: Informational Interview Preparation and Questions

Hopefully, informational interviews were one of your three ways in Exercise 2 to get more exposure. If it wasn't, I urge you to make them number four and actively pursue them.

Here are some strategies for identifying who you want to interview, preparing for success and questions you can ask.

Identify industry trends and research specific roles and organizations that match your interests and talents. Identify a person in one of those roles to interview. Find out if there is anything you have in common with this person. If you are both alumni from the same school, mention it. Ask for a small amount of their time (30 minutes is a solid starting point) and tell them why you are interested in conducting an informational interview with them. If possible, have the interview in person, and if they aren't open to that, ask to do it over some form of videoconferencing.

Preparation

Research the person's background, professional history, role, and accomplishments. Do some homework on their organization, departments, and recent developments. Learn about some of the challenges they are facing.

- Dress professionally, as appropriate for the type of organization and as best you can.
- Prepare your questions and prepare your elevator speech.
- Sometimes, an informational interview can turn into a real interview and you can talk about what you are doing and what you are interested in. You should also have your resume with you. Don't take it out unless they ask for it, but you should be prepared in case they do.

During the interview

◆ Keep to the time. If you have agreed upon 30 minutes, stick to it. When 30 minutes have gone by, point it out and provide the opportunity for the interview to end. If the person wants to continue, they can continue, but you should initiate an ending.

◆ Try to make a good connection with them. Ask them about their interests and career path, and talk about common interests where you can find them. Make consistent eye contact, have positive and open body language, and practice active listening.

◆ Take notes! Have a pad of paper and right down the insights and connections the person shares with you. It shows you are listening, care, and will follow through. I often wonder how the person will remember all the advice and the seven organizations and contact names I gave them when they don't write anything down.

◆ Before you leave, ask them for the names of two or three other people they suggest you talk to or do informational interviews with. Ask if they can introduce you or if you may mention that they referred you in an outreach email.

After the interview

Be sure to send a follow-up handwritten thank-you card (preferable) or a professional but heartfelt email. And keep in touch with them beyond this one act of thanks. Ask them to connect on LinkedIn if it feels appropriate. Send them an email every now and then to update them on your progress, that doesn't necessarily require a response. Be sure to let them know them how the information or connections they provided helped you.

And now, do some research and identify three people with whom you can do an informational interview:

1)

2)

3)

If you're feeling a bit intimidated by the thought of reaching out to these people, we're going to help you get started and gain some informational interview confidence. Here are some simple steps you can take to make your informational interviews run smoothly:

Step 1: Develop your 30-second elevator speech. Who are you, what are you doing, and what do you hope to get from the interview? Write that here:

Step 2: Write out the questions you want to ask each person. You will have to tweak your questions to fit each interview, but here are some sample informational interview questions:

1. Could you tell me a little about your goals and your journey in achieving them?
2. What are your organization's top priorities right now?
3. What do you think are some of the major health trends that will influence your profession, your role in the organization, and your role in it in the future?
4. What kind of education, skills, and experience would someone like me need in order to get a job and be effective in your organization?
5. What are the things you like and don't like about your job?

6. What advice do you have for me as someone who is interested in and passionate about the work you and your organization do?

7. Are there other people in your organization or network that you recommend I speak with to get more information about career opportunities in areas that I'm interested in? Would you be willing to introduce me to them or allow me to use your name when contacting them?

Add some questions of your own:

8.

9.

After the interview, be sure to thank them and let them know how their advice will help you move forward in your career direction.

4

ASSESSMENT AND DISCOVERY

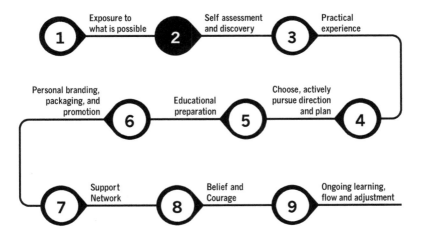

*"As you become more clear about who you really are,
you'll be better able to decide what is best for you—
the first time around."*
—Oprah Winfrey

"Life isn't about finding yourself. Life is about creating yourself."
—George Bernard Shaw

Assessment and Discovery is the second step in the Life and Career Planning Framework. This chapter will provide you with insights, tools, and exercises to assess and discover who you are, what you want out of your life and career, and your many strengths as they relate to your authentic health career. This chapter will help you uncover your "Why."

Assessment is a vital step on the path to finding your authentic health career. So many people make costly misaligned career choices and end up in careers they don't like or invest significant time and money going to graduate school only to find out (too late) that it isn't for them. The stakes are particularly high in the health field given the high and rising cost of health training programs and the intensive years and energy involved in preparing for, applying to, and completing programs. There are also alarmingly high and growing trends of physician burnout and suicide.

According to the Association of American Medical Colleges, the median debt for medical school graduates in 2018 was $200,000.[21] Many graduates also have considerable debt from their undergraduate education. One of my former student's brothers graduated from a prestigious medical school with $300,000 in debt and decided he would really rather be a "beer brewmaster" rather than a doctor (though he couldn't because he now couldn't afford it). In addition to the financial burden, graduates have often worked extremely hard in high school to get into a top college, survived an intense four-year or more undergraduate premed experience, invested months and resources in getting a great MCAT score, and persevered through the medical school application process. Many have also had to complete post-bac programs or other academic enrichment programs in addition to securing appropriate research and clinical experience and navigating gap years. All of this is BEFORE the intensity of medical school event starts!

---

[21] AAMC, "Debt."

Many of my students at UC Berkeley and in Health Career Connection hate it when I tell students that to become a doctor, they must give up their twenties—a pretty special and fun time in life. I tell them if it is their authentic health career, it is worth it! One of my favorite Health Career Connection alums, who is living and fully enjoying her authentic health career, recently told me, "Jeff, you know how you tell us that becoming a doctor requires giving up your twenties, you are wrong.... it's your twenties and early thirties." She finally completed residency and started her dream job at the age of 33. She wouldn't trade it for anything but said, "Please be sure that students know what they are getting into and it is really what they want to do with their lives and careers."

49% of doctors surveyed would not recommend
medicine as a career to their children.[22]
—The Physicians Foundation

We need you to be a doctor if it is who you are and what you truly want to be. However, **you don't have to be a doctor**, and there are hundreds of other rewarding health and non-health career paths that you can follow to lead the life and make the difference you were born to make.

Assessment is very important because if you don't know yourself and what is most important to you, you will have a harder time choosing your authentic path. You have the power to create the life and career you want; you should first assess your aspirations and your superpowers and how those fit with the multitudes of emerging health career options.

---

[22] Physicians Foundation, "2018 Survey."

WHAT IS ASSESSMENT?

Assessment is the process through which you define and understand your authentic self more clearly and determine how who you are and want to be align with potential health career options. Assessment has three major components:

1. **Self-Assessment:** This includes who you are, what you value, what are your goals, what you're good at and enjoy doing, and what your passions, preferences, and aspirations are. How do you want to serve? What kind of person do you want to be?
2. **Assessment of health career option requirements and rewards:** Which of the hundreds of health career options are you interested in? What are their rewards? What are the requirements for entry into and success in the field?
3. **Assessment of how you "fit" with specific health career options and potential health work environments:** How do the requirements and rewards of the health career paths you are interested in align with who you are, what you are good and enjoy, and what are your goals and preferences? Which seem like the best "fit" for you if you are being your best and most authentic self? What do you want in a work environment and how does that influence your choices?

SELF-ASSESSMENT

Going back to our Life and Career Alignment Triangle, Self-Assessment encompasses the bottom two corners of the Triangle, which are (1) defining your passions, values, and goals and (2) what you are good at and enjoy doing.

With the knowledge or at least direction of what you want, you can make more well-informed choices about your life and health career options and educational programs that are aligned with it.

Health and Employer Needs and Opportunities

Being

Searching

Purpose

Fulfilling Work

Impact

Financial Rewards

Satisfaction and Happiness

Surviving   Health and Wellness

Passion, Values, Goals   **Good at/Enjoy**

Authentic Alignment

To build the life you want, create the work you love.

—Marsha Sinetar

I encourage you to develop and make choices from the mindset that YOU can build the life you want and create the work you love by discovering, achieving, and enjoying your authentic health career path. While COVID-19 has created daunting economic challenges, overall the world is an abundant place, not a scarce place. There are so many opportunities out there that you can and must create the life and the work that you want. How do you do that? Well, first, you have to start with *self-assessment* and *define* what you want. The content and exercises that follow in this chapter will help you do that now and then adjust over time as your life, self-awareness, and circumstances changes. You will also work to identify or create the work you love through the exposure strategies in Chapter 3 and learning from your experience as described in Chapter 4 and lifelong adjustment in

Chapter 11. I am confident you will succeed in creating the life you want and work you love. Let's start defining what you want.

ASSESS AND DEFINE YOUR CORE VALUES

Self-assessment starts with assessing, defining and prioritizing your core values. This is an important part of the foundation for determining the life you want and work that will enable you to fulfill them. Your core values are a key element in the Life and Career Alignment Triangle because you want to be sure the benefits you realize from engaging in work aligns with them. Of the thousands of students and colleagues I have worked with, I have found that the ones who work in career paths, jobs, and health organizations and communities aligned with their values are often the happiest, most fulfilled, and most successful.

There are many definitions of values, for purposes of choosing your authentic career I define values as the things that are most important to you and would bring you the most meaning and fulfillment through your life and work. You and others significant in your life will need to make many choices and trade-offs as you pursue the life you want and work you love and deal with what life presents you. I believe and have found that the clearer you can be about your values and how you prioritize them, the more conscious and better life and career choices you can make aligned with who you are and what you want.

Assessment includes defining your core values from among three categories of career-related values:[23]

◆ **Intrinsic values** are related to the **intangibles** about the career. These are the values that motivate you and help you feel fulfilled. Examples of intrinsic values are giving back to your community, healing patients, and expressing your creativity. I have found

---

[23] Loffredo, "Values."

many people in the health and public field have intrinsic values, such as service, social justice, equity, health as a right, access to quality, and affordable healthcare.

◆ **Extrinsic values** relate to the tangible rewards derived from your career and your work environment. Some examples of extrinsic values are pay, job security, working as part of a team, autonomy, and providing influence.

◆ **Lifestyle values** are what you do for a career and where you work to produce a certain type of lifestyle. The type of lifestyle you desire can help complete the picture of what you value. A few examples of lifestyle values include living in a big city, traveling extensively, having a flexible work schedule, being able to meet family obligations, and living simply.

As you identify values in each of these categories, you can begin to identify and assess the core values matter most to you and that you want to prioritize when choosing your authentic health career. There are many sources you can reference for lists of values and several sources with practical steps for defining your values.

Here are three that may be useful:

1. **Mindtools—What Are Your Values?**
   https://www.mindtools.com/pages/article/newTED_85.htm
2. **Six Ways to Discover and Choose Your Core Values:**
   https://www.psychologytoday.com/us/blog/changepower/201811/6-ways-discover-and-choose-your-core-values
3. **Seven Steps to Discovering Your Personal Core Values:**
   https://scottjeffrey.com/personal-core-values/

APPLYING YOUR CORE VALUES IN THE HEALTH FIELD

Many professionals in the health field successfully align and live their work with their life values. I was recently at a conference with people whose life work has been leading community health centers. Their core values include healthcare is a human right and that everyone deserves quality healthcare. Their values also include equity and justice. These are personal values that permeate through their lives, but also through their careers.

An important part of assessment is determining if and how you will be able to live according to your personal and professional values in your chosen future path and what trade-offs might be involved. For example, in the past, many people who became doctors were motivated by a core value of autonomy. Autonomy meant the independence to run their own practices, set their own compensation, and make medical decisions as they determined to be in the best interests of their patients.

Over the past two decades, many doctors would say that changes in the practice of medicine have reduced doctors' autonomy. It has become more common for doctors to practice in larger medical groups, many no longer owned by doctors, who set individual providers' schedules and compensation and expect them to adhere to clinical guidelines and authorization processes for patient care. Many doctors might feel that these changes have conflicted with their core values of autonomy. Others might feel that the trade-off of having less practice autonomy may have resulted in more personal autonomy (less time on call, potential to work part-time, treat only outpatients, less burden, a risk of running a practice). How someone views the change and the impact on their satisfaction and lifestyle is a personal decision. I encourage you to clarify your values and assess how you will be able to fulfill them given the changing way that health will be provided and paid for at the beginning and throughout your career.

Many people in the health field have a strong desire to work in a setting that enables them to operate in alignment with their personal values. What are your values? You can stop and clarify your values now or through the exercises at the end of the chapter. You can also use the links provided to websites on page 69. Most of these resources help you clarify your values. I encourage you to take the additional step to define what it means to *live* your values. The more specific you can be about how you will know if you are living and fulfilling your values the better you can make life and career choices that align with them. For example, if you list family as a core value, what does this mean *for you?* Does it mean that you visit your grandparents every weekend? Does it mean that you want to start your own family? If so, by when? How much time and in what ways do you want to spend with your family relative to your career obligations? Being clear about and prioritizing your values as they relate to your life and career choices is a vital step in determining your authentic health career path.

Assess the Implications of Core Values on Your Health Career Options and Timing

Now that you have identified, defined and prioritized your values, there are three key related considerations:

1. What is the window of time in which you want to be working toward, living and fulfilling your values?
2. What are the implications of your values and the window of time in which you want to be living them relative to your career choices?
3. Will the lifestyle and central functions associated with the health career I intend to pursue or am pursuing enable me to sufficiently live according to my values?

FINDING YOUR WHY

In addition to assessing and defining your core values, it is important to be sure you fully understand and own your "why" you want to pursue a specific health career direction and if you already have one, why you want to pursue that one and/or change to another job or path. I have been told many reasons *why* the students and health professionals I worked with wanted to pursue health careers. Some of the most common and compelling why's have been:

- Called to care for and heal people who are ill or suffering
- Passion for prevention of disease and promotion of health and wellness
- Burning desire to serve my community or people from similar backgrounds
- Love of science and the human body
- Commitment to social justice
- Desire for status and prestige
- Motivated to secure a profession and employment with solid income, stability, and security.
- Drawn to specific aspects of the role that align with your passion and skills
- Family expectations
- Have "known" since an early age or an important life event
- Stimulated by a personal, family, or community health experience

The last three why's are particularly common among the pre-health students, graduate students, and health professionals I have worked with. While they are legitimate reasons, it is useful to examine them, and all of your other why's, in more depth as you refine your authentic health career direction.

The more conscious and clear you can be about *why* you want to pursue specific health career, job, and educational paths the more your why's can guide your path and choices. Your why's can serve as a North Star to inform and filter your choices and as a powerful source of motivation and strength/resilience to return to when you encounter hard work and challenges on your journey. Your journey to health careers will most likely be time-consuming and expensive and while rewarding the work can be very challenging. There are also so many different options to choose among. For maximum guidance and motivation, it makes a difference if the why's are deeply rooted in who you are and what you want and not weighted more toward external factors or other people.

For example, one of my former students—Juan—was really struggling between being a doctor or becoming a leader in health policy. He graduated from college and still wasn't sure, yet he felt he had to make some major decisions about applying to medical school or pursuing a job in health policy. During our life-career planning workshop, he was visibly anxious and confused. He came up to me afterward, and during our discussion it seemed that the primary reason he wanted to be a doctor was to realize his mother's dream. She was a single mother who came to this country as an immigrant and had worked three jobs and made tremendous sacrifices for him to become a doctor. Another why is that he wanted to be able to take care of her and provide her with a comfortable lifestyle. He was also passionate about improving health for low-income and minority individuals and populations, but, at the time, he seemed to believe that his skills and interests were more aligned with advancing health policy change. At that point, I thought he would shift his focus to health policy.

Juan wisely chose not to apply for medical school or graduate programs in health policy because he wasn't really sure about what he really wanted and why. He took advantage of an opportunity to work on policy and other non-clinical aspects of health as a gap year after college to figure out his why and what he really wanted to do. During that year, he ended up deciding that he really did want to become a doctor, not just to live up to his mother's dreams but also because he really did feel called to care for sick patients and empower them to take charge of their own health. He also believed that being a physician would give him the knowledge and credibility to be a leader in changing health policy and that he could gain the necessary skills by securing an MPH while attending medical school. With his why now clear, he ended up applying and getting accepted to a dream medical school where the values and population served aligned with his, and where he got a full ride. He is very happy and doing quite well in medical school and will soon be pursuing an MPH in health policy and management. Juan will be an amazing doctor and policy champion who is very clear on his why.

What are your why's? Take the time to consciously assess and define them. One way to get at your health career why's are to do an assessment called the 5 Why's which is Exercise 2 in the End of Chapter Exercises.

PURPOSE

A major reason why you may want to pursue a particular health career is because it aligns with your core career purpose. I define core career purpose as your primary reason being and/or for doing the work you do or want to do. Your core career purpose can encompass your why's and may be more specific about your reason for being.

Clarifying your core career purpose can have the same powerful benefits as businesses defining their core purpose. Collins and Porras define a core business purpose defines an "organization's fundamental reason for being which serves as the foundation for driving decisions and assessing success."[24] They described that when properly conceived, **purpose** is broad, fundamental and enduring; a good **purpose** should serve to guide and inspire the organization for years, Collins and Porras studied the most successful companies and found that having and acting upon a clear purpose, along with core values—as you worked on earlier in the chapter—had greater chances of enduring success and adaptability.

---

[24] Collins and Porras, "Vision."

Businesses have core purposes from which everything else flows. Disney's purpose, for example, is to make people happy. Disney has pursued many different business and entertainment opportunities and designed all their initiatives to help make people happy. They have also been incredibly successful financially. You can too.

If you believe that everyone has a purpose, then defining your own can really be helpful in deciding what you want to do in your career. For many of us, defining your core career purpose may be easier said than done, particularly at a young age and/or early in your career. Don't sweat it. It's okay. It is something to reflect on and work toward refining over time or, as with me, it might just come to you when you have a breakthrough moment of knowing. If and when it does come, it can be liberating and very useful for your career choices, even more so if you choose to pursue it.

After years of struggling and searching, I found that my purpose was to empower others to realize their full potential. With the clarity of and a commitment to living this purpose, I eventually used it to guide my career and job choices. For some, a life purpose may come from a spiritual place or a higher power, but for others, it can come from getting in touch with your passions, experiences, perceived injustices, or commitments and, for some, from strategic thinking. Regardless of where it comes from, defining your purpose can help you choose and achieve a career that enables you to have the life and impact you want and are meant to have and filter choices and adjustments along your path throughout your journey.

ALIGN YOUR CAREER PATH WITH YOUR VALUES AND PURPOSE

At the peak of my career as a senior health executive, I had a very well-paying job with lots of influence and autonomy for one of the top academic medical centers in the world. I was also teaching at Harvard. On paper I should have been extremely happy. I also had a wonderful wife and marriage; two healthy, happy children; and a beautiful home.

Unfortunately, I was miserable. I grumbled all the way to work and all the way home. I went to the doctor with a sore throat only to be asked if I was depressed. My body and soul were telling me that while I liked and was challenged by the work I had done for 20 years, it was time to do work fully aligned with my purpose and values. After more than three years of soul-searching and confronting my fears about making a dramatic change when I "had it so good," I found the courage to take a 70% salary cut when my third child was on the way and move our family across the country to fully pursue work that aligned with my purpose and values. Although it was financially challenging for many years, it was the best career decision I ever made, and it enabled me to have almost two decades of fulfillment and advancement of my purpose and core values on so many levels.

With your core values, why's, and purpose clarified, you can assess how different health professions, jobs, and organizations would enable you to live them and achieve your values and definition of success. It is also important to understand your preferences and style.

UNDERSTANDING YOUR PREFERENCES AND STYLE

Distinct from clarifying your values and purpose is understanding what you are good at and enjoy (there are many things you can do but deep down don't really want to do) and how you work best. One way to identify preferences and style is to take different assessments and have them interpreted by a qualified person. Assessments can provide key insights into your strengths, passions, and preferences that you bring to your work and career. While people with all styles and preferences work in the full range of health career options, understanding yours can be beneficial as you assess your fit with the choices you are considering.

There are dozens of different career-related assessments. Examples of some proven personality and career assessments used by students, health professionals, and career-changers are listed below. Many of them have a cost for the test and interpretation, some are free. Check to see if your school, college, health professions school, company, or professional association offer any of these tests and a career-related interpretation. I encourage you to review the primary objective and descriptions of the assessments and intended target audiences to see which are most relevant and resonate with you.

◆ CliftonStrengths (formerly StrengthsFinder) https://www.gallup .com/cliftonstrengths/en/strengthsfinder.aspx
◆ Mapp Career Test https://www.assessment.com/
◆ Meyers-BriggsType Indicator https://www.myersbriggs.org/my-mbti-personality-type/mbti-basics/home.htm?bhcp=1
◆ Riso-Hudson Enneagram Type Indicator https://www.enneagram institute.com/rheti
◆ Self-Directed Search (SDS) http://www.self-directed-search.com/
◆ True Colors https://truecolorsintl.com/the-four-color-personalities/
◆ Who Am I—VisualDNA Quiz https://you.visualdna.com/quiz/ whoami#/quiz

These assessments can be excellent tools for you to use in defining what you are good at and what you enjoy. The assessments do not define who you are and what you should or shouldn't do. They are simply tools for helping you identify your strengths, passions, and preferences.

I encourage you to find someone to help you interpret your results and how they relate to your life and health career decisions. For example, there are certified Meyers–Briggs practitioners who will help you interpret your results as they relate to your health career options. In general, you can usually find someone in your school's career counseling program who can help you understand various assessments and what they might mean for you. Life and career coaches are also very common now, but make sure to check references and certifications before taking advice from anyone. There will be some people who give you advice that discourages you from your authentic path instead of guiding you to it, so it is very important to reflect back on your own values, purpose, and passions and make sure that any person mentoring you is aligned with your values.

YOUR HEALTH CAREER PREFERENCES AND PASSIONS ASSESSMENT

I know that it can be a challenge, particularly early in your life and career, to know yourself and what you want. However, you are faced with critical "choice points" about majors, experiences, career paths, jobs, and graduate education preparation. The clearer you can about your preference and passions, how they relate to specific career paths, and/or taking steps to clarify the answers, the better you will be able to make well-informed decisions in advance of or at critical choice points.

As you advance in your life and career, you may also find that your passions, preferences, and values change. This is natural as we progress through different life stages and we learn, grow, and discover who we are (this is an ongoing life process). Personal, health, family, and relationship circumstances change, which also may lead us to re-evaluate our direction and options.

Changes in the world and industry and work environment can also present new opportunities, needs, and challenges that we may want to pursue or necessitate a change in our direction and path. It is normal for people to have many cycles of change that cause us to re-evaluate our situation. It can either be exciting or painful, depending on how you look at it. Mid-career or midlife crises are common and normal and often occur when we least expect or don't want them. Making adjustments in your health career path or jobs as your needs change is discussed in depth in Chapter 11, which covers lifelong learning and adjustment, and its End of Chapter Exercises.

Remember: Wherever you are, you are exactly where you are supposed to be. The key is to make good choices going forward based on what is important for you.

ASSESS THE KIND OF PERSON YOU WANT TO BE

Brendon Burchard is one of the world's leading personal productivity authors, trainers, and coaches. He coaches and trains many of the top-performing business, entrepreneurial, and social change leaders in the world to be their best and achieve their desired impact. My friend Tony Faulkner connected me to Brendon's trainings, and it transformed my life.

I had already had a successful life, career, and family but was coming off a very visible, major project that didn't work out as planned, and it took a lot out of me. I also realized that while I had been working hard for so many years to live my purpose, help others achieve theirs, and do great things, I was way overextended and wasn't being the kind of person I wanted to be for myself, my family, and my friends. I was also undermining my professional reputation, credibility, and relationships. For example, I had continued to avoid working on this book. Some of my projects were behind. I was working hard and rushing through every day and seemed to only be falling further behind, getting more discouraged and more down. A key turning point came when my wife lovingly gave me feedback that my grumpy, irritable moods; frustration with work; and busy schedule that always had to be accommodated was affecting our relationship and having an impact on my relationship with our children. She was more emotional and serious than I had seen her. I initially resisted and was defensive about her feedback but decided to look in the mirror and face the truth.

While my life circumstances were truly blessed, my experience of them, my behaviors, and my personal and professional relationships were not aligned with the person I wanted to be. I was not sleeping, constantly hurried, was stressed and anxious, and was not enjoying the amazing life I was given and helped create. Things were not going in the right direction. I lacked clarity, focus, discipline, and accountability. Despite all my mindfulness and meditation training, I was increasingly doubtful and was avoiding the things I knew would serve me well. I was suffering from not being the person I wanted to be and was born to be. My success and all I had taken on had come at a significant cost.

A person often meets his destiny on the road he took to avoid it.
—Jean de La Fontaine

Fortunately, I had signed up for an online course from Brendon on Personal Productivity Mastery. I had let it sit for months because "I didn't have time." Watching it—like many things (books, people, experiences, insights) in my life—provided just the insights and inspiration I needed at just the right time. I needed to hear and be willing to answer three fundamental questions that Brendon emphasized. As part of our high-performance plans, we should all ask ourselves:

◆   What kind of person do you aspire to be?
◆   How do you want to show up personally, professionally, and with family?
◆   How do you want to connect and interact with others?

He emphasized the importance of prioritizing our answers to these questions as part of our long-term goals. He also emphasized the importance of asking and reflecting on these questions daily and having the intention, commitment, and accountability to live accordingly. This was a life-changing breakthrough for me just when I needed it.

I had worked hard for decades to create a great life for my family and me, to help others, and to live according to my purpose, but I had never explicitly addressed these questions. I strove to be a nice, caring, positive person who was there for people, and I cared about what they thought of me. However, while I was giving it my all to be that way and do work aligned with my values and purpose, I wasn't conscious of the toll and cost of what it took to do the huge amount of work I was doing on myself and others. I hadn't explicitly answered those questions, nor did I regularly reflect on them and get feedback from people who mattered to me personally and professionally. I now follow Brendon's approach of being intentional and committed to showing up and being the kind of person, I want to be for myself and others. It is a work in progress but has already been transformative. For more information about this and to access all of Brendon's powerful work see his website at https://brendon.com/.

So how do you want to show up in your work and personally? Which among the hundreds of health career paths and jobs will allow you to show up in your overall life the way you really want to? While much of how you show up is a choice that you will make each day regardless of your occupation or job, what you pursue will have a significant impact on what is required of you to do your work and fulfill your personal commitments. I encourage you to be explicit and up front about the kind of person you want to be and choose your path and job with your eyes open about the opportunities and challenges involved in living according to your vision and intention.

> *My mission in life is not merely to survive, but to thrive;*
> *and to do so with some passion, some compassion,*
> *some humor, and some style.*
> —Maya Angelou

ASSESS JOB REQUIREMENTS AND REWARDS

Exposure strategies in Chapter 3 will help you become more aware of the hundreds of health career options. Each will have a defined scope of responsibilities and its own set of educational and professional requirements for entry into training programs, securing jobs, and for advancement in the field. Each also has different associated paths. Each has its own set of opportunities, challenges, and rewards.

As you consider various options that interest you, I encourage you to thoroughly do your homework to fully understand the associated scope, requirements, and rewards including the following factors:

- Prerequisite course work
- Required competencies to secure employment and be effective in your role (current and future)
- How workers in this role spend their time and what they are responsible for each day and associated sources of satisfaction, stressors, and frustration
- Level and nature of patient or community interaction
- How the work will get done in this profession now and in the future
- Role that technology and data will play and how they will shape health careers and jobs in the next 10 years
- Steps involved and average time to enter and advance
- Length of time and cost of educational requirements
- Hour and lifestyle requirements
- Current and future levels of compensation and associated requirements

A practical example of a resource you can use to assess if a particular career path is a fit for you are insights from the California Institute for Behavioral Health Solutions (CIBHS) regarding if Behavioral Health is right for you. Behavioral Health careers are some of the fastest growing and most needed in California and nationally.

Here is what CIBHS suggests are some of the characteristics of people who would meet the requirements and be a good fit for behavioral health careers: "People with strong skills and traits in the following areas might be well-suited for a career in mental health, including excellent listening skills, advanced verbal and written communication skills, having empathy and compassion toward others, possessing clear and healthy personal boundaries, belief in people's capacity to change, comfort, with ambiguity, critical thinking, being non-judgmental, the ability to be discrete, authentic, and self-aware and the ability to recognize and seek out help when you need it for yourself."[25] There are many technical and training requirements in addition to these skills and traits that behavioral health workers need that you would want to become aware of before you pursue one of them.

Another example of how to assess your fit with a specific career path is to look at the competencies that have been established for the profession you are considering and the education and training programs you will need to complete. Most health professions are becoming competency-driven. You can review the competencies to assess if, with training, you could and would want to develop proficiency in them to be enter the field and be an effective professional. You can assess if training and working with these competencies would be something you would be good at and enjoy. Keeping with our behavioral health theme, the Substance Use and Mental Health Services Administration (SAMHSA) and Health Resources and Services Administration have established core competencies for integrated behavioral health and primary care (a major healthcare improvement focus being implemented nationally and locally).[26] Competencies have also been established for many other health professions including public health,[27] nurse practitioners,[28] and physician assistants.[29]

---

[25] CIBHS, "Careers."

[26] SAMSHA, "Core Competencies."

[27] PHF, "Public Health."

[28] Nurse Practitioner Schools, "NP."

[29] AAPA, "Competencies."

ASSESS FAMILY CONSIDERATIONS

Many people of all genders, ages, and backgrounds identify family as a priority value. I encourage you to consider how your health career and job choices will influence your ability to full your family values. Having enough time to enjoy and meet family responsibilities in a way that you fulfill that value can be a challenge in some health career paths and jobs while others may offer significant time and flexibility. For example, hospital CEOs, partners in health consulting firms, and doctors in busy medical practices have demanding schedules and responsibilities that will make it a challenge for them to have enough family time. However, their income and levels of influence can provide their families with tremendous life opportunities and privileges. Advanced practice or registered nurses, pharmacists, or radiology techs have impactful jobs and may be able to do shift work and have a part-time schedule that fits with their other responsibilities and still make high levels of compensation. I encourage you to know what you are getting into professionally and which types of work environments within those professions best align with your family goals.

When my first son was born, I made being a great father and fulfilling my family goals top priority core values. My goals were to be actively involved in their lives, be there when they needed me, and have a strong relationship with them. I also committed to being a solid partner with my wife in taking care of family responsibilities in addition to meeting our financial needs. My commitments to fulfilling these values were key factors in my decision to leave my senior health executive job to become a consultant and educator. I went from working 70-plus hours per week, including 7 a.m. meetings and 6 to 9 p.m. meetings two to three days per week to working for myself at home and being able to take my son for morning walks, feed him lunch, and help my wife make dinner in the early evening. I returned to be a health executive a couple years later to take advantage of an amazing career opportunity and fulfill a commitment made to my wife to try to live on the East Coast. However, as we were blessed to have two additional wonderful children, I once again left being a health executive to become an educator at UC Berkeley, which provided me with the autonomy and schedule flexibility to coach sports, have nightly family dinners, attend dance recitals, and enjoy wonderful family vacations. While I made less money, my family experience and living according to my values was priceless.

When Do You Want to Have a Family?

People of all gender preferences and identities face considerations about whether or not to have a family and, if so, when. These choices can be particularly challenging given the timing, cost, and long length of education and training required for many health professions. Many professions also require major work and time commitments to advance and achieve important levels of status and income, such as becoming a partner in a medical practice, a senior health executive, or a tenured professor. Your age, stage of education, professional standing, required work commitment, and level of income are all important to consider when making decisions about children and family.

I encourage you to consider you and your life partner or family as a system when making these decisions. One thing to keep in mind is that you actually don't know until you have the child. If you already have children, then you will have to consider and balance what is in their interests and yours. One thing is for sure: you only get one chance to spend time with your children, enjoy them, and give them a good start in life. It goes by faster than you think.

Caring for parents and/or family members is also an important consideration, especially for those of us in the sandwich generation or who want or need to financially and emotionally support their families. I know several people who need the time, energy, and flexibility to care for aging parents and their children. I know people, particularly students and early careerists, who struggle to provide financial support to their families and want to earn a great living in order to provide a better life for their parents. These are important income and lifestyle considerations as you choose and actively pursue your authentic path and plan future jobs. I commend those of you who are committed to financially supporting your parents and families. I encourage you to remember that to fulfill your goals, you still need a health career through which you can be successful, happy, and healthy. Make good life and career choices now and along the way so you can meet your core family values.

Assess How Potential Career Paths, Jobs, and Employers Align with Who You Are and What You Want

After you have assessed and defined your core career values, why's, purpose, and aspirations for the kind of person you want to be, you can use these powerful insights as a filter for choices about the health career paths and jobs you pursue and the places where you work. Your work on the exposure and experience elements of the Framework will increase your awareness and knowledge of health career options and those that most interest you. Armed with this knowledge, you can then assess how the nature of the career path and future job roles that interest you will fit with who you are and what you want. Be very honest because you are the one who has to devote all the effort, time, and energy along the journey to enter the field and potentially spend more time with your work than with your family and other things you enjoy doing. It's critical to assess if there is alignment between who you are and what you want and the nature of the career path **before** rather than after you enter a health profession. You also want to be sure that the jobs and employers you choose will enable you to live the life you want.

It's okay if you don't know the answers to these questions now. The key is to build time into your career exploration plans to be sure you can develop answers and find aligned careers. Strategies for you to gain exposure to the nature of health career options, how they align with your core career values and their lifestyle implications are detailed in Chapter 3.

Getting practical experience—through the strategies in Chapter 5—and reflecting on it will also give you much more information about the work you are considering doing and position you to make better choices and make the case for you to advance.

WHAT ARE EMPLOYERS LOOKING FOR?

In addition to assessing your own preferences and values, it is important to understand what employers in the health field you want to work in are looking for now and in the future. Based on my extensive work with employers in the healthcare, public health, and behavioral health fields, in addition to profession- and position-specific technical requirements, they are also looking for the following critical essential competencies that apply to all workers:

◆ Critical thinking and problem-solving
◆ Written and oral communication
◆ Team leadership and followership
◆ Analytical skills and knowledge of Excel
◆ Interpersonal skills and navigate organizational culture
◆ Project management
◆ Initiative and independence
◆ Adaptability and flexibility
◆ Enthusiasm
◆ Ability to deal with ambiguity
◆ Resiliency

I encourage you to assess your interests and capabilities relative to these competencies in addition to the technical requirements of your field when determining your path forward. From both categories consider which you are truly good at and enjoy doing now and which you authentically have the aptitude and desire to develop. As indicated in the Life and Career Alignment Triangle, the more aligned what you are good at and enjoy doing are with what employers need and your values and goals, the more motivation and power you will have to have the success, fulfillment, and impact you desire.

ENSURING YOUR JOB IS ALIGNED WITH YOUR PRIORITIES

The assessment considerations outlined in the first half of this chapter focused on helping you choose your authentic health career path. Once you are pursuing a particular path you also have to make well-informed choices about jobs and advancement. The considerations outlined in the remainder of this chapter will help you make good choices about jobs and organizations that are aligned with your values and goals.

WHAT DO YOU WANT IN A WORK ENVIRONMENT?

In addition to clarifying the work you want to do, I encourage you to also define what you want in a work environment. I have known many people who choose their authentic health career path based on jobs and work environments. Work environment considerations include bosses, work pace, co-workers, travel, family friendliness, and more.

Having a good boss is always an important factor in your job satisfaction but is especially critical when you are just out of school and taking one of your first career-focused jobs. If you have a boss who can see you for what you are capable of and can help you get the right kind of experience and challenges, they can help open many doors for you and aid in your professional development. That is worth a lot. On the other hand, there are bosses who see you only as a way to get the job done for them. They do not notice your potential or see ways to help you grow. Early in your career, you really need a boss who cares about your development and can help you progress in the direction that is best for you.

The other reason it is so important to have a good boss is pure job satisfaction. If you got your dream job but it came with a boss you didn't like or didn't work well with, you would most likely not be happy in your position. Countless studies cite dissatisfaction with bosses as the *number one* reason people quit their job. If you don't like your boss, it makes it very difficult to do your job well.

I was very lucky when I came out of graduate school to have a boss who gave me exactly the right kind of responsibilities to help me grow. She knew what my goals were, gave me perfect experience to pursue those goals, challenged me, and promoted me, and within three years, I was vice president of the organization.

Work pace is another important consideration. What kind of work pace do you like? I have some students who get bored easily and need a fast-paced, constantly changing role. I knew a woman who worked in a department at Kaiser that was very good, but very slow. She was high energy and wanted to be challenged, so although this was a good position, she was not happy in this job; it drove her crazy working at such a comfortable pace. On the flip side, I know many students who are more laid-back and like completing projects and tasks at a slower pace. Some individuals get anxious with a fast-paced, hectic work environment. What is the best pace for you?

The **mission and values** of a company you choose to work for will ideally match and align with your own mission and values. Working according to your values is priceless. However, it might not be the most important consideration for you when finding a job.

I hope it is becoming vividly clear that this chapter is not just about assessing yourself regarding your passions and strengths. Half of assessment is about assessing *which things are the most important to you* when searching for a job. It would be impossible to go through this chapter, answer all the questions, and find a job that fulfills every single one of your preferences. The reality is that no job is perfect.

I believe that there is a job that is *right* for you, a job that is a *very good fit*. I am not asking you to keep searching until you find a job that aligns with your values, gives you a perfect boss, goes at exactly the right pace, deals with things you are passionate about, utilizes your strongest assets, *and* gives you high pay and excess vacation time. It's simply impossible. I am asking you to go through this chapter and make a list for yourself, your own list. I am asking you to evaluate yourself and your options and go from there.

Moving on, another work environment issue regards **family friendliness**. Some work environments, companies, and bosses are much more conducive to having a family and spending time with them than others. There are some jobs that will eliminate you from consideration immediately if during the interview you so much as mention vacation time. Some jobs don't want people who even think about time off. And maybe that's you. Maybe it is important to you to work hard and challenge yourself, and having a family is not something you are thinking about. Maybe, however, you are someone who wants to start a family in a few years. This is something you should think about when applying for jobs now. There are many jobs where the hours, type of work, or bosses work very well with a family-focused person, and if this is you, those are the types of jobs you might want to look at.

A more obvious work environment consideration is your **co-workers**. I have had some students whose top criterion for a job was having co-workers who stimulate and challenge them and have the same values. Being in a supportive, friendly, and helpful work environment is important and will ultimately make you happier.

Countless students I have talked to tell me the same thing that they *know* they don't want in a career: **to be behind a desk all day**. This is a common consideration that many people find out very quickly about themselves, but it is something you have to be careful with. Sometimes, even if you know that you don't want a desk-ridden work environment, you must pay your dues and temporarily do work that might put you behind that desk all day. This is sometimes the way that early stages of many careers work, but as you progress and advance, your job will evolve into something less contained and singular. After a certain promotion or change of focus in your job, you might be running around and going from meeting to meeting and no two hours will be the same. You would probably consider my job, for example, a desk job. And I do, in fact, have to sit at my desk and get certain things done, but I am also out in the community speaking, teaching, traveling, and more. My job is constantly changing.

On that same note, **travel and adventure** might be very important to you. Some people want a job that allows them to see the world. They want a job that involves adventure and movement and excitement. However, the other side of this is that if you are traveling constantly for work, you will live in hotel rooms and eat out all the time and be far from family and friends. Maybe this is something you want now but will not want for 10 years straight. You can look at a job and see what the advancement is like. Maybe you will be traveling for the first two years in this job but then you can get promoted to a more stable role.

Finally, you should look at the **opportunity for growth and advancement** and the **experience** that a job will give you. You should always assess what type of experience you will get from a job, what skills you will learn or how it can build your resume and make that part of your overall strategy. This means that you do not have to enter your dream job right away if a different job gives you the experience to help you advance toward a more preferred job. On the other hand, you can look at the growth and advancement within a company you are striving to work for. Maybe the position you take at first is not what you are dying to do, but you can see that there is a lot of opportunity in the company for you to advance, learn, and grow into larger and better roles that you are much more passionate about.

A big consideration is your **work–life balance**. How much of your life energy do you want to be devoted to work? It is something that will probably change over your lifetime, but this is something you have to pay close attention to. Always keep in mind that you can create the life you want and the work you love.

OTHER CONSIDERATIONS ALONG YOUR JOURNEY

As I mentioned earlier, many people don't know exactly what they are passionate about or what types of issues, jobs, or organizations they want to work on. You might not know what kind of boss or co-workers you want, and you may have no idea whether you would enjoy a desk job. The good news is that you don't always need to know. **Sequencing** is a way to help relieve this all-encompassing pressure of needing to know. One part of sequencing involves taking a step even if you aren't sure that it's in the exact right direction. I know a recent graduate who is interested in public health, education, and writing but doesn't know the specifics of what she wants to do, who she wants to work with, and so on. She took a job teaching in an after-school program for underprivileged kids, and she learned that she likes working with kids, but that this particular work environment isn't right for her. She still hasn't figured out exactly what she wants to do, but she has begun the process of narrowing it down.

Another form of sequencing involves knowing what you want but not being able to pursue it for various reasons. Another student of mine graduated from UC Berkeley and knew exactly what type of job she wanted. She applied for positions in her field both in the Bay Area as well as in Washington, D.C., where her family lived. A main concern for her was moving back to Washington, D.C., after being away from her family for four years, so when she was offered a job in both places, she had a difficult decision to make. She was offered a job in the Bay Area that wasn't exactly what she wanted but paid significantly more than the D.C. job. The D.C. job was more aligned with her preferences and values. In the end, she chose the job in the Bay Area because it would allow her to pay off her student loans.

She never lost sight of her goals and eventually made it to her family and the job that she wanted in D.C., but she was much more financially secure when she made the jump.

Another student I had grew up poor and ultimately wanted to work with underprivileged individuals, and she came to me and asked if it would be wrong to take a different job that made more money first, before she went on to pursue what she was passionate about. This is absolutely okay. Your authentic path will not always be a smooth straight road. Sometimes you have to take on an experience that will move you forward even if it isn't exactly what you want or if you don't yet know what you want.

While some individuals do not yet know what they are passionate about, others are overwhelmed with the number of things they might want to do. If you have multiple passions, you could look for **multifaceted roles**. Multifaceted roles are ones that allow you to do a combination of things. For example, individuals who work in academic medical centers are able to teach, see patients, do research, and more. Because of the nature of the position, they can decide which of those things they want to focus on more and which fits with their lifestyle at that particular time. It is important to remember that you can have different emphases over time. There may be times in your life where it is more important to make money, so you focus on the part of your job that will make you more money. Other times, you may want a stronger focus on your own family values, so you can take the role that allows for that.

Another way to address the issue of having many passions is the **portfolio approach**. This means that you don't have to get everything from your job. You can fulfill some of your passions and desires through volunteer work or hobbies. An example of this is a woman I know who was very passionate about international health issues. She wanted to work on health issues in Africa but decided that having a family was not conducive to this kind of work. She ended up taking a job working with a student health organization, something that aligned with her family values, but then every summer she volunteered in Africa for three weeks. That was not part of her job, but she wanted to make an impact in a specific way that her job did not focus on, so she was able to make her impact through volunteer work in the summer.

In line with these ideas is **centrality**. Centrality is how central you make one specific part of your life, an idea from Greg Hicks and Rick Foster's book *How We Choose to Be Happy*. They found that people who are truly happy find what makes them happy and then make that thing central to their life and work. It's quite simple, really.

> *Centrality is happy people's nonnegotiable choice*
> *to pursue the greatest passions of their minds and*
> *hearts. In other words, they make central to their lives*
> *that which brings them the greatest joy.*
> —Greg Hicks and Rick Foster

Sometimes, of course, this isn't possible. Depending on life circumstances, you may have to make that passion secondary or fulfill it through volunteer work. Other times, the opportunity arises for you to bring the thing that makes you happiest into a more central role. For example, when I was a health executive I started teaching on the side at Harvard, but my primary job was as a health executive. Over time, I realized that what I really love and what really makes me happy is teaching and working with students, so I decided to make that part of my life more central. I took the job at UC Berkeley because it made working with students more central. Centralizing is not always an easy thing to do, but it will always bring you greater fulfillment and happiness.

One way to do this is to find a work setting that enables **self-direction**. If you are in a position where your organization dictates everything you do, it may not be as easy to shift your focus to the thing that you are most passionate about. This is something that I considered in my own journey. When I chose to work at UC

Berkeley, I was able to focus on the kinds of issues I was passionate about and align my work with my values. Being in a self-directed role gives you the power to decide where to focus your energies and passions. Many people do this by having their own business, such as a health consulting business. The more you can align yourself with your values, goals, and passions, the happier and more successful you will be.

However, that being said, you also have to take another thing into account: **paying your dues**. Many students think that they should go right to the role of responsibility, directly to the position they want, without having to take the smaller steps. I had a student who, right after graduating, was offered a job after interning at a prestigious hospital. Any job at this hospital would look very good on a resume, and on top of that, my student was working with well-esteemed co-workers who could really help him pursue his goals. Two months into the job, he came to me very frustrated because all he was doing was data entry. It bored and frustrated him, and he really thought it was demeaning work. He asked if I thought he should quit. I told him definitely not. Even though it wasn't glamorous, and it wasn't very much fun, an entry-level job like that is part of paying your dues, part of helping where there's need and using it as a chance to make connections and get experience. He stuck with the job for a year, applied to med school, and got into the top school of his choice. The experience he had gained, combined with the letters of recommendation he received from his co-workers, helped him get to where he wanted to go. That is what is important to remember when you find yourself in a place that may not be where you want to be or where you think you deserve to be. You sometimes have to take on those responsibilities and positions to pay your dues, make the connections you need, and get experience that will ultimately help you.

There are dozens of stages that you will go through in your career journey, and as I said before, this is not a linear road you are embarking on. The important thing is to be really clear about what kind of life you want and make clear choices aligned with your preferences and values. If you do these things, **your life and career will become integrated**. It may not happen right away and it will change with your changing life circumstances, but you should be moving toward an integrated life-career balance no matter what stage you are in. Remember that you can have a career and lifestyle that enable you to live exactly how you want to live.

HOW TO ASSESS YOURSELF NOW

Now that you have learned about the key self- and career-path assessment considerations and tools described in this chapter; it is time for you to do the work. I encourage you to carve out time in your schedule to develop your answers to all the assessment questions or at least those that will be most helpful to informing your health career or job decisions. Many of the questions may not be easy to answer and may take some reflection and further exploration over time. Be patient but persistent in working to develop clear answers to guide your choices. It's okay and normal if your answers change as you increase your self-awareness and gain more life and work experience. The key is to do the work, develop definitive or working answers and actively pursue additional assessment as needed given where you are in your life, career, and educational journey.

As you conduct your assessment, you may find it helpful to engage and get appropriate feedback from trusted mentors, advisors, coaches, colleagues, friends, and family. Their insights, experience, and perceptions of you can be beneficial input for you to consider. However, remember that only you can truly know and decide who you are and what you want and that often it may be different than what others want for you based on their interests, values, fears, and comfort. Chapter 10 on belief and courage contains many insights and practical tips on how to decide on and go for what you really and deal with challenges you encounter with important others who may not support your authentic path.

Your time is limited, so don't waste it living someone else's life. Don't let the noise of other's opinions drown out your inner voice. Most important, have the courage to follow your heart and intuition. They somehow already know what you truly want to become. Everything else is secondary.
—Steve Jobs, Stanford Commencement Speech, 2005

In addition to addressing the assessment questions in the chapter and getting feedback from others, you can also pursue the assessment tests outlined on page 77 of this chapter and get support from trained counselors or coaches who can help you interpret them. There are also paid or free assessment exercises you can do online or workshops you can attend. These can provide helpful structure, questions and feedback for you to do and reflect on the work.

Assessment exercises are similar to assessment tests in that they will help you reflect and discover things about yourself that you might not have known or thought of before. Assessment exercises are designed to get you thinking and to inspire you to come up with your own answers. They will ask you questions that require a great deal of reflection and digging deep, but the result will be very satisfying and authentic, because you will come out of it with answers that *you* discovered. One example of an assessment exercise is that might be useful to you is my **Life-Career Planning Questionnaire**:

Drawing on my 35 years' experience helping students and career-changers find their authentic path, I have developed my own life-career planning questionnaire to get you thinking about all aspects of your life, preferences, values, and so on and how they can relate to a career. It is an eight-part questionnaire with questions and organizational charts that will help you find your authentic career path. It is divided into sections based on discovering WHO you are, WHAT you want, and HOW to align the many factors involved in your self-discovery. To learn more and to access the questionnaire, please visit my website, Jeffoxendine.com.

END OF CHAPTER EXERCISES

Exercise 1: Assessing and Defining Your Core Career Values

I encourage you to complete the table below as a tool to clarify your core career values. Identify up to seven values that will guide your personal and professional choices and way of living (see list of values on my website). For each one, define what living according to that value means to now and when you are living your authentic life and health career. Rank them in priority order as a what to help you understand their level of importance and as a basis for making trade-offs.

Value	Define	Rank

Value	Define	Rank

For those of you who want to go into further levels of specificity and the tradeoffs involved in what you value and the benefits you can gain through your authentic health career, I encourage you to go to my website and complete the Benefits of Your Health Career Assessment (Jeffoxendine.com). I developed and utilized this tool with physician groups to decide and prioritize what they wanted to get of their practice, so it is particularly relevant and well suited for those of you who are or want to be a physician or another type of clinician that can operate their own practice. It is also useful for consultants, entrepreneurs, coaches, or others wanting to start their own business.

Exercise 2: Finding Your Why

Why do you want to pursue the role and impact you are intending?

◆ 5 Why's
   ☐ Write down *why* you want to pursue this direction.

   ☐ Continue to answer why four more times

□   Share your answers with a mentor, peer, or friend

Exercise 3: Six Words to Describe Your Authentic Health Career Path

This exercise is self-explanatory and very simple, but it can be motivating and interesting to see what comes to mind for you. Here are some examples that students of mine have come up with in the past:

"Devoted to serving underserved populations."—Student
"Won't let anyone stop me."—Student
"Seeking the fullest expression of self."—Oprah Winfrey
"Empower people to realize their potential."—Jeff Oxendine

What are the six words that describe you or your authentic health career?

Exercise 4: What do you want in a job?

As I talked about earlier in the chapter, everyone will have different things that are more important to them when searching for a job. After reading what some of those things are in this chapter, I want you to look through the list below (everything in the list is contextualized and explained within the chapter), pick the top five most important things to you when looking for a career, and then write them next to the numbers provided.

Work Environment:
Boss
Work pace
Mission and values
Co-workers
"Not behind a desk all day"
Travel and adventure
Work–life balance
Experience
Opportunity for growth and advancement

Other Considerations:
Sequencing
Multifaceted roles/Portfolio approach/Different emphasis over time
Centrality vs. secondary or volunteer roles
Settings that enable self-direction and values
Paying your dues
Life and career become integrated

1)

2)

3)

4)

5)

Now that you have made your own list, write out your preferences for each consideration you chose. For example, if you wrote "Work pace" as your third-most important consideration when finding a job, describe what your ideal work pace is. Do this for everything in your list.

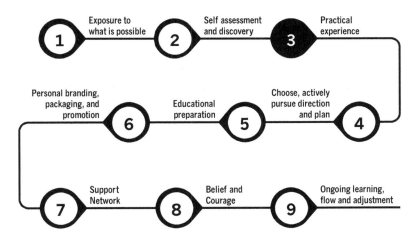

FRAMEWORK STEP 3

PRACTICAL EXPERIENCE

The only source of knowledge is experience.
—Albert Einstein

There is no substitute for experience.
—Proverb

Practical Experience is the third step in the Life and Career Planning Framework. This chapter will help you understand the value of practical experience as a way to validate and expand your health career options, gain valuable skills, and strengthen your positioning to advance toward achieving your authentic health career. It will provide you with an understanding of what type of experience matters and several strategies for gaining valuable experience.

While it is essential to gain exposure to health career options and assess how they fit with who you are and what you want, there is no substitute for practical experience. By gaining more practical experience you can have firsthand knowledge of the health professions you are interested in, develop key competencies and relationships, and establish a track record to strengthen your competitiveness for jobs, health training programs, and career advancement.

Practical experience matters a lot in the health field. In many professions, such as public health, most graduate programs want you to have at least two years of paid post-undergraduate experience before even applying. Public health also requires each student in an MPH program to have a practicum or internship experience during their program. Physician assistant programs require a minimum number of clinical hours before you are eligible to apply. Many behavioral health careers, such as licensed clinical social workers and marriage and family therapists, require hours of practical experience to be eligible for licensure. Even medical schools are increasingly favoring people who can competitively meet the entrance requirements *and* have relevant post-undergraduate work experience. In fact, according to the American Association of Medical Colleges, the average age of students entering medical school is now 24 years old.[30]

Health employers are also increasingly prioritizing the quantity and quality of candidate work experience. If candidates meet the educational and licensure qualifications for a position, relevant work experience through which skills, responsibilities, and accomplishments aligned with job requirements are demonstrated is often a key determining factor in who gets interviewed and hired. In many large

---

[30] AAMC, "Age."

urban areas and desirable suburban and rural areas, there are ample applicants who meet the educational qualifications for health jobs so experience pre and post health professions training can be the differentiator among candidates. Even with high-demand jobs like nursing and nurse practitioners, where graduates have excellent training and are licensed, employers are often looking for candidates with experience to ensure that they are able to function effectively in complex patient care environments.

I have increasingly found that very talented graduates from top health professions training programs who lack much pre-training program experience are having a harder time competing for internships and post-graduation jobs, residencies, and fellowships if that don't have enough pre-, during-program, and post-internship experience.

WHY DOES EXPERIENCE MATTER SO MUCH?

In my extensive experience working with health professions programs and health employers, I have found that work experience matters so much and continuously becomes more important because it enables them to more confidently assess your:

- Understanding of and commitment to what you are pursuing
- Ability to effectively handle the responsibilities, workload, and dynamics
- Knowledge, skills, and expertise aligned with success requirements
- Maturity and professionalism
- Resourcefulness, problem-solving, and experience you bring to known and unknown challenges
- Ability to get things done independently, with supervision and working with others
- Perspective and wisdom you bring and will contribute to others and the organization

◆ Differentiate and strengthen the reputation and performance of the organization

In addition to how it will help strengthen your attractiveness and competitiveness for health professions programs and health employers, experience also enables you to:

◆ Assess and make better-informed choices about your life, authentic career direction and corresponding education and training needs
◆ Discover what you don't want to do before making significant investments of time and money
◆ Demonstrate your qualifications, skills, and capabilities relative to your authentic path
◆ Contribute more to health professions schools and employers
◆ Get accepted to better health training programs and secure more funding
◆ Secure better jobs and get paid more and advance faster and farther

ELLIOTT'S STORY

I met Elliot when he was a Health Career Connection summer intern. He had a unique combination of an undergraduate degree in nursing and business. He served in the Army during a conflict, which gave him experience international experience, and saw firsthand the need for improved health support for people in refugee situations. When he completed school, he had a choice to make about the kind of experience to pursue. He chose to first work as a clinical nurse to gain experience and credibility in patient care. After a couple years of clinical experience, he decided it was time to pursue his passion for providing healthcare to refugees displaced due to conflict.

Elliot spent a year treating refugees in the Sudan. He was part of a team of people who were experts and did this work all over the world. He highly respected them and found the work very rewarding. However, he also learned that the people who did it were "lifers," meaning they were so committed to the work that for their life, they went from conflict to conflict, caring for refugees in different parts of the world. Most didn't have families or home bases they spent a lot of time in. His experience made it clear to Elliott that while he loved the international work, he wanted to have a family and enough time to be with them. He also wanted to have work that allowed him to have a base in the United States. His clinical experience was great, and he now wanted to transition more to the management aspects of health. His experience helped him get accepted to a prestigious MBA and MPH program. He came home and got engaged to his fiancée. He completed his graduate program, during which time he did an internship with a healthcare consulting firm to get firsthand experience with consulting. He found he liked it, and it got his foot in the door for his job when he finished graduate school. He now is happily married, has two young daughters, and loves his consulting job. Practical experience informed his life and career choices and helped him secure his authentic health career.

GETTING EXPERIENCE CAN BE CHALLENGING

While work experience is increasingly important, it isn't often easy to get in the health field. In some cases, such as public health, there is a catch-22 whereby having experience is required to get into graduate school but it is more difficult to get the necessary experience without the graduate degree.

THE WHAT, WHERE, WHY, AND HOW OF EXPERIENCE

Early in your education and career, any kind of health-related experience is valuable. Even better if it is aligned with one of the potential health career paths you are seriously considering or want to explore.

An important step is to find out from employers and health training programs in the health career directions you want to pursue what kind of experience they value and recommend. Career Centers, advisors, and faculty can be helpful sources of this information but don't always have the most up-to-date and accurate knowledge. They may also see if through the lens and network they are most familiar with, like faculty promoting research experience, while employers or health you are interested in may value practical experience more. Seek out information from employers firsthand through informational interviews, in-person and online career fairs, talking with recruiters, and attending conferences and professional association meetings. You can also learn what employers are looking for by reviewing online job postings and descriptions.

Gaining experience also provides you with the opportunity to apply what you learned in school, develop practical skills and technical knowledge needed in your field, and demonstrate your competency with them. You will also have specific examples of work you have done, the results, and what it took to create them that you can share in interviews. For example, my son is pursuing a career in quantitative biology and was able to apply the knowledge he learned in course work in a research lab. He also developed technical skills in the lab that are valuable in both academic and industry roles he can pursue. He demonstrated his ability to use those techniques and the latest equipment and has solid references from lab leader and faculty to attest to his skills. He will be able to put his experience on his resume that will help him get more interviews and then talk about his work and accomplishments in his graduate school and job interviews.

FEEDBACK FROM HEALTH PROFESSIONS SCHOOLS OR OTHER GRADUATE PROGRAMS

One way to learn what kind of experience matters is to speak directly with health admissions staff, faculty, and alumni of health professions programs you want to pursue. They will know what kinds of experiences their programs value and may have suggestions for how and where you can obtain it. For example, many medical schools have broadened their view of relevant experience beyond the traditional research and clinical experience. Hands-on work in community health, health policy, consulting, or global health are examples of the types of experiences that medical schools may value. Gap years are encouraged, and different kinds of experiences are embraced. Experience before med school, rather than going straight through, is increasingly valued and may make you a more well-rounded and attractive candidate. It may also help you be better prepared and have more clarity about what you want. The break from being in school may help you be more mentally and physically ready.

> *I highly recommend having work experience before going to medical school, it was invaluable to me and helped me get where I am today. My medical school classmates who got experience or took time off before medical school were glad that they did and those who didn't wish that they had.*
> —Ashby Wolfe, MD, MPH, MPP

WHAT KIND OF EXPERIENCE?

Many kinds of experiences are valuable, but paid experience is preferred for many reasons. When you are paid, often the work is more meaningful, and you have more formal responsibility and expectations for which you are accountable to superiors and co-workers. Fortunately, there are more options available than ever to gain paid internships and post-undergraduate work experience. There are more roles for undergraduate students during and after school. Clinical examples include scribes, health coaches and navigators, and medical assistants. Non-clinical roles include consultants, population health or quality-improvement analysts, project coordinators, and research assistants. Not only do you get more meaningful experience, but you also get paid (which we all need and deserve).

Employers and health professions schools typically prefer relevant paid experience. They also like to see that through your experience you have had progressively increasing levels of responsibility (project, complexity, people, and budget). Paid experience aligned with the field and organizations you want to pursue can make you a more competitive candidate.

So, given the importance of experience, how do you get more experience at each stage of your career development?

Experience during school:

◆ Volunteer with a community or health-related organization, if possible, one that is relevant to your interests and the career direction you are seeking

◆ Internships—summer or academic year (paid preferred, unpaid okay). Remote internships will likely become more common.

◆ Paid full- or part-time job (health-related preferred if possible)

◆ Work study—work in a health-related role if you can

◆ Work with an instructor or professor in a lab, classroom or in the field (e.g., research assistant, teaching assistant, program assistant)

◆ Class projects focused on real-world health issues on campus or in the community

◆ Enrichment programs that provide practical or research experience

◆ Clinical simulation experience in nursing and allied health fields

◆ National or regional community health-related programs (e.g., Health Leads, Peer Health Exchange, COPE Health Solutions)

◆ Leadership role or active engagement in a student organization (health if possible)

◆ Training and certification program, such as medical assistant, certified nursing assistant, health coaches or navigators, and community health workers

◆ Team or individual project challenges sponsored by companies, professional associations or campus departments (e.g., American College of Healthcare Executives Case Competitions)

◆ Hackathons

Post College Experience (pre-health professions training):

◆ Secure jobs through on-campus recruiting and more broad job search

◆ Internships (many can lead to you being hired for a job afterward)

◆ Fellowship or associate programs (Capital Fellows, CDC Associates)

◆ Corps participation (Peace Corps, Health Corps, Global Health Corps)

◆ National programs (Teach for America, City Year)

◆ Transition to practice programs (recent nursing graduates)

◆ Behavioral health specialist roles

◆ Serving as a medical scribe

Experience during health professions training or graduate school:

◆ Internships

◆ Practicum projects

◆ Course-related projects

◆ Capstone projects or thesis

◆ Graduate student researcher, assistant, or instructor

◆ Part-time or full-time jobs (if you can manage the workload of both)

◆ Special program participation (e.g., Leadership fellows or consulting teams)

◆ Clinical placements

◆ Student-led health programs or initiatives (e.g., UC Davis Student-Led clinics, Suitcase Clinic)

Post-graduate health professions school training:
- ◆ Health administration fellowships (Mass General, Mayo Clinic, Sutter Health)
- ◆ Public health fellowships
- ◆ Postdoctoral fellowships
- ◆ Residencies (nurse practitioner, mental health)

> **If there is one key take away you get from this chapter**
> **is that experience really matters and there are more**
> **options than ever to secure what you need!**

Chapter 6 details all the reasons it is important to get paid work experience prior to applying for graduate health professions school and provides tips on how to convince your parents this is the case. You can also get a quick summary from my blog post at http://myhealthcareernavigator.com/profiles/blogs/the-importance-of-paid-work-experience-before-graduate-school

LIFE EXPERIENCE AND MATURITY SUPPORT SOUND DECISIONS

Getting more paid work experience after college and before applying for health professions schools also helps you gain more life experience and develop more maturity before you have to make major career and graduate education choices. You will likely be in a position to more about who you are and what you want. Studies show that our brains reach maturity about age 25.[31] The parts of our brain that are not fully developed until then are the areas that help us make more rational decisions and struggle less with peer pressure and what others think. Thus, taking time to get paid work experience after college also helps you gain more life experience and more maturity, which

---

[31] Mental Health Daily, "Age."

helps you make better career and graduate education choices that are in your best interests.

UNDERSTAND AND MAKE THE CASE ON HOW YOUR EXPERIENCE IS TRANSFERRABLE TO POTENTIAL NEW DIRECTIONS

As health employers become more specific about the types of experience they want for particular positions, it is more important than ever to be able to be clear about and communicate how your experience is relevant to your career direction and the roles you are pursuing. This isn't always easy to do, and it is a step that many people avoid or don't do well.

This can be particularly challenging is when someone early in their education or career doesn't have much related experience at all. It is common for people to have retail or other types of experience in order to pay the bills and/or support families. Some students also primarily have sports-, music-, art-, or dance-related experiences as that has been their focus for many years. Others have limited experience because they had to focus on education and/or didn't have access to employment. Whatever the situation, you have what you have and need to leverage it the best you can do to get where you want to be.

Good places to start are:

◆ Find someone who will provide an opportunity for your potential not what you have done.

◆ Pursue programs that take into consideration and value the distance you have traveled to get to where you are and will be open to how your experiences apply.

◆ Identify skills and perspectives and wisdom you have gained through your work and lived experience—for example, customer service, teamwork, problem-solving, project or people management, and/or an initiative—that are aligned with what employers are looking for and learn to tell your story. Be able to provide examples.

◆ Draw upon lessons from your experience. Find ways to relate to others.

◆ Establish relationships with mentors and through faculty and informational interviews.

◆ Join professional associations.

◆ Volunteer or get paid experience in the field you want to pursue and with a well-known brand or in which you can get experience beyond your qualifications. Be willing to pay your dues to get in a better position and gain experience for your long-term goal (I started out as janitor in the hospital). You do not have to start out in your dream job.

◆ Find a boss who sees what you can do and will develop you over time by providing you with the right kind of experience at the right time.

THE VALUE OF A BOSS WHO SEES YOUR POTENTIAL AND SUPPORTS YOUR DEVELOPMENT

I went to graduate school without significant previous work experience. Everyone else in my program had several more years of experience. It was a struggle to feel like I belonged and comfortable throughout the program. However, at 25 and fresh out of the program, I was fortunate that, my boss, the CEO of two newly merged hospitals, including one where I had interned, saw the potential in me and hired me to be her Assistant to the President and Chief of Staff. It was an amazing role because I got to see what the CEO's role was like day in and day out (I decided I didn't want the job; talk about the value of experience!) I also was in on all the key meetings and decisions. I got to see how an effective health leader conducted herself and dealt with the many challenges she had to confront. She also knew just how to develop me as a health executive. She listened to my aspiration of being a VP of Operations and gradually, over time, gave me progressively increasing stretch responsibilities as I was almost/barely ready for them. I started by managing the administrative assistants in administration and things such as space and the capital budget. Within three years, I was Executive Director of Clinical Services with more than 500 employees and a $250 million budget. I am deeply indebted for her mentorship and the opportunities provided. Find your Ellie. There are many of them out there in the health field.

HOW IS YOUR EXPERIENCE TRANSFERRABLE TO YOUR NEW PATH?

I am looking for resourceful, innovative problem solvers.
—Susan Ehrlich, CEO,
Zuckerberg San Francisco General Hospital and Trauma Center

If your authentic health career path is different from the ones you have previously pursued and in which you have experience, be confident that you will succeed and that you can make the transition, secure jobs, and have your desired impact. However, sometimes the transition can be challenging and take time. The key is to learn what employers in your new path are seeking and develop a compelling story of how your experience and skills are transferrable and have prepared you to meet and exceed those requirements. As the quote above indicates, many health employers are seeking people who can be innovators and problem-solvers. Solid critical thinking, interpersonal, team, and customer service skills are also in high demand in most health professions. Many types of education and experience prepare you with these kinds of skills, not just traditional health career paths.

Become good at telling the story of how your experience makes you an excellent candidate for the path you want to pursue and get the additional education and experience you need to gain the specialized knowledge, skills, and credentials to be even more competitive and effective.

For example, many of my colleagues in business school, my MPH graduate students at UC Berkeley, and colleagues I worked with in the field had significant experience but not in the new field they were transitioning into. This included engineers with technical expertise trying to become managers, previous biology majors going into biotech marketing, and nurses becoming health administrators. It also included people with years of clinical research experience trying to transition into management roles. It was a challenge for some of them to make the transition and package themselves in a way that employers wanted to hire them. However, with creativity and perseverance, all were able to make the transition when they got better at telling their story and how their experience and skills translated to their new direction.

MIKE'S STORY

Mike was a very bright MPH student in Health Policy and Management. Prior to the HPM program, he had more than 10 years of progressively increasing experience in clinical trial research and management. I could see how bright he was, and his potential. However, employers hiring interns and post-MPH students were becoming extremely narrow in what they were looking for in terms of experience. Mike was not getting interviews, and when he did, he would not get selected for the position. We worked hard on having him better tell his story about how his past experience translated to the roles he was seeking. He learned to communicate how his research team people leadership, project management skills and grant budget responsibilities prepared him well for a job in health management. He wanted more analytical roles, so we focused on how we could have him demonstrate his analytical skills. Mike improved his interviewing skills and the examples he used in behavioral interviews. It was still a challenge. He finally got a break from a large health system, successfully made the transition to health administration, and is thriving in his role.

WHAT ARE YOUR NEEDS FOR EXPERIENCE?

Whether you are a college student seeking post-graduation experience before graduate school, a college graduate making choices about and positioning yourself for your next career move, a graduate student getting ready to hit the job market, an experienced health professional, or career-changer from another industry, you have needs for additional experience. I encourage you to assess the kind of experience that would help you most to discover and/or advance toward your career. The End of Chapter Exercises will help you assess your experience strengths and areas that you need to strengthen. You can include your next steps for gaining more experience or translating yours into a new path into your overall action plan to be developed in Chapter 12. You can go directly to the action plan now if you are ready to take action.

END OF CHAPTER EXERCISE

Assess Your Experience Relative to Your Career Direction(s)

1. If I had to choose today. my authentic health career direction or up to three potential directions are:

2. I have ___[insert amount]___ of work experience through the combination of my jobs, internships, research experiences, and other relevant paid opportunities? Relevant volunteer experience?

3. How much of my work and volunteer experiences are relevant to the career directions I am now pursuing?

4. How does the combination of my work experience compare to what employers in the health career direction and specific next jobs I am pursuing are looking for, for me to be a solid candidate given the competition in the geographic areas and programs I want to pursue?

5. How does the combination of my work experience compare to what the graduate health training programs, clinical training, or certificate programs in the health career direction I am pursuing and specific programs I am pursuing are looking for, for me to be a solid candidate given the competition in the geographic areas and programs I want to pursue?

6. What are the strengths that my work experience provides me to get into the programs or jobs and/or advance toward my goals?

7. What are the areas I need to strengthen?

8. How can I best tell my story about how my experience translates to and qualifies me to be effective in my next step? How can I link it to the specific requirements of the program or job? Which examples will I use? How can I make them compelling?

9. What are the options for me to gain greater experience in the areas of my strengths and/or strengthen needed areas?

10. What are three action steps I will take in the next three months to secure this experience?

FRAMEWORK STEP 4

CHOOSING AND ACTIVELY PURSUING YOUR DIRECTION(S)

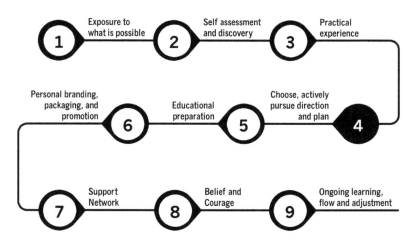

The most difficult thing is the decision to act, the rest is merely tenacity. The fears are paper tigers. You can do anything you decide to do. You can act to change and control your life; and the procedure, the process is its own reward.

—Amelia Earhart

This chapter is the fourth step in the Life and Career Planning Framework. It will help you understand the importance of choosing and actively pursuing one to three career directions aligned with the live you want to lead and your many strengths and goals. Your directions help focus your pursuits and filter your decisions. It provides you with a powerful seven-question tool to help you clarify your directions. It also provides you with insights into how to make your choice.

> *Your power to choose your direction of your life*
> *allows you to reinvent yourself, to change your future,*
> *and to powerfully influence the rest of creation.*
> —Stephen Covey

One of the most important, and often one of the most challenging, steps in achieving your authentic health career is **choosing and putting a stake in the ground to actively pursue your authentic health career *direction*.** I define your authentic career direction as a career and educational path that is going toward the health profession, role, type of organization, and personal and professional impact that align with who you are and want to be. A direction can serve as your North Star to filter, prioritize and navigate among the numerous health career and educational choices you can pursue. Knowing and being committed to a direction can provide clarity, focus, and inspiration. Armed with a clear, compelling direction, you can determine and act on the steps, relationships, and preparation required to achieve your authentic life and career goals.

Actively pursuing your direction will result in you successfully developing it and advancing toward your goals or discovering a different direction based on opportunities that arise that open new doors to your future and are even more aligned with who you authentically are.

If you don't know where you are going,
any road will get you there.
—Lewis Carroll, *Alice in Wonderland*

If you lack a direction or are paralyzed to actively choose and pursue one, it is like you are treading water (which we all need to do sometimes). However, it makes it difficult to make progress and make good decisions about the many educational, career, and life choices we still may need to make. A lack of direction can also undermine our confidence and make us feel bad about ourselves (I know, I have been there). It can also make it more challenging to get the help you need and secure opportunities that will help you move forward and strengthen your qualifications. Finally, it may also make it harder to deal with many others who are constantly asking you, "What you are doing now?" or "What are you going to do when you grow up or graduate?" and more subject to parental or peer pressure.

Please know that lacking direction is very common and is actually a normal and important part of the life-career decision-making process. Remember and accept that wherever you are is exactly where you are supposed to be and is okay. Sometimes we are simply in the surviving or searching stage of your career journey as discussed in Chapter 2. The key is to set the intention to develop a clear direction on a path and/or to a destination aligned with who you are and what you want. Depending on your situation you can be either working toward clarity or actively pursuing a direction with all you have. Keep the faith that wherever you are, you will establish a clear direction.

BECOMING A HOSPITAL ADMINISTRATOR

During my first year and a half of college, I floundered without direction. I had no idea what I wanted to be, partly because I was underexposed to what was possible and had very limited course work and experience. I also didn't have mentors or role models to inspire and guide me. All this is typical and normal for someone early in college, particularly someone from a working-class community with insufficient academic preparation.

My situation may have been even more extreme than others, I was a PE major because I loved sports and valued physical activity and challenge. I really didn't know what I would do. Fortunately, although I lacked direction, I was enjoying college, learning a lot and discovering more about myself and what was possible.

Then one day, at the beginning of the second semester of my sophomore year, after a particularly confusing and painful period during which I felt more lost than ever and more pressure to decide, everything suddenly clicked and began to flow. I had one of the most powerful "moments of knowing" in my life. I can still remember the incredible moment of clarity and awakening followed by a deep knowing and cautious but growing sense of optimism. A direction emerged that felt as though it suited me and aligned with what was needed in the world.

This moment of knowing about my career direction altered my life in a positive way forever. I was never the same and was squarely on the path to my authentic health career and a life of service, impact, and success far beyond what I could have ever imagined.

The breakthrough insight was a blessing and a convergence. It was a tremendous blessing that it occurred, just when I needed it, and was really aligned with who I was. I can't explain how and why it came about. It felt like a was a convergence of factors and my background and perhaps the result of numerous things I had been exposed to and experienced over time. Perhaps a higher power and/or the universe intervened.

I believe going through the searching stage and working through the confusion, with the intention to discover my path, played an important role. Perhaps it was just part of the normal process of being in college and maturing as a person. These kinds of breakthroughs happen to many people in college as through a natural process of greater exposure and experience and new life developments. Regardless of how and why it occurred, I was totally pumped and have been eternally grateful.

My clear direction that emerged was to become a hospital administrator. The convergence was an eclectic combination. I had worked in a hospital as a janitor for three summers and liked the hospital environment and people. Hospitals are like small cities and communities, and I could feel myself belonging there. However, I never once thought of being a doctor or clinical professional. My mother sent me an article on the "hottest" future careers, and hospital administrator was third on the list. The salary was solid, and it required a master's degree which somehow intrigued me even though I knew no one, other than my professors, who had one. My father was a hospital administrator as an enlisted man in the Air Force (although he had not gone to college until his forties), but it had never dawned on me to consider it, and he had never encouraged me at all to even consider it. In fact, when I shared my new direction, he strongly discouraged me from pursuing it. He said it was it was a very challenging job; the number of jobs were limited, and there was intense competition for them. He wasn't confident I would be successful. However, I was still excited and proceeded knowing I would succeed.

Another factor that attracted me to hospital administration was that I liked things that combined a variety of knowledge skills and of disciplines. Hospital administration incorporated a combination of knowledge of medical and community health issues, without having to be a clinical person, understanding political and social issues, and business and management. I had no interest in general business because it seemed to have no social value and was part of the problem, but the business of health seemed interesting. Health administration and public health also had a social justice aspect, and I quickly became motivated to improve access to care for underserved and minority population and believed deeply that healthcare is a right.

I had picked up brochures in the admissions office about different majors and looked at the description, curriculum, and requirements. One of the majors was community service and healthcare management. I loved the courses and the description, and graduates could pursue hospital administration. Something inside of me said to go for it.

I called the program director on the phone. He happened to be in the office and answered. He told me to come right over to discuss the major. After our conversation he enrolled me in the major on the spot! I suddenly and quite unexpectedly had a compelling new career direction and aligned major. Classes had started, but I was able to enroll in two of the required major courses, including the core course. The next day I started. The session focused on increasing access to care for underserved populations. I walked out of class as if walking on a cloud. I had found my passion and calling and direction. I was going to become a hospital administrator in a hospital that served the underserved and improved health access and care.

I am blessed to have had this moment and many others. I almost always follow them and have regretted it when I didn't. Armed with my direction I had similar moments when I went to a pre-public health conference at UC Berkeley and had a moment of knowing that I wanted to be like the professor and students who spoke and to attend UC Berkeley School of Public Health. This was a long shot given my background and undergraduate institution. However, having a clear direction and knowing inside made it seem possible. I had a clear focus on my goal, total determination and as much discipline as a 20-year-old in college in the early 1980s could have. I had learned about focus from playing sports when I set my sights on achieving different goals and, through hard work and discipline, was able to achieve them. I applied that knowledge to my career direction.

Things really began to flow, snowball, and accelerate. The more I followed my direction with determination, the more opportunities and key people who could assist and believed in me appeared.

Doors would open and I would enter. Each one seemed to lead me closer to by dreams and gave me more confidence (though I still had plenty of self-doubt and fears). I ended up with a terrific internship that I happened to find the night before it was due and just got it in. It changed by life and really launched my health career. It connected me to Berkeley, where I ended up applying and getting accepted to the brand-new MBA, the MPH Program in Health Services Management. I chose that program because given my career direction as a hospital administrator, my mentors suggested I should get an MBA. This was a major directional shift as I had previously gone on record multiple times saying I would never get an MBA. But given my direction, I chose it as the best path. It was the best possible decision. Upon graduation, I became a hospital administrator in a community hospital in Berkeley, just like the one I envisioned. I met my goal! It felt sooo good.

> *When you are actively pursuing a direction, it will either*
> *develop or another more suitable option will appear.*
> —Gayle Peterson

I believe that choosing a direction and giving your all to actively pursue it will increase your chances of success. If it is aligned with your passions and goals and how you want to serve and what you are good at and enjoy (the bottom of the Life and Career Alignment Triangle, described on pages 13 and 67), you will find happiness, fulfillment and financial rewards. You also get into the flow along the way and can enjoy the journey of following the path. Some of my most fun and fulfilling moments were following my path and having new and exciting developments, people, and doors open like a growing snowball and my belief that I could do it strengthening all the time. It was exhilarating. The momentum and clarity helped me overcome the numerous struggles that occurred along the way as I knew they were part of the journey, too, and that I would get to my desired destination. As I write this book as part of my new direction, I am feeling the same.

YOU MUST CHOOSE

If you choose not to decide you still have made a choice.
—Rush, "Freewill"

It can be difficult to choose just one direction, particularly if you have many different interests and not much exposure and experience to know which will be best. It can be hard to get enough exposure and experience at a young age or early in your education or career. It can be particularly challenging to choose a direction when you are unsure and not really ready. Some people also just like to keep their options open and wait for more information, opportunities or clarity. Some fear that choosing will have them miss out on other opportunities. Choosing one direction can is also challenging for someone like me who is interested in and good at several separate but related things. I have passion for each and can see the connection among them. I have a compelling rationale for pursuing each of them, it feels right and great when I do them. I also have a hard time letting go of options and putting a stake in the ground. Sometimes for good reason as it might be premature to let go.

For all these reasons, if you are not sure and/or ready to fully commit to actively pursuing one direction, I encourage you to choose up to three directions to actively pursue. I have worked with thousands of students and colleagues to choose and actively pursue one and up to three directions.

Most people have the capacity to pursue three directions. Pursuing them involves (1) gaining more exposure, experience, connections, and support to help you make a well-informed decision within a span of time that best suits you and (2) strengthening your qualifications, preparations, and opportunities to pursue one or more of the options.

This can include actions that would help you position yourself for multiple directions. For example, gaining more paid experience in an area and/or developing a certain skill could help you regardless of the direction you choose and inform your choices.

You can define your time frame for conducting and completing your pursuit, with milestones along the way, based on decisions you need to make or when you want to successfully transition to your next step. Next steps can include selecting and getting accepted to a new major, securing a great internship, having a job upon graduation, matriculating to a health profession training program, or changing jobs. Your chances of making a well-informed choice and accomplishing your desired next step are greatly increased by choosing and actively pursuing a direction as early as you are ready and able.

For those of you who are unsure of your authentic path, I encourage you to select your one to three directions strategically and with careful discernment and then commit to a plan to take specific actions over a defined period of time to explore and gain experience with each of them.

A related approach that many companies use when selecting strategies is scenario planning. Companies use scenario planning when there is significant uncertainty about the future environment they will operate in, and as a result, they need to consider and prepare for a few—typically three to four—different alternative future scenarios. In some cases, to hedge their bets against the uncertainty, companies choose strategies that position them well regardless of the scenarios. You can take a similar approach. For example, you can explore multiple career direction scenarios and choose a path and next steps that will position you to either be successful in any of the scenarios and/or make a more solid commitment to one of the directions, and perhaps a backup, and make a firmer choice when you have more knowledge and clarity.

For example, if you are unsure if you want to pursue medicine or public health or a combination, you could pursue an undergraduate major in public health and complete your premed requirements. This approach would give you the option to learn and think more about each direction before you choose, provide you with knowledge and skills that would be beneficial in either path you choose, and position you with the qualifications to be a competitive candidate for either path (or a combination of both). It will take more time and effort to pursue both than it would to simply focus on one direction, but since you are not sure, it still gives you a solid plan and helps you advance rather than being stuck in indecision or being limited to one path.

WHERE DO YOU START OR BUILD ON WHAT YOU ALREADY KNOW?

If you don't already know your one to three options, there are several approaches you can take. One option is to begin by brainstorming potential career paths that you are aware of and have some interest in without pressure to be perfect or decide. Go with what you know about health industry needs and trends (top of the Life and Career Alignment Triangle). Revisit your why's; your values, passions, and goals; and what you are good at and enjoy doing (the bottom of the Triangle). If you haven't done that work, I encourage you to go back and do it now. It is tempting for people to just blow past that and feel like they want to choose and then have a harder time deciding. Do the hard work to clarify and have the discipline to stay true to these important factors, which are uniquely you, is a way to filter and prioritize your options. It is a way to not only help with your decision but also ensure that the direction(s) you choose are authentically in alignment with who you are and want to be.

After you have done your exploration of trends and personal reflection, list out potential paths that you might want to pursue or at least explore further. Commit to the next steps, which involve doing more research to explore these and other paths, and set a time or two when you will return to consider and prioritize options.

A very effective approach that has helped thousands of people I have worked with is to start by completing the 7 Questions to Assist You in Clarifying Your Authentic Health Career Direction(s) exercise described in the next section and included in the End of Chapter Exercises.

Another approach is to choose one path to fully pursue and see how it develops and commit to continuing to be open to and explore other options (but not at the same level of effort).

A final approach, if you have the time, would be to identify two to three promising paths and plan to strategically pursue experiences that will help you choose among them. For example, you could focus on premed course work, clinical shadowing, and lab research experience during your sophomore year and summer and then focus on public health-related course work (along with premed), volunteering, and practical internship experience your junior year. You could then decide which area or the combination that you want to pursue during your senior year as you plan for a post-graduation job and graduate school. You can plan on two gap years with different kinds of experience to help you decide on your ultimate direction. At that point, you would have five years of actively pursuing your directions to help you make a well-informed choice.

PURSUING DIRECTIONS IS NOT PERMANENT AND HELPS YOU LEARN

When I encourage you to choose your one to three directions, I am not asking you to commit to your ultimate health career goal. I am simply asking you to map out your options and put a stake in the ground to actively pursue them toward making a well-informed decision when you are ready. You don't have to decide and shouldn't until you know. Though there are choice points, like college graduation or taking a promotion or going back to graduate school, there is no set time clock for when you must decide. Experienced professionals will tell you there is no rush to go to graduate school and that it is better to take the time to gain experience and actually enjoy your education and health career exploration.

The key is to put a stake in the ground and actively pursue your one to three directions to narrow your options and start learning by doing and gain momentum toward more well-informed clarity.

INACTION IS COSTLY

Taking action to clarify, choose, and advance your directions is much better than inaction. Many people I encounter are understandably concerned or discouraged by not knowing their direction, but instead of actively pursuing a direction, they tread water in indecision. Others know more about what they want to do and may even have certainty but delay or avoid moving forward (I know this one all too well). I encourage you to act rather than being "stuck" in your thoughts, if–then thinking, or and habits of hesitancy and underlying avoidance to move forward. Defining your direction, letting others know, and taking action raises expectations and accountability for yourself and others. Having and staying stuck in the story of not being sure or still evaluating your options allows more time for indecision and gives you a pass for a while. It's okay if you really don't know and you need more information or time. However, choosing and actively pursuing one to three directions buys you that time, gives you some focus, and gives you some momentum moving forward toward clarity and progress.

Describing your one to three directions and taking action to pursue them (even small steps) gives you something to say when you are asked the inevitable and uncomfortable questions about what you want to do (particularly in interviews or by people who matter to you). Letting people know your directions allows influential and supportive people to know how they can help you decide or advance.

MARY'S STORY

Mary graduated from UC Berkeley as a biology major with all her premed requirements completed. Premed at Berkeley is challenging and left her feeling beaten down, burned out, and less confident in her ability to realize her dream of becoming a doctor. She needed to take some time off to recover and to study for the MCAT.

Mary took on a job at a local hospital as an administrative coordinator in a clinical area. She felt it would provide her with the time to study and planned to take the MCAT and apply in a year. One year turned into two and then three. She wasn't really sure of her direction but would tell people being a doctor was still her plan. The more time passed, the harder it was for Mary to reboot and apply herself in the way she needed. She stopped actively pursuing medicine as a direction and didn't choose or pursue alternatives. She had some major family issues that left her depressed and made it even harder to start up again. Her confidence continued to diminish. Fortunately, she found a relationship that she was very happy with and ended up having a wonderful family. She chose to focus on her family instead of pursuing her career, which was a great life decision and gave her children a solid life foundation. However, she still has some regrets that she did not pursue medicine. She sometimes thinks about what her life would have been if she had fully applied herself to go to medical school. She loves her family and may have chosen the best path for her, but she will never know if she had fully chosen and put a stake in the ground whether or not she also could have become a doctor or some other type of health professional.

> *There are two kinds of pain, the pain of discipline*
> *and the pain for regret, it is up to you warrior,*
> *to choose which you will live with.*
> —A Navy SEAL saying relayed by Bo Eason
> from his Personal Story Power workshop

I encourage you choose the pain of discipline to go all in to explore your directions and then fully go for and do what it takes to achieve the one that you know is best for you. The progress you will make, what you will accomplish, and the rewards you will reap will be well worth it!

So How Do You Choose Your One to Three Directions?

So choose and begin actively pursuing your directions and believe that you will succeed and that regardless of how things go, you will figure it out. So how do you choose?

If you are a student, I encourage you to add another class to your schedule called My Life and Health Career Exploration 101. Treat it like a one- or two-unit class, which means devoting the amount of time you would spend in class and outside class for that number of units actively pursuing your one to three directions. Unlike other classes, you are the instructor and can set the hours. But be sure to build at least the number of course hours into your weekly schedule and show up prepared and as an enthusiastic learner for them. Use the time in whatever way will be most beneficial in pursuit of your health career direction. You can use the time to research health career options and their requirements, conduct informational interviews or shadow a health professional. You could also meet with mentors, work on your resume and complete the seven questions exercise below. Just like a regular course, I would encourage you to set objectives and deliverables and have checkpoints on your progress. Since there is no grade you can take the pressure off and just be present for and enjoy the process. I am confident it will be one of your most enjoyable, productive, and enlightening courses, and you will like the results.

If you are not a student, you can still add time to your weekly schedule to explore your directions and next steps. Treat the scheduled time like an important meeting with your boss that you would prepare for and not miss. Have deliverables and timelines and be open to the possibilities that arise. You could use the time for assessments, coaching, informational interviews, attending professional development events and conferences, and networking with mentors and colleagues You could also use the time for graduate-school test prep or studying or taking a course to learn a new skill or certification to position you for your next move.

Begin with the end in mind.
—Stephen Covey

7 QUESTIONS TO ASSIST YOU IN CLARIFYING YOUR AUTHENTIC HEALTH CAREER DIRECTION(S)

I have designed seven questions that, regardless of the stage of your career and educational path development, can help you clarify your authentic health career direction(s). I developed these questions through my experience choosing and reinventing my own authentic health career direction four times and through assisting thousands of students and colleagues to successfully pursue theirs. Everyone I have worked with has found them very practical and helpful.

The questions and considerations under each are described below. Please give some thought to each question from the perspective of your authentic self. You can either make the time to answer them now or answer them in the exercise at the end of the chapter. I am confident the answers will provide you with greater clarity of your direction(s), building on what you already know. There are no right or wrong answers as long as they are authentic and motivational and provide clarity for you.

It's okay to have several answers to the questions and some different scenarios of how they all fit together to form your potential one to three career directions. It's okay if you can't answer them all. You will then know where you need to do the work to answer them and gain more clarity and focus.

1. **Population(s):** There are many populations you can impact by working in the health field. Which populations do you want to work with? For example, you might be particularly interested in working with people from certain socioeconomic, racial, ethnic, or educational backgrounds. Perhaps populations in your hometown or a similar area or more globally. You might be interested in working with different age groups, such as older adults, teens, or young children. You might also consider people with specific acute or chronic diseases, such as cancer or heart disease, or those with mental health conditions, or you may consider working with people at risk to prevent these conditions. You could work with people at certain stages of health and illness such as healthy babies, crisis intervention, acute care, emergencies, recovery and rehabilitation, or death and dying. Perhaps you are interested in working with people in challenging life situations, such as refugees, immigrants, victims of natural disasters, or people with addiction. Choose one or more groups that you would most like to work with now and/or when you are fully living your authentic health career.

You will also benefit from defining which geographic region(s) you want and are willing to work I now and at various career stages. This may influence where you want to attend school, seek employment, and build networks. You also want to be aware of the trends, health and health workforce needs in those regions, and the requirements to be a competitive candidate in your desired profession.

At the start of my career, I was most motivated to work with low-income and minority populations in underserved communities. I still have that commitment and focus on undergraduate and graduate students, recent graduates, and people at all stages of their health careers seeking to discover and live their authentic path.

I chose to live and work in Northern California and the San Francisco Bay Area but to have an impact on local, state, and national populations. I also lived in Boston, which I loved, to honor a commitment to my wife to try living on the East Coast. I still work extensively in Boston but from Northern California. I also do work in North Carolina—where my family and Lumbee Indian Tribe are based—on health issues.

2. **Health issues or determinants of health:** Which health issues or determinant of health do you want to work on? There are many health issues and factors that have an impact on the health of populations and individuals that need talented people like you to address. Health issues or determinants of health could include one or more of the following three categories:

- Prevention, primary care, treatment or recovery from specific health conditions or injuries—such as diabetes, cancer, Alzheimer's, gun violence, sports injuries, depression, oral health
- Policy, management, systems change or programmatic issues that impact health outcomes, patient experience and cost—such as health coverage, access to care, quality improvement
- Determinants of health such as health behaviors (smoking, healthy eating and active living, sexual behaviors); environmental conditions (exposure, global warming, safety, access to healthy food); individual and healthy community condition; (housing, transportation, employment, education; and access to quality, affordable, healthcare and health homes)

If you are interested, list and prioritize the health issues or determinants you would be working on as part of your authentic path.

Early in my career I was most motivated to improve health coverage and access to affordable, quality healthcare. I was also motivated to improve prevention and primary care and strengthen the responsiveness of hospitals to meet documented community needs.

I still care deeply about those issues and work to improve them more indirectly through policy, systems change, programs and education to ensure we have a supply, distribution, and diversity of health workers to prevent illness, promote health, and provide access to quality care for all populations. I also am committed to increasing the cultural and linguistic appropriateness of program and care. I inspire, empower, and professionally prepare you and other health leaders and professionals to be better educated, employed, and compensated and healthier as you live your authentic lives and careers and to have the impact you are meant to have on the health of populations. I am also passionate about increasing my impact on promoting mental health and self-care.

3. **Health organizations:** Which specific type of health organization(s) do you want to work in? One of the exciting things about the health field is that there are so many different health sectors and types of organizations you can work in to have the life and impact you desire (go to my website for a list of different types of health organizations: Jeffoxendine.com). You might already have a plan for which you want to pursue and/or definitely not want to pursue, or you may need to gain some exposure and experience to help you decide. Deciding which types of organizations you want to focus on or explore is an important step in defining your direction. Examples and considerations include:

◆ **Sectors:** healthcare, public health, mental health, biotech, pharma, devices, community health, technology, research, academia. Across these, there are public- and private-sector organizations that do work locally, nationally, and globally.
◆ **Types of organizations:** examples include hospitals, community health centers, clinics, physician groups, biotech companies, global health organizations, policy and advocacy, consulting firms, health plans, disease management, health technology, digital health, and start-ups.

◆ **Size and stage of development:** health has organizations that are small, medium, and large. Examples of large employers include health systems and hospitals, academic medical centers, health plans, and private-sector health corporations, such as pharmaceutical, biotech, and equipment companies, often some of the largest employers in their communities. Government agencies that implement programs and administer policies and governmental public health and behavioral health are also larger employers. Health IT and consulting firms are also larger employers. The trend toward increasing consolidations in many of the health sectors, including mergers and collaborations with Google, Facebook, CVS, Amazon, and Walmart, will have more health-related services and products delivered by large companies or their affiliates.

However, much of health is local or regional, which includes large and many smaller firms. There are also small and medium-sized health organizations in the categories earlier. It is also common for community-based organizations, medical groups, community health centers, advocacy groups, foundations, long-term care facilities, and social service providers to be small or medium-sized.

The reason why you might care about this that size may matter when it comes to you having the type of work environment, resources, compensation and benefits, ability to get things done, and level of impact you want to have.

The stage of development of an organization and its financial resources may also be factors. Many health organizations are well established, some for more decades or than a century. However, there are also many kinds of growing, emerging, or start-up companies that could offer stimulating, innovative, and rewarding experiences at some stages of your career. Early in your career, it may be an easier time to make a risk as you have less to lose. Alternatively, it may be easier when you have more experience to contribute and have resources to withstand challenging financial times.

If you don't know which sectors and organizations you to work in over the longer term, you can focus on the sector, type of organization, and size/stage that you want to pursue for your next step.

4. **Role or function:** Which roles or functions do you want to play within the health field and/or the type of organizations that you want to work in? Roles and functions refer to the specific kind of health professional that you want to be and role and function you want to play. These can include clinical professions such as doctors, nurses, pharmacists, psychologists and physical therapists, and non-clinical professions, such as administrators, policy advocates, epidemiologists, and health IT specialists. Like many professionals, you can have a combination or roles and functions, such as being a nurse practitioner and a medical director or a licensed clinical social worker and mental health program manager. One of the exciting things about the emerging health field is that there is an abundance to new roles and functions emerging and opportunities to combine them. Here is your chance to do your homework, through exposure, assessment, and experience, to envision the role and functions that will best suit you.

Within each professional path category there are numerous role and function options. For example, within the health administration path you can work in line management roles overseeing operations or staff expert roles such as marketing, finance, business development, or health IT. The more specific yet open you can be the better to both help you focus your educational and employment choices as you actively pursue your direction yet seize new opportunities that align with who you are that present themselves along your path.

I have been fortunate to have many different roles and functions and combinations of them throughout my career. I started as a hospital administrator in operations who because of my MBA and MPH training also effectively took on business analysis and development roles. I became a medical group executive and served as the Executive Director of a statewide physician coalition. I served as executive director of a large radiology foundation at one hospital, the executive director of a radiology initiative that spanned an entire health system, and an instructor at an affiliated medical school. I was a faculty member and an associate dean at a school of public health and an external consultant. I am an educator, author, and nonprofit CEO.

Please envision and describe what you want to do. I encourage you to expose yourself to all the different roles available within particular organizations, as discussed in Chapter 2. You can also find lists of different roles on my website (Jeffoxendine.com). It's okay if you don't know yet, but it really helps when you do.

5. How close do you want to work with individuals and the community? Some of us want and need to work directly each day with patients or clients and/or do that work in a community setting. Others do transformational work to improve health through policy, programs, resource allocation or research but do not often engage with individuals or communities. There are many roles that have some aspects of client or community interaction and some that do not. For example, someone can be a physician that sees patients three days a week in a community health center and then is a policy change leader and researcher for two days a week.

You may already know your answers to this question, or you might have to discover and refine it through more exposure and experience. For example, I had a student who needed the experience of an internship to answer this question. Prior to graduate school, she had worked with low-income individuals and families to find health coverage. She loved the work but came to graduate school to pursue health policy to make a larger-scale impact. During her summer internship, she worked on health policy issues in an innovative county health department that had recently transformed access to care for more than 50,000 people. When I asked her what she learned from her internship, she said, "I need to work with families and individuals; I need to interact with them every day. I want to work in the community; working at a desk in an office building and not connecting with people is not for me." Her internship supervisor was part of the conversation and responded that she understood but had the opposite preferences. Her entire career was dedicated to helping low-income people have better healthcare access, quality, and outcomes. She was a national innovator who led the effort to provide the 50,000 people with better access and outcomes. She said she doesn't need to work with people or communities directly to have the impact she wants to make and can, in fact, make a larger scale impact that someone who works with 10 to 20 clients per day. The point is that there is no right or wrong answer. You just have to answer the question for yourself. And one of the cool things about health is that, as previously mentioned, you can often have both kinds of roles or do one for a part of your career and another at a different stage. It's for you to decide where you want to start and where you want to be at each stage of your journey.

For the first 20 years of my career, I was a health executive who cared deeply about patients and the community but worked at the level of managing the organizations, programs and people who served them. I would frequently walk through the hospital to see patients and remind myself why I did the work and occasionally engage patients to learn about their service, I was not directly involved with them. I felt good about my work and the impact I had. As I began to teach and mentor students, I became increasingly drawn to more satisfied by working directly with individuals and groups. As a result, I ended up adjusting my career path and roles and functions to work with students and teach classes and workshops. I now still spend a significant time doing this and working on policy, systems, and program change. I really like my combination and the impact I have.

6. What professional impact do you want to have?

Whether your impact as a health professional is far in the future or you are already having the impact you want to make, it is important to be clear about your intentions and how you will know. The journey to becoming a health professional can be long, challenging, and expensive. Your journey and your work as a professional can be very demanding and require all you have to give and more. Depending on the choices you make, most of us may end up spending more time on our work than we spend with our families. Given all you will invest in your health career, you want the impact to be worth it! I encourage you to define your intended impact as clearly as possible and use it to guide your career direction, educational preparation, job, and lifestyle choices.

You can start by visualizing yourself doing the job you ultimately want to have and how you will be impacting people, populations, or organizations. You can define your vision and goals regarding the impact you want to have on the health issue, populations and organizations you care most about. You can also consider your "why" for pursuing a health career and your values that you defined as part of the assessment in Chapter 4.

An example one of my student's intended impact was "I will reduce the rates and burdens of diabetes and violence on the Latino population in the Central Valley of California; particularly in the community I grew up in and similar ones. I will empower residents to make policy, systems and community changes to create healthy communities in which these and other health and equity outcomes can be sustained." His *why* was that he wanted to prevent others from his community suffering from the severe life and health challenges he and his family had endured and to give people more hope and opportunity to lead safe, healthy, and prosperous lives.

You don't have to wait until you are the health professional you ultimately want to be so you can also think about how you will impact people throughout your journey (i.e., I want to make a small difference every day in the life of individuals by giving them more hope, opportunity and mentorship).

When I started my career, I was guided by the value that health is a right. My intended impact was to increase access to quality, affordable care for everyone, particularly low-income and minority populations, so that we all could lead happier and healthier lives an be productive members of society. I still work to achieve that impact and fulfill my life's purpose of empowering as many people as I can from all backgrounds to discover and fully live our authentic lives and careers and have the impact we were meant to have. Empowering more people to live their authentic health careers, particularly people from underserved communities struggling with health access and outcomes, is how I will now achieve large-scale impact on both my desired goals.

7. What are your personal and professional definitions of success? This is a critical question that I find most people don't take the time to answer and utilize to guide their life and career decisions. Many people set career and educational goals based on preferences or opportunities that are presented without a clear definition of success. Over the years, I have found tremendous value in defining success for my life and career and for my jobs and projects. It seems obvious and vital to define success. However, I find many people and organizations charge ahead with assumptions about outcomes and success that are not as clear as would be beneficial. More health organizations have moved to define success and associated specific metrics so that they can track and more likely achieve intended outcomes. This approach focuses everyone to work toward a clear, shared definitions of success. I encourage you to define what success means to you, as specifically as possible, to give you a clear end point to work toward and as a filter for choices along your journey. I encourage you to ask how this choice, such as your career direction, next job, or graduate degree, will contribute to your definition of success.

Key factors to consider in your definition of success include:

◆ Physical and mental health and well-being
◆ Happiness and fulfillment
◆ Spirituality and religion
◆ Service goals
◆ Family size, timing, goals, relationship quality, personal time devoted to them
◆ Quality and time spent with important relationships— significant other, friends, parents, family, community
◆ Annual income and overall wealth
◆ Amount of time off
◆ Days worked per week and hours per day
◆ Lifestyle
◆ Status
◆ Experiences—travel, arts, adventures, hobbies
◆ Home or other physical things you enjoy

Armed with a definition of success for clarity, focus, and motivation, you can assess and chose specific career directions and educational paths that will enable you to achieve your desired outcomes. For example, if success for you is the ability to have a large family, spend significant personal time to nurture, and enjoy them and have enough time to pursue your passions for music and hiking, you will need to either have a career that will enable this in addition to the work you do or have a partner with whom you can organize your lives to make this happen. It also may involve you living in certain geographic areas with proximity to family and an affordable cost of living for the amount of work and level of pay you want. If your definition of success is to make a million dollars per year, do work that is fulfilling to you, and provide your family with your definition of the best in education, life experiences, and opportunities, then you will need to choose a job that enables you to accomplish this. Hopefully being happy and healthy for as long as we can are part of all our definitions of success.

A medical group I worked with used a clear definition of success to make important strategic and operational decisions. When we started the process, each of the 60 doctors had their own goals for the group and themselves, which varied widely. We developed a shared group definition of success for the group as providers of care to patients and as a business. With providing the highest level of patient care quality as a given, the group prioritized security, stability, and autonomy as the most important elements of group success and defined what each meant. We also defined success for how individual group member physicians would benefit and the quality of their work life. This included how much money group members would make, how much time off they would have, and the intensity of their workdays. The group used these definitions of success to determine their strategy, who they hired, and how and with whom they developed partnerships. One of the most important examples of how the group used their definition of success to make a decision was their decision to not merge with another large group, which made tremendous strategic sense for them to do, because the other group had a vastly different definition of success for the merged group and its members.

If you don't define what success means to you, you might end up some place that is different (better or worse) than you expected and that may or may not fulfill your needs and preferences. You can't predict the future and the many positive and challenging developments that life will bring you, but if you have a definition of success to guide you, which you can change any time, you will be more likely to no what you want when you have a choice and end up where you want to be. You can also use it to prevent costly, misaligned career choices.

Defining success for your life can be a daunting task as a student and early in your career and even at more advance stages. I encourage you to dig deep and do your best. It's okay if you don't know yet. Set the intention to define success over time when you feel ready and have life, career and educational experiences to help inform you. Understand that your definitions may also change over time and at different life stages. Don't put undue pressure on yourself. Choose a draft, live life, and see how it goes, and if the definition you use serves you well. Just make conscious choices about who you are and what you want. If it is easier, just focus on the definition of success for what you are doing now and perhaps your next step. Life may guide you to develop the rest when it's time.

If you have a sense of your definition of success, you can refine it further in the End of Chapter Exercises or over the next span of time.

If you are very clear about your definition of success, then use it as a filter to make good choices about your life and career. A definition of success allows you to work backward to make choices and live now to get you to where you want to be.

I began to develop definitions of success during my junior year in college. Early in my career, my definition of success was to achieve my goal of becoming a hospital administrator, complete my education, marry if I found the right person, earn a good income, and enjoy my life to the fullest. I wanted to travel the world and experience as many new places and meet as many interesting people as possible.

Despite having a few long-term relationships, I waited a long time to get married because I was committed to a definition of success for a life partner that came from a line from a Joni Mitchell song, "All I really, really want our love to do is to bring out the best in me and in you." When I had given up hope, I was blessed to find my wonderful wife. We have brought out the best in each other since for more than two decades. I am glad that I held out until my definition of success was fulfilled.

When I had children my definitions of success changed dramatically. Being a great father and partner with my wife in raising our children to be "awesome human beings" who are happy, healthy, and successful (based on their definitions, not ours) became the core of my definition of success. I also shifted my professional focus to be on fulfilling my core purpose of empowering people to realize their full potential and having the autonomy and flexibility to be there for my family.

My definition of success now still includes the family and professional elements described earlier and includes being fully supportive of my aging parents; living much more from my highest, best, and authentic self; and fulfilling my spiritual and service goals. My definition also includes living as much as possible in the present moment with greater awareness and compassion, surrender to what life presents and helping others to do the same. It includes completing this book and supporting it to have the largest-scale positive impact (though just publishing it is success in itself). It includes having a level of income and assets in the next five years that allow me to retire if I want to and live where I want to, including for extended periods of time at the beach!

What's yours?

Combining Your Answers Into a Vision of Your One to Three Directions

If you can answer these seven questions (or a subset of them), you can envision one to three compelling career directions. Clarify your directions and actively pursue them as discussed in this chapter. You can start acting on your direction(s) now by completing the action plan in Chapter 12 and moving forward with next steps.

If you can't answer these questions, it's totally normal and okay; this is where getting more exposure, experience, and mentorship come in, along with more self-awareness and personal reflection. Even with the benefits of more time, experience, and awareness, not everyone is going to have an epiphany about their directions. The important thing is to identify the things that you DO know about yourself and your preferences and explore career directions that align with them. Some things will unfold and reveal themselves to you as you go. The seven questions are just a tool to help you decide.

You might end up with multiple answers to the questions above. That is okay too! Most people come up with one to three directions in which they might be interested in going. This is still narrowing your options down and making great headway.

Please remember that directions are just one to three paths you are pursuing. They are not set in stone. YOU can always CHANGE directions as you discover more about yourself and your fields of interest.

How Do I Choose and Actively Pursue My Direction?

Once you have done the work to identify your one to three directions, you have to choose and actively pursue them. As mentioned previously, a direction, by definition, brings clarity, focus, and commitment to fully pursue one to three career paths that align with your authentic life and career. However, it is not set in stone, so you can change your mind and pursue other things that emerge as you are pursuing the direction.

The acts of choosing and actively pursuing set in motion important forces within you, your networks, and the universe to help your path develop and you succeed. It also gets you unstuck and feeling better about yourself and allows others to provide greater support to and believe in you. Aren't you tired of everyone asking you, "So what are you doing now or what are you going to do when you graduate?" and then being disappointed and you feeling discouraged when you give an unclear answer. (Not that there is anything wrong with not knowing—you are exactly where you are supposed to be.) For some of us, it can be a reminder of not being good enough or where you want to be compared to what you or others think. Having one to three directions you are pursuing provides useful clarity to you and to them. It allows them to better understand and support you. Most importantly it allows people to assist you and flow to occur.

Choosing and actively pursuing enables you to step into, with intention, and take full advantage of and contribute to the abundant flow of people and opportunities that can emerge to assist you on your journey. Choosing can give you a shot of positive reinforcement and confidence that you have and are acting on a direction. You no longer need to hide or hold back. It can be liberating and joy-producing. It helps you enjoy and the journey, in some cases very long ones to health careers, along the way, and as Brendon Burchard says, "bring the joy" and "honor the struggle" along the way and deal with inevitable success and challenges. It feels great to be unstuck and have direction.

How Do You Choose?

There are many different approaches and no perfect answers. I encourage you to find the approach that works for you so that you feel good about. What works for you may be influenced by a number of factors:

- Your personality type
- How your brain is wired—more left- or right-brain orientation
- Decision-making style and experience
- Confidence and trust in yourself
- Self-esteem
- Self-knowledge and awareness (accuracy)
- Comfort with risk and uncertainty
- Willingness to follow instructions, surrender
- Other

Many people may like formal, structured decision-making techniques:

- Clarifying your goals, values, definitions of success
- Defining your priority objectives and outcomes
- Thorough research of your options so that you can make a well-informed choice
- Deliberate steps to validate what you are thinking about
- Sufficient practical experience and exposure
- Analyzing your options
- Developing and applying decision-making criteria—including forced ranking of options
- Other

Alternatively, many of us may be less structured, more spontaneous, or more spiritual in our approach:

- Following your intuition or "gut"
- Going with what feels right, inspired, or good
- Prayer
- Being open and surrendering to what is presented (see the alchemist or surrender experiment)
- Seizing moments of knowing
- Going against your normal tendencies
- Following your passion and purpose and trusting it will take you where you want to be
- Going for something even if you are not sure
- Having faith and trust

Many of us may do a combination of the above. I encourage you to consider a combined approach. Many of my most important and successful life decisions have been through a combination including my decision to pursue health administration, my shift to leave my executive job and go to UC Berkeley and marrying my wonderful wife of 23 years. As I said to her when I proposed, "my heart and head are in agreement."

HOW DO YOU KNOW WHEN YOU HAVE YOUR AUTHENTIC DIRECTION?

So how do you know when you have found your authentic health career direction? Once again there is no right or wrong answer. It depends on how you are wired and what works for you.

Below are some things I have experienced myself or heard from others:

- Heightened feeling when you are doing something aligned with your direction
- A sense of greater connection or knowing when you do what you want to do
- Being in state of "flow" and consistently building momentum through accomplishments, people and opportunities
- Feeling a sense of ease
- Time flies by when you are doing the work
- Excited to get up in the morning and get to work or class
- Path and opportunities will develop, snowball effect
- Feeling like you would do want you want to do for free (though you don't have to)
- Being sure you are not just doing something for status or ego gratification
- Considering what is your highest and best use
- Happiness and satisfaction

A former student of mine said that he knew he wanted to pursue health policy "when he couldn't stop talking to women about it when he was at parties." It didn't help him find a significant other but affirmed his career direction.

When it is time to choose, I encourage you to do so from your highest and best self, not your more small or limited self. Believe the positives about yourself and see the incredible things you have to offer as others see you.

> Remember that it's ok to go against your rules
> and preferences when you know it is right.
> —Michael A. Singer, *The Untethered Soul*

HOW DO YOU KNOW IF YOU WANT TO BE A DOCTOR?

Over the years I have had thousands of students struggle with the huge life and career decision about whether they really want to be a doctor. I am not a doctor, so to assist them, I have asked some of my most esteemed and experienced physician colleagues for advice on how to advise students.

Here are the major factors that they recommend people consider:

◆ Be very clear about and committed to your *why* for being a doctor.
◆ Make sure your why is aligned with who you authentically are.
◆ Be sure you want to spend a significant part of your life treating individual sick patients and spend a minimum of seven-plus years deeply immersed in training to do it.
◆ Be well informed of the future trends that will shape the role, work life, opportunities, and compensation of physicians (10 to 20 years out) and be sure you still want to make the time and investment and you are up for the changing role and requirements.
◆ Be willing to live the lifestyle and have the demands of medical school, residency, fellowships, and practice.
◆ Be clear that being a physician is the best fit among all your options with your values, skills, and desired impact.

ACTIVELY PURSUE

Whether you choose to be a doctor or pursue another health profession as your authentic health career direction you must actively pursue it to achieve your dreams. Active pursuit of your direction has many components, starting with truth and accountability.

TRUTH AND ACCOUNTABILITY

In their book *How We Choose to be Happy*, my friends Rick Foster and Greg Hicks describe the nine characteristics of the happiest people. Speaking and living according to the truth and being accountable are two of the nine. Their research indicates that we as humans are wired to have positive biochemical reactions when we tell and live by the truth which contributes to our feeling of happiness. We are also happier when we are accountable for our commitments and being who we are. I encourage you to embody/take to heart, both behaviors when it comes to choosing and actively pursuing your direction.

The more truthful you can be about your authentic direction, as opposed to directions that may not truly suit you and/or that others want you to pursue, the more likely you will succeed and find happiness and fulfillment. I know this can be very challenging, particularly when you may be letting go of a long-held dream or vision of yourself and when people who you care about will be disappointed or angry. I discuss how to better address both in the chapter on belief and courage. It can also be challenging to admit that you may not have the aptitude, talent, or skills required for a particular health profession that you want to pursue. This is not a reflection on your intelligence or capabilities; you are likely very well suited for another career path in which you will excel and have great impact. It may just be that the requirements for entry and/or practice are not a fit or at least not at this point in time. Perhaps with more preparation and strengthening of needed skills you can do it. The key is to be truthful about whether, with the hard work and preparation, you will truly be able to enter and be good at and happy in a specific profession.

I cannot emphasize more strongly that this decision needs to be made by you, with consultation from many well informed, honest and supportive people, rather than getting derailed by comments from someone acting from a biased, self-interested, or inaccurate view of who you are and what you can do. Be honest with yourself, and from your most confident and capable self, not from your small sense of self or limiting beliefs, and go for what is true for you to the best of your knowledge. If you are not sure, then keep actively pursuing a direction until you have more knowledge and clarity to help you choose. No rush!

Once you decide what is true for you, then I encourage you to be accountable for actively pursuing you chosen direction(s) with all that you have. Many of us, myself included, have gained clarity about which direction to pursue and then not actively pursued it or done so according to a time frame we desire or that would serve us and others well. We find many reasons why not to pursue it and choose less challenging, risky, or more immediate directions or we stay "stuck." Particularly when we have to put ourselves out there and risk being wrong, embarrassed, or failure. Sometimes the stakes feel higher when you have chosen something that is highly personal and that you really want which makes it harder to act for fear of disappointing yourself and/or others. In his book *The War of Art*, Steven Pressman identifies the most common reasons people don't act on their dreams. He also lists ways that you can. I will discuss in more detail belief and courage about how to overcome these factors. Having the mindset and commitment to be accountable is an important first step. Utilizing for holding yourself accountable for actively pursuing your authentic direction, getting the support you need, and engaging others to help hold you accountable are critical for making progress.

Remember accountability can lead to goal attainment and happiness. Making progress and being accountable feels much better than "being stuck" or "in limbo" and talking about rather than acting on your dreams. It will also show others in your life that you mean business, are making credible progress, and are well suited for and on your way to your authentic career. This will help them become more supportive and excited overtime. It will also help you be more qualified for opportunities to advance when they arise and help you do better in interviews. Clear focus, acting on a plan, and making progress build momentum, and people will want to be part of your journey.

Be accountable to your ancestors and family. They worked very hard and made huge sacrifices for your life, opportunity, and success. It is tempting and admirable to go for what they want you to do, but more valuable ultimately to be accountable for your unique impact and a happy, successful life. Have this accountability drive you.

Finally, accountability for actively pursuing your authentic health career is also important for our communities and the people you want to serve. We need more of all kinds of health professionals and leaders, particularly those who are acting in alignment with their unique talents, passions, values, and service goals. Be accountable for the impact you are supposed to have on the world and all of us. Think of how powerful it will be when more and more people are actively pursuing and achieving their authentic health careers and having the impact they are supposed to have and that we need. Be accountable for your contributions.

Life takes on meaning when you become motivated, set goals
and charge after them in an unstoppable manner.
—Les Brown

END OF CHAPTER EXERCISES

Exercise 1: 7 Key Questions to Clarify Your Authentic Health Career Direction

The following seven questions have assisted thousands of people I have worked with to assess their health career passions and preferences and develop a vision of their authentic health career direction. For a more detailed explanation of the questions you can refer to page 135.

Set aside some time to think about who you are and answer these questions from your authentic self and what you are or want to be doing in the health field—not what you think you should do or what others want you to do. Answer them as honestly, freely, and specifically as you can. As you answer them, tap into your passions and what light's your soul on fire. There are no right or wrong answers and they will not be set in stone. It's okay if you don't know all the answers yet (though you may be surprised about how much you do know). Answer the ones you can and list some ideas and options for those that you are not sure about. You have time to figure out the others and the other chapters in the book provide you with the process to do so. It's okay to have several answers to the questions and some different scenarios of how they all fit together to form your potential one to three career directions.

If you are not ready to answer these questions about your major life directions (or feel too pressured to do it from that perspective), then the answers can be about your next steps.

Please answer these questions from your authentic self:

1) Which **population(s)** do you want to work with (e.g., elderly, low income, teenagers, pregnant teens, Latinos, community where you're from, etc.)?

2)   Which **health issue(s) or determinant(s) of health** you want to work on? (e.g., diabetes, cardiovascular disease, education, improving environmental exposure, etc.)?

3)   Which **kind of organization(s)** do you want to work in (e.g., hospital, clinic, physician group, biotech company, global health organization, etc.)?

4)   Which **role(s) or function(s) within that organization** that you want to work in (e.g., doctor, administrator, sales, marketing, etc.)?

5)   How close to the **patient** or to the **community** do you want to work?

6)   What **professional impact** do you want to make? (e.g., I want to reduce the rate of diabetes so people suffer less in the community where I'm from)?

7) What is your personal and professional **definition of success** (e.g., make a certain amount of money, have a family, travel the world, etc.)?

Exercise 2: Choosing Your Direction(s)

Utilizing your answers to the seven questions above, choose one to three directions that you will actively pursue. Specify the time frame you will pursue them and desired outcome. Write them down here:

1)

2)

3)

List three to five key steps you will take in the next six months to actively pursue the directions you have chosen.

If you want a more in-depth tool to assist you with discovery of who you are and your directions, you can complete the life-career planning questionnaire on my website at Jeffoxendine.com

FRAMEWORK STEP 5

EDUCATIONAL PREPARATION

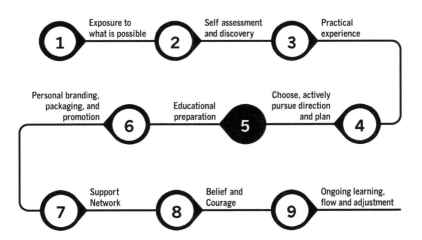

*Education is the most powerful weapon
you can use to change the world.*
—Nelson Mandela

*Education is the passport to the future, for tomorrow
belongs to those who prepare for it today.*
—Malcom X

Educational Preparation is the fifth step in the Life and Career Planning Framework. This chapter will assist you to understand how your educational preparation (undergraduate and graduate health professions training and health certificates). It describes the four key things you get out of health professions education and training and discusses how you can use them to filter and decide on the options that best suit you. It also helps you consider which degree, school, and program would help you advance toward your goals and when is the best time for you to pursue your training.

When I ask college students, "What is your current health career direction?" the answer often is, "To get my MPH," or "To go to medical school." These are totally normal and legitimate responses for someone focusing on their next educational steps. However, as you know if you have completed the previous chapter, my question regarding their direction is to understand the specific health professional path and the types of organizations, populations, health issues, and impact they want to have. Getting an MPH or MD or any other health professions degree or certificate is part of the education and training required to enter, effectively function, and succeed in your desired direction. They are not a direction or destination in themselves. This is a critical paradigm shift I encourage you to embrace.

While education and training are very important and rewarding as individual experiences and achievements unto themselves, they should be directly aligned with your authentic life and career direction to have the maximum benefit to you and society and the highest return on investment. Yes, I said return on investment because your education requires a significant and growing investment of not only your money but your time and life energy as well. There is also the resulting life and career path you will be on and the opportunity cost of pursuing those paths instead of others. Remember how I have said that becoming a doctor will cost you your twenties and early thirties.

You will notice that in the Life and Career Planning Framework that education comes after exposure, assessment, experience, and career direction. This placement is intentional because in my experience with thousands of people pursuing health careers, you will make a more well-informed choice of your educational preparation if you have done the work in the other steps first. You will know what is possible for you, what you want, and what best suits you; have the experience to validate and demonstrate your preparation for your direction; and make a better-informed choice about your direction. Armed with this knowledge and awareness, you are then ready to choose the educational preparation that best aligns with your direction and who you are. You will also be a more competitive applicant; a better-prepared, more-able-to-contribute student; and a more attractive graduate for further training or employment.

ALIGN YOUR EDUCATION WITH YOUR AUTHENTIC HEALTH CAREER DIRECTION

Alignment of your educational preparation with your career direction is critical. You want to be sure that through your undergraduate, post-bac, and graduate training you obtain the following five key elements in a manner that empowers you and increases your probability of entry and success in your chosen, authentic health career direction.

They should be specialized to fit your career direction. I will use examples of each that I gained from my undergraduate and graduate degrees my chosen direction of health administration:

Specialized knowledge: you will need as a foundation for and to have the necessary expertise in your chosen field. For example, in health administration, I gained theoretical and practical knowledge in health economics, health policy, health planning, the US health system, epidemiology, and management of hospitals and health systems strategy.

Skills: practical and/or research skills that professionals in your direction need to enter and advance in the field and utilize to be effective. In my field, it included "essential skills"—leading and working in teams, making effective presentations, negotiation, interpersonal skills, giving feedback, and "hard or technical skills"—data and financial analysis, people management skills, strategic management, and market research. Skills I wish I had learned (that they don't teach in school) are time and energy management and project management. Learn what kinds of knowledge and skills employers are seeking in your field and assess which programs will best help you develop them.

Credentials: Which credentials will employers in your field and desired sector value and will make you competitive for jobs and advancement in the near and longer term? I chose to secure both an MPH and an MBA because employers and my mentors in hospital administration told me the combination would be very powerful and help differentiate me. This has been the case for my entire career!

Practical training and experience: What kinds of practical experience and professional development will you be able to obtain to prepare you for employment and effectiveness in the field? This could include internships, practicum, residencies, fellowships, community projects. Look at the quality of these experiences offered at different schools, degrees, and programs offer. All are not created equal and may not give you what you need. You should examine how easy it is for you to obtain the kind of experiences you want and get paid and how satisfied students with your background are with their experience. I also encourage you to assess the level of support the institution provides for you to obtain your experience and how much it is valued and supported by faculty.

Practical experience and professional development were top priorities and strengths of both my graduate programs. I had two excellent and well-paid full-time internships that led to and prepared me well for jobs during and after my program that were perfectly aligned with my goals.

Connections: As you will learn in Chapter 8 on networking, it's either network or not work. I encourage you to engage in a school, degree, and program that will provide you with strong connections and networking skills and opportunities that will serve you well throughout your career. I can't tell you how critical strong alumni, employer, faculty, and fellow student networks will be during and after your program. There are many people who will have the "same" education and degrees that you have, so strong connections that can open doors, support and provide opportunities for you are invaluable. Jobs, internships, and mentorship can come more easily through faculty and professional connections than having to do it on your own. The school, degree, and program affiliation you share with them can be a huge differentiator and advantage in accessing and maintaining connections that will benefit you. Connections are most important for upper-division and graduate students to get solid advice and position you for success in your next steps. It is important to have specialized connections that can help you discover and achieve your authentic health career path.

One of the reasons I chose UC Berkeley School of Public Health was because at the time 70% of the hospital CEOs in Northern California were graduates of the school. I knew that these and other senior leaders were very dedicated to Berkeley and committed to helping UC Berkeley graduate students and fellow alums. My decision paid off; by the time I finished my degrees, I had met and been supported by dozens of UC Berkeley alumni and had multiple job offers without having to apply for a job. I secured these offers through informational interviews with alumni and support from a formal mentor assigned by the program. Every day since I started the program, I have benefited from connections with other Cal Bears!

WHICH SCHOOL, DEGREE, AND PROGRAM COMBINATION WILL BE THE BEST FIT FOR YOU?

I encourage you to prioritize choosing the best school, degree, and program combination for your graduate education. Rather than just focus on the reputation of the school, the type of degree or the nature and quality of the program, it is important to consider how all three elements will be integrated to meet your unique needs and goals. It's the combination of these elements that provide you with the specialized knowledge, skills, training and connections you need to succeed early on and throughout your career.

An MPH in Health Policy and Management at the University of Michigan is very different from an MHA (master's in health administration) at the University of North Carolina Chapel Hill, which is different from the UC Berkeley MBA, MPH Program in Health Management, even though all three are focused on health administration. Which will be the best fit for you depends on your authentic path and which will provide you with the best combination of the four things you get from a program?

You may also want to consider the following:

◆   The geographic location relative to what you want to study during the program and where you want to work and live afterward
◆   The quality and accessibility of faculty and how their research, practical work, and connections align with your goals
◆   The degree of and commitment to diversity, equity, and inclusion
◆   Student and employer satisfaction
◆   Life experience and adventure
◆   Full-time, part-time, and online (or hybrid) nature of the program relative to your goals and what you can do

You will notice I did not include the rankings of the school or how much financial support you are provided. If the program isn't a great fit for you on all the other factors, then neither of these things matter. The rankings may have nothing to do with what matters to you or to employers. Reputation with employers, residency programs, and others you care about does matter but may have nothing to do with rankings. If you are in a program that is in the top 25 or so that most will have strong reputations and serve you well. You may also have a strong regional or local program that doesn't have a high ranking but suits you just fine, particularly if you have a lot of work experience already and/or it is your second graduate degree.

While I know that financial support is critical to many of you, you will have a much greater return on investment over the long term by going to a best-fit school aligned with your authentic path rather than one that doesn't serve you as well but provides more funding. I have many students who have taken the risk to go to a school that provides less support but is their top choice that find the ways to get the financing they need and end up with the experience and ultimate success they seek.

EXPERIENCE FIRST!

One way to make a well-informed choice about your graduate education and to get accepted to the best fit program is to get more experience prior to graduate school. As discussed in Chapter 4, experience can increase your knowledge of what you want to do and what you want to get out of graduate education or a health professions training program. You will also be better positioned to get accepted to your best-fit program. During your education you will have more to contribute and may feel a greater sense of confidence and belonging since many of your classmates will be older and have experience.

If you are intent on going straight through to graduate school without experience or tempted by one of the many four plus one programs being offered by universities I encourage you to stop and consider if you really know what you want and what you want to get out of your graduate education and if the degree school and program will best suit you in the near, mid, and long term of your career. Please also consider the potential benefits of gaining more work experience. For most people, particularly those of you coming out of college, there is no hurry to go to school. I know it is tempting to stay in school when you are in the studying mode and you want to advance toward a rewarding career. Graduate school can also seem like a promising option if you don't know what you want to do or have job options. I also know that many parents also promote and sometimes pressure their children to go straight through. These are common dilemmas that hundreds of students I have worked with have faced. My advice is to take your time and go to graduate school when you know what you want, are ready, and are sure that the degrees, school, and program are a great fit and will serve you well over the long term.

DIANA'S DILEMMA

Diana was a Health Career Connection (HCC) Intern about 10 years ago. During our Graduate Education Workshop, she looked stressed. She rushed up to me afterward and said she really needed my advice. Diana had a major dilemma. She understood my strong advice about getting experience first before attending graduate school. She also understood the importance of alignment between her life and career direction and the graduate degree, school, and program she pursued. Her dilemma was that besides her HCC internship, she hadn't gotten post-graduation experience, and in three weeks she was scheduled to start a graduate program at an Ivy League school that she felt was no longer aligned with her authentic career direction. She felt compelled to re-evaluate her decision. The clock was ticking.

When she began the HCC internship program, Diana wasn't sure what she wanted to do. She had graduated from Cornell with very good grades and leadership experiences. HCC was her bridge to the working world. Motivated to have a post-college plan and feeling pressure from her parents and peers to have certainty, Diana applied to jobs and graduate programs that were aligned with her interests. While she really wasn't sure what she wanted, her primary interests were nutrition and health administration. She hadn't had much exposure to or experience with either, so she struggled to know if she really wanted to pursue them.

Diana had chosen to participate in HCC so that she could obtain first had experience in health administration. Her choice had been rewarded. She discovered that she was passionate about health administration, enjoyed it and did a great job on her projects. She got feedback from her boss that she had solid potential to succeed in the field. She still wasn't 100% sure it was the path for her but felt it offered more potential than nutrition. Diana was excited to explore the possibilities and asked her boss if she could continue to work for the organization after her internship. Her boss said they would love to hire her but didn't have an immediate opening. However, she would pursue funding and thought that a job could potentially become available in the next three to six months. However, it was not a guarantee, so she encouraged Diana to continue to pursue health administration and pursue jobs with other health employers. The problem was, the Ivy League program was scheduled to start soon, and Diana didn't have a solid plan if she didn't enter the program.

Diana's parents were also putting pressure on her to attend the program. They thought it was an amazing opportunity. She could have a master's degree from a prestigious school in just one year. During that time, she could figure out what she really wanted to do. Worst case, if she didn't want to pursue nutrition afterward, she would still have a master's from a top school. They were also concerned that she didn't have other tangible options.

While Diana understood and respected her parents' perspective, she was uncomfortable about going to a program if she wasn't sure she wanted to pursue nutrition, especially given it would cost her $65,000 in tuition plus living expenses for a year in an expensive city. She already was $60,000 in debt from her undergraduate education. Her parents were not able to provide her with any financial support, and her school only offered loans. Diana thought this was a high price to pay for something she wasn't sure she wanted to do. But she didn't have other options.

Diana asked me what I thought she should do. Though the deadline was rapidly approaching, I recommended she do some additional research to help inform her decision. She reached out to her graduate program to find out what students did post-graduation. It turned out that most of them were on a track to get a PhD in nutrition and became research assistant's for faculty members post-graduation. As research assistants they were groomed to become doctoral students and made about $45,000 per year before they started their six-plus-year PhD program. I asked Diana if she wanted to pursue that path. She said no. She was much more interested in health administration and didn't want to go into further debt to become a researcher in nutrition. It wasn't even public health nutrition that was the area she was most interested in. However, she still wasn't sure she could let go of the tangible graduate-degree option, particularly given her how her parents felt. She had also already made a commitment and put down a deposit.

After a stressful week of soul-searching, Diana ultimately decided to not attend the graduate program. She was scared she wouldn't find a job and her parents were upset, but it was the right thing for her to do.

The next few months were rough. Diana wasn't having much luck with jobs, and she was starting to regret her decision. However, when things seemed most bleak, she got an email from the HCC electronic mailing list with posting for a job at Kaiser Permanente in Oakland California. She applied and got the job! Her courage, persistence, and patience were rewarded. Diana ended up working for Kaiser for three years and got experience that affirmed she wanted to pursue health administration. Her experience positioned her well to get into an MPH program in health administration at Boston University. After her degree, she has had a very successful career as a health administrator and is living her authentic life and health career.

I encourage you to have the clarity and courage that Diana demonstrated so that your graduate degree, school, and program will position you to achieve your authentic health career. Also, to be sure that you obtain the exposure and experience and do the assessment work and research you need to make a well-informed choice and gain entry into the school and funding!

Graduate degrees are a huge financial and opportunity cost. They can be one of the best life experiences and investments you can make in your life. You will have limited opportunities to get your degree and want to be sure you get what you need. The degree, school, and program you pursue will shape and be your calling card the rest of your life, so choose wisely. Just do all you can do be sure that the choice you make will serve you well in the near term and throughout your career.

To help inform your choice, answer the questions in the End of Chapter Exercise.

I encourage you to take advantage of excellent resources available to through professional and educational associations help you make well informed health professions school choices including:

◆ The Premed Navigator from the American Association of Medical Colleges: American https://students-residents.aamc.org/navigator/

◆ Association of Schools and Programs of Public Health: https://www.aspph.org/study/before-you-apply/

◆ American Dental Education Association: https://www.ada.org/en

◆ American Association of Physician Assistants: https://www.aapa.org/career-central/become-a-pa/

◆ American Association of Nurse Practitioners: https://www.aanp.org/education

You can also visit my website, Jeffoxendine.com, to obtain more information. On the website, you will also be able to access other resources to help you choose, get entry into, and pay for your graduate education.

END OF CHAPTER EXERCISE

From your authentic self, answer the following questions:

1. What is my authentic health career direction?

2. Why graduate school and why now?

3. Do I have enough exposure, experience, and self-assessment at this time to make a well-informed choice? Be confident that my chosen path aligns with who I am and the life and career I want to have?

4. What are employers who hire people from my authentic health career direction looking for in the candidates they hire? What will they be looking for by the time I finish my training? Ten to 20 years into my career?

5. Given my experience and educational background, what additional specialized knowledge, skills, credentials, practical training, and networks do I need to prepare, be effective and meet my goals?

6. Which degree, school, and program offer me the best opportunity to secure what I need? What do graduates of these programs do? Where do they work? How hard is it for them to secure a job in the path I want to pursue? To advance?

7. What other considerations are important to me in choosing a school, degree, and program that are a good fit for me? (Establish a list.)

8. How competitive will I be for entry into that program at this time? What do I need to do to increase my competitiveness? My preparation for success?

9. What criteria will I use to select a program?

10. What are my action steps for strengthening my preparation and competitiveness? List networking, test prep, and other steps. Where will I get the support I need?

FRAMEWORK STEP 6

PERSONAL BRANDING, PACKAGING, AND PROMOTION

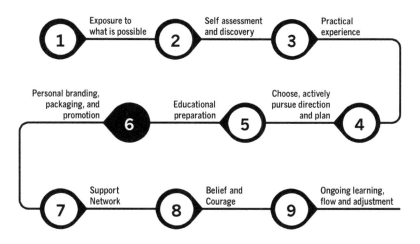

You too are a brand. Whether you know it or not.
Whether you like it or not.
—Mark Ecko

This chapter on Personal Branding, Packaging, and Promotion, step six in the Framework, will assist you with strengthening your personal branding and your corresponding packaging (resume, cover letter, interview skills, elevator speech, LinkedIn profile, etc.) and promotion. Personal branding, packaging, and promotion are critical to your ability to meet you job and educational goals.

Having a clear career direction and acquiring the corresponding education you need for entry and success are necessary but not sufficient. You must also effectively brand, package, and promote yourself to get the experience you need, get into your top choice educational program, and secure jobs aligned with your life and career goals. Packaging and promotion are also essential to networking and advancement throughout your career.

Whatever your health career path, including physicians and other health providers, you will also need effective personal branding to differentiate you from competitors and allow you to build trust with prospective clients.[32]

> *Your brand is what people say about you*
> *when you're not in the room.*
> —Jeff Bezos, the founder of Amazon

WHAT DOES PERSONAL BRANDING MEAN?

"The term 'branding' used to be reserved for businesses, but with the advent of social sites and the gig economy, *personal* branding has become fundamental. A personal brand is the unique combination of personality, skills and experiences that make you who you are. It is how you present yourself to the world and has become more important than ever."[33] It also includes your overall strategy for communicating who you are and why you should be selected for and will succeed in your authentic health career.

---

[32] Castrillon, "Branding."
[33] Castrillon, "Branding."

If you Google personal branding, you will find numerous resources with advice on how to develop and promote your personal brand. Google yourself to see what prospective employers, co-workers, or graduate schools will consider to be your current personal brand. Here are some useful resources: https://www.syedirfana-jmal.com/brand-yourself-for-success and https://hbr.org/2013/09/personal-branding-for-introverts.

Branding considerations and strategies vary by your goals, niche, target audience, and reason for branding (e.g., securing a job, getting into graduate school, attracting patients/clients, transitioning to new career directions, or establishing trust and expertise). The following approach seems most relevant to people seeking a job or positioning themselves for graduate school:

1. Be clear about who you are and what you want.
2. Define who you are trying to influence, why, and what outcomes you are seeking. Understand what is important to them and what is the best way to engage them.
3. Determine your unique purpose, values, and strengths and what differentiates you from others relative to the outcomes you are seeking.
4. Decide on what persona and value proposition you are trying to communicate and how the unique elements of my personal story support it.
5. Identify the best channels for you to communicate your value and story to your audience and the tools you will use.
6. Strengthen your packaging (resume, cover letter, social media presence, etc.) to be sure it is congruent with your story and desired outcomes.
7. Develop and follow an action plan and timeline for implementing and maintaining your brand. Determine your networking strategy.

This article from Entrepreneurs.com offers another five-step process for you to consider in developing your personal brand; you can find it at https://www.entrepreneur.com/article/298513.

As part of the branding process, I encourage you to assess your personality strengths and how you will brand yourself given your background and objectives. Sally Hogshead has an online assessment that you can utilize to help determine how to take advantage of your unique characteristics and strengths.[34] Her website also includes other valuable personal branding resources.[35]

> *You never get a second chance to make a first impression—*
> *make it one that will set you apart and reflect who you are.*
> —Caroline Castrillon

Physicians and other health providers, consultants, and entrepreneurs in the health field rely more and more on branding to attract clients, enhance their credibility reputation, and communicate their value. These resources provide personal branding advice for health professionals: https://bankershealthcaregroup.com/blog/personal-branding-for-healthcare-professionals/ and https://www.medelita.com/blog/personal-branding-healthcare-professionals/

YOU ARE READY!

The good news is if you have done all the work thus far on the elements of the Framework that precede the personal branding and packing step, then you are well prepared. You have already done your homework to clarify who you are and what you want, what makes you unique, and what you are good at and enjoy doing (the bottom of the Triangle). You have already identified what the world needs and

---

[34] Hogshead, "Test."
[35] Hogshead, "Fascinate."

what employers are looking for (top of the Triangle). You have already gained experience aligned with your passions to inform and make the case for the authentic life and career direction you have chosen (if you haven't done it, go back and do it before you work on branding and packaging). Armed with this information, you can follow the steps outlined earlier and use the resources provided to develop and implement your personal brand strategy. You will be working on utilizing it through networking in the next chapter.

PACKAGING COMPONENTS

With clarity about your personal branding strategy aligned with your authentic health career you are ready to strengthen your packaging. Solid packaging is particularly important for you to secure the next step in your authentic career path—such as a job, promotion, internship, fellowship, or entry into graduate school. Your packaging "portfolio" includes a combination of the following components. The description of each component includes its role in helping you meet your goals, tips for success, and links to resources to further strengthen your packaging.

1. Resume

A resume is a written compilation of your education, work experience, credentials, and accomplishments. Most professional positions require applicants to submit a resume and cover letter[36] as part of the application process.[37,38] Many graduate schools also require or encourage a resume as part of their application. Resumes are often the first thing that recruiters or hiring managers review to assess your

---

[36] Doyle, "Cover Letter."
[37] Doyle, "Application Process."
[38] Doyle, "Resume."

qualifications. Initial employer screenings of resumes are increasingly done by an automated system so it is important to learn and apply how to make your resume get selected through these mechanisms.

More research- or academic-oriented jobs or graduate programs may prefer a curriculum vitae (CV) instead of a resume. A CV also summarizes your qualifications and includes more details related to your relevant academic and research experience, presentations, and publications. When applying for a position, you should be clear whether a resume or CV is preferred by the employer and, if a CV, the level of detail desired.

Given that the purpose of a resume or CV is to get you an interview and you get the job based on your qualifications and how well your interview and references support the fit between you and the position and organization, your resume should by designed accordingly. Keep in mind that the average time spent on an initial resume review is approximately seven seconds,[39] so be sure your most important qualifications and key words aligned with the position description are quick and easy for the reader to access.

7 KEY RESUME TIPS FOR HEALTH PROFESSIONALS

1.   Keep it to one page (I know you have lots of valuable experiences and awards, but remember how quickly employers read resumes).
2.   Be sure the content, format, and tone align with the personal brand you want to convey.
3.   Focus the descriptions under each experience on your objective, actions you took, and the results (OAR) rather than a summer of your responsibilities. Use active verbs (*led, analyzed, wrote*) to describe your action and use the correct tense.
4.   No need to include an objective or "references available on request"

---

[39] O'Donnell, "Recruiters."

5. Highlight key skills relevant to your field and the position—including technical and essential skills (working in teams, interpersonal skills, initiative, customer service) and have experience to support them. Specify key language skills and computer skills.

6. Include health-related volunteer and leadership-related experiences (student clubs, professional associations, community, church, etc.).

7. Be sure the key points you want health employers or health professions schools to see quickly jump off the page.

Additional Resources

For more in-depth advice on resumes visit my website (Jeffoxendine.com) and watch this webinar: http://myhealthcareernavigator.com/video/how-to-write-a-resume-and-cover-letter-that-gets-you-a-job.

2. Cover Letter

You typically submit a cover letter with your resume when you apply for a position. In your cover letter, you make a concise, compelling case about why you are interested in and qualified for the position and why you should be chosen for an interview over other candidates. Your cover letter also demonstrates your writing skills and ability to be persuasive. Like your resume, the content and tone of the cover letter should be aligned with your personal brand.

5 KEY COVER LETTER TIPS FOR HEALTH PROFESSIONALS

1. Start with strong topic sentences that convey your enthusiasm for and fit for the position and sets up the rest of the letter. Don't start with something like "attached is my resume for your position."

2. Be very clear about what the employer is looking for in a successful candidate and concisely make the case about why and how you are a solid fit. Highlight your unique qualifications.

3. It should be no more than half to three-quarters of a page that is easy to read and reflects your best writing (with no spelling or grammatical errors).

4. Convey your passion for the position and how it aligns with your goals and values and your education and experiences.

5. Summarize your story in a way that makes the reader want to learn more and meet you!

Additional Resources

For additional resources visit my website (Jeffoxendine.com) and watch this webinar: http://myhealthcareernavigator.com/video/how-to-write-a-resume-and-cover-letter-that-gets-you-a-job

3. Writing Sample

Solid writing skills are increasingly important in the health professions, particularly in public health, health policy, health administration, consulting, research, and evaluation-related positions. Many employers are now asking for a writing sample as part of the application or if they consider you a serious candidate. You should have a few writing samples that serve as examples of your best writing. Ideally, the format and content of the samples you submit would align with the nature and the level of the work you would do in the position you are seeking. For example, if you are applying for a health policy analyst role, it would be ideal for your sample be a policy brief, report, or well-written academic paper related to health policy. If you are a student or recent graduate, a relevant academic paper, or at least one that demonstrates the quality of your writing, will often suffice if you don't have a professional writing sample. However, I encourage you to find opportunities in your courses, internships, student club work, or community advocacy work to work on practical examples that would be relevant in your authentic health career directions.

3 KEY WRITING SAMPLE TIPS FOR HEALTH PROFESSIONALS

1. Anticipate that you will need writing samples at some point in your job search or graduate school application process. Select and refine examples that you already have and seek out and develop additional samples aligned with the types of positions you will pursue.
2. Have professors or colleagues review and provide feedback on samples and how to strengthen so that you put your best work forward.
3. Put your writing samples in an attractive format and package that can easily and quickly be sent to employers upon request. Have a note to include your rationale for sending the samples and how they demonstrate your qualifications.

Additional Resources

For additional advice on submitting writing samples, see https://www.indeed.com/career-advice/interviewing/guide-to-submitting-a-writing-sample.

4. Interviewing Skills

Once you get the interview, it is important that you can effectively communicate your qualifications, strengths, and fit for the job in order to get the offer. You will be well served by strengthening your interview preparation and skills.

Interview preparation starts far in advance of an interview. It starts with knowing how to communicate your personal brand. It also includes knowing and having a concise, compelling way to communicate your career direction and how the position you are interviewing for fits. You also need to effectively convey and give examples of your strengths and experience relative to the position goals and requirements. You even need to be able to discuss your areas for further growth and development.

Interview preparation also includes finding out and preparing for the format of the interview and with whom you will be meeting. Interview formats range from an initial phone screening interview with a recruiter to an in-depth one-on-one interview with a hiring manager and/or series of co-workers to a three-hour case study interview with a panel. An interview process may involve all the above. Medical school interview formats vary by school and can include a combination of in-depth interviews and short five- to seven-minute interviews with multiple people. You need to find out ahead of time so you can be mentally and physically prepared and develop effective strategies and skills.

Case study interviews are becoming more common in the health field, particularly in health consulting, management, or policy but also in other areas. They are designed to have you demonstrate your critical thinking, problem-solving, and communications skills under time pressure and without complete information. Case studies can be challenging and stressful. Obviously, you want to know in advance if you are going to have a case study and be prepared. Fortunately, there are many resources and training available to hone your case-study interviewing skills, and you can learn from many people who have survived them and secured great jobs.

Here are some helpful resources:

https://www.preplounge.com/en/case-interview

https://igotanoffer.com/blogs/mckinsey-case-interview-blog/
115672708-mckinsey-case-interview-preparation-the-only-post-youll-need-to-read

https://www.themuse.com/advice/ace-the-case-7-steps-to-cracking-your-consulting-interview

Practicing in advance is an important way to prepare for all kinds of interviews and to enhance your skills. You can practice on your own by anticipating key questions, preparing your answers, and articulating your answers. You can do this in the mirror or videotape yourself. I also encourage you to practice with mentors, friends, or colleagues and ask for their positive and constructive feedback on what you conveyed and how you can be more effective. A potentially uncomfortable but enlightening experience is to do a mock interview and have it videotaped. Some campuses have a service through which you can be interviewed by a career center counselor or, in some cases, a machine and then review your interview tape afterward. Why not see what the interviewer sees and be sure you are communicating in the best possible way. However you approach it, be sure to be well prepared and strengthen your interview skills.

7 KEY INTERVIEWING TIPS FOR HEALTH PROFESSIONALS

In addition to the preceding tips, consider these tips:

1. Be sure you are dressed appropriately. Find out the dress code in advance.
2. Know where you are going and give yourself significant extra time to get there early. If a video or online interview, be sure you have the necessary software and can connect in advance.
3. Prepare your opening statements or elevator speech in anticipation of being asked something like, "Tell me about yourself and why you are interested in this position." Be focused, concise, and enthusiastic.
4. Prepare your answers to behavioral interview questions by having solid examples of your strengths and skills relative to the position requirements and discussing the impact and results of your actions.
5. Be sure to make a positive connection with the interviewers through eye contact, firm handshake, smiles, and body language. Practice active listening.

6. Go in with the mindset that the interviewer will like you rather than the fear that you will be rejected.

7. Always follow-up immediately with a thank-you note, handwritten preferably, and/or professional email.

Additional Resources

For more resources on effective interviewing skills, go to my website (Jeffoxendine.com) and see https://www.monster.com/career-advice/article/boost-your-interview-iq and https://www.glassdoor.com/employers/blog/interview-questions-healthcare/.

5. Elevator Speech

Having an effective elevator speech or pitch is important for effective interviews, networking, and gaining support for your goals and ideas. An elevator speech is a clear, brief message or "commercial" about you. It communicates who you are, what you're looking for, and how you can benefit a company or organization. It's typically about 30 seconds, the time it takes people to ride from the top to the bottom of a building in an elevator.[40] Elevator speeches are also important in health professions school interviews and to start out your informational interviews. I encourage you to develop elevator speeches of longer or shorter lengths (e.g., the number of floors of the elevator ride) so you can tailor it in the moment to fit the purpose and amount of time you have for the interaction and the person you are connecting with. For example, your opening elevator speech in your informational interview will be shorter if you have 15 minutes with the CEO of the hospital you have not met versus an hour with a colleague of a mentor who attended the same undergraduate institution as you.

---

[40] UC Davis, "Elevator Speech."

Just like with interviews, it is important to prepare for and practice your elevator speeches in advance. You may want to start by writing down your answers in a template that is practical for you. For example, a simple elevator speech template I use with students is included as part of End of Chapter Exercise 2 on page 194.

Armed with your answers you can practice and then experiment in your interactions. Over time you will find out what works best for you.

7 KEY ELEVATOR SPEECH TIPS FOR HEALTH PROFESSIONALS

In addition to the earlier tips, consider the following:

1. Be sure you have open and engaging body language, eye contact, and facial expressions.
2. Be confident in yourself but not cocky.
3. Tailor your comments to the objectives you have for the interaction and the person you are speaking with.
4. It's more about making a positive connection and getting the conversation started than being perfect. If you make a mistake just smile, recover, be nice to yourself, and keep going.
5. Be specific about your health career direction(s), yet if you are not sure or if the opportunity isn't a perfect fit (or you don't know what the person does), leave an opening, such as, "I am currently focusing on being a psychologist or social worker, but I am also exploring other paths in the mental health field."
6. Briefly discuss how your experiences, education, and passion align with the person's role or the opportunity you are pursuing.
7. If appropriate, end with an "ask" or "request" of the person, such as, "I would like to explore opportunities aligned with my interests in your organization" or "I am hoping we can set a time for an informational interview."

Additional Resources

https://www.thebalancecareers.com/elevator-speech-examples-and-writing-tips-2061976

https://www.indeed.com/career-advice/interviewing/how-to-give-an-elevator-pitch-examples

https://healthcaresuccess.com/blog/physician-marketing/elevator-speech.html

6. LinkedIn Profile and Engagement

You must also have a LinkedIn Profile that effectively communicates your personal brand, interests, and strengths and must be a highly skilled and engaged user. More companies are searching for talented employees through LinkedIn and using your profile to assess your qualifications. Internet-based recruitment, by people and artificial intelligence, will play a larger role and will become more specialized and sophisticated.

LinkedIn is also a powerful networking tool for leveraging and expanding your relationships. I am amazed at the access that LinkedIn provides to people in your network and in theirs. You have endless, large-scale opportunities to promote yourself and work and connect to people who can assist and/or hire you.

I recommend strengthening your LinkedIn profile, navigating skills, and engagement to advance toward your next steps and authentic career direction. If this isn't already a top strength for you, make it a core part of your action plan.

7 KEY LINKEDIN TIPS FOR HEALTH PROFESSIONALS

1. Have a picture that communicates who you are aligned with your professional brand.
2. Align your profile with your resume and ensure that both effectively communicate your personal brand. Have mentors,

recruiters, and hiring managers in your chosen field give you feedback.

3. Connect with people you know and others within your sphere of influence—such as alumni from your school, people who have worked for the same employers, and/or key players in professional associations or your community. Reach out with requests to connect or have an informational interview.

    Join relevant groups.

4. Secure testimonials related to skills you highlight and that are most relevant for the career paths you are pursing and positions you are applying.

5. Craft a concise, compelling message to request people to connect with you.

6. Carve out a solid portion of time each week or day to engage.

7. Post regularly on interesting things you are doing or learn related to your authentic health career direction, passions, and plans. Highlight your milestones, accomplishments, and new jobs.

Additional Resources

https://www.dummies.com/social-media/linkedin/10-tips-leverage-linkedin/

https://www.linkedin.com/pulse/20140425191634-27848656-5-tips-for-leveraging-linkedin-to-raise-your-visibility/

https://www.topresume.com/career-advice/14-ways-to-leverage-your-linkedin-profile-during-your-job-search

7. Social Media Presence

According to a 2018 CareerBuilder survey, 70% of employers use social media to screen candidates during the hiring process, and 43% of employers use social media to check on current employees.[41]

---

[41] Career Builder, "Social Media."

Graduate programs are also using social media as part of the admissions process. So guess what? It is in your best interest to be sure your social media presence, history, and content present you in the way you want employers and graduate schools to see you (before and after you get the job). Please go through all your sites and be sure to clean them up in advance of when you need them.

STORYTELLING

In addition to these seven components of packaging, you must be able to tell your story verbally and in writing.

> *Your ability to follow through and execute on your greatness*
> *comes down to how effectively you can communicate your*
> *unique story. There is unbelievable power in the skill of*
> *storytelling because it is what ultimately creates trust*
> *and builds confidence with those around you.*
> —Bo Eason

All of us have a unique and powerful story. Your story and how well you communicate it may make the difference in your ability to get into health professions training programs, graduate school, secure jobs, and advance in your field. Being able to tell your story will also lead to the ability to secure support and funding for your dreams and ideas.

Storytelling is an art and a skill. It is a skill that can be developed and perfected.

I was fortunate to be trained by Bo Eason to strengthen my personal storytelling ability. I have benefitted ever since. Bo's training and book can be found at https://boeason.com/.

Your essays and personal statement for graduate school and cover letters for jobs all involve telling your story. Your in-person or video interviews are opportunities to differentiate yourself by telling your story. I encourage you to develop your story aligned with your personal brand and designed to help you connect with and advance toward your authentic career. Refining your story also helps you get in touch with your deep reasons for wanting to pursue your authentic health career. It helps you develop the ability to be real and vulnerable in a way that enhances personal connection and trust.

> *We can tell the box checker's a mile away.*
> —Panel of Admission's Deans

My colleagues who are admissions deans at medical schools have made it clear that there are many students who have done all the right things to get into medical school, such as getting a good science GPA, solid MCAT scores, research experience, and a publication but in their interview can't communicate in their authentic voice why they want to be a doctor. Be sure you can. Here is an example of a story from a doctor colleague of mine who is associated with medical school admissions.

WILBUR'S STORY

Wilbur grew up in the South Side of Chicago, the city's toughest neighborhood. He was the youngest of four children raised by his single mother. His family moved apartments frequently and three times were homeless. He played sports and worked to keep off the streets and out of trouble, but it wasn't easy to stay safe. He had a passion and was very good at science. Since his grandmother died of cancer and his grandfather of diabetes, he had always wanted to be a doctor. He would have to overcome many challenges to reach his dream, but it kept it alive. One of the challenges was having a young child while in high school. With the assistance of teachers, mentors, and coaches who saw his drive and potential he went to college and pursued premed studies. His girlfriend, mother, and sisters helped him raise the child. The organic chemistry and physics classes he encountered were initially event more challenging than expected due to his high school preparation. Fortunately, he learned to ask for help from TAs, professors, and tutors. He also formed strong study groups with classmates and persevered. He ended up doing well in those courses and finishing with strong grades in his biology and African American Studies majors. He did well on the MCAT. His next biggest challenge was getting into medical school and being able to pay for it.

Wilbur had to work 30 hours per week during school to support his family and help pay for housing and tuition. When he finished school, he had to take a full-time job as a transporter in an inner-city emergency room (ER). One day, he almost was shot by a patient who returned to the ER unhappy with not getting the pain medication drugs he needed. Wilbur wondered when his challenges would end.

Wilbur ended up meeting a mentor who advised him that his challenges and how he overcame them were major strengths. His mentor helped him craft a story of Wilbur's experiences, resilience, and lessons learned and how they contributed to him being a strong candidate for medical school and promising doctor. He practiced his story in writing and verbally. He learned to connect with people through his story and inspire them. He incorporated it into his statements of purpose for medical school and his interviews. Wilbur ultimately not only was accepted to a strong medical school that was a great fit for him but also received a full-ride scholarship. The school was impressed by his story, academic performance, life experiences, and resilience and how he clearly and compellingly articulated how they prepared him to be an effective doctor for under-resourced communities like the one he came from. He became a family medicine doctor who also led pipeline programs for youth interested in health careers and became a strong role model and mentor. He now uses his storytelling to raise money for the programs he leads for inner-city youth and the clinic where he practices. He is now also part of the outreach and admissions process for a medical school he teaches at and helps other students develop their stories to assist them in advancing in their journey.

What's your story? How will you tell it to advance toward your health career dreams?

END OF CHAPTER EXERCISES

Exercise 1: Personal Branding

Utilize the seven tips and the resources to begin to define your personal brand. Be as clear as possible about your objectives, target audiences, value proposition, personality types, and messaging.

Exercise 2: Elevator Speech

Use this template or another that you like to write down your elevator speech. After you write it down, practice it on your own and in the mirror, and make any necessary adjustments. When you are ready, begin practicing it with friends or family. Then try it out at a networking event or for in an informational interview. Continue to review and practice it. Have different versions for various lengths of time and settings you will have to use it. See how people react and if it helps you succeed in your pursuits. Ask for feedback. Continue to refine and reap the benefits.

I am (full name) _____.

I am a student or an alumnus of _____.

I am majoring in _____, working at _____, or a member of _____ (what best applies).

My current health career direction(s) or interests are _____.

I am in the process of/am here because _____.

I would like to speak with you or learn more about _____.

Exercise 3: LinkedIn

Update your LinkedIn profile and engage with it at least twice a week. Have friends and professional colleagues give you feedback. Ask for feedback from recruiters in your field. Review profiles and activities of others in your field. Reach out to and connect with alumni from your school who are in your chosen path and set up informational interviews.

FRAMEWORK STEP 7

NETWORK OR NOT WORK

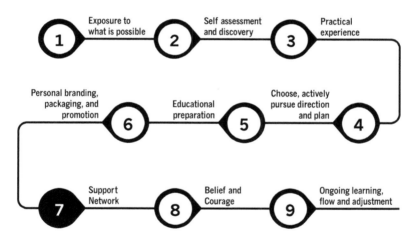

It's either network or not work.
—Harvey Bichkoff, former CEO, Marin Oncology

Networking in the seventh step in the Framework. In this chapter, you will learn why networking is essential to discovering and achieving your authentic health career. You will also learn to adjust your mindset about how to approach mentoring, even if you are uncomfortable with it, and gain practical skills that will help you become a more effective networker in person and electronically. You will learn how to put yourself in the flow of people and opportunities and expand and maintain your network over time for personal and professional success.

My good friend Harvey's quote, which opens this chapter, is one of the most important pieces of advice I have ever heard. Since I heard him provide this sage advice to my MPH students at UC Berkeley many years ago, I have delivered his message to inspire thousands of students to strengthen their networking skills. Whether you like it or not, networking is **necessary** for you to achieve your authentic health career and secure jobs and entry into health professions schools along the way. Networking is also essential to success in your chosen field because it is a way to build and utilize relationships that enable you to secure the information, funding and team members you need to get things done and meet your goals. I found the company that published this book and decided to work with them through networking. All my jobs, program funding, and accomplishments in my more than 30 years in the health field have come from networking.

> *Your network is your net worth.*
> —Tim Sanders

WHAT IS NETWORKING?

I have found that people have a wide range of definitions and perceptions of networking and that many of us, because of our background or experiences, may not be familiar with what is involved. I define networking as developing, utilizing, and maintaining mutually beneficial relationships through which information, connections, and support can be shared for mutual benefit.

I find the following definitions of networking practical and useful for people pursuing their authentic health careers. Hopefully some elements of them will resonate with you:

> Networking is "a supportive system of sharing information and services among individuals and groups having a common interest." For example: "Working mothers in the community use networking to help themselves manage successfully."[42]

> "Networking is the exchange of information and ideas among people with a common profession or special interest, usually in an informal social setting. Networking is used by professionals to expand their circles of acquaintances, to find out about job opportunities in their fields, and to increase their awareness of news and trends in their fields or in the greater world. Networking helps a professional keep up with current events in the field and develops relationships that may boost future business or employment prospects. Needless to say, it also provides opportunities to help other people find jobs, make connections and catch up on the news."[43]

> "Networking simply means making connections and forming relationships with other professionals in your field. Many graduates view professional networking as the gateway to obtaining job offers. While networking and knowing the right people often provides access to career opportunities, there is more to be gained from successful networking than just finding a job. Through networking, professionals share a wealth of knowledge, resources, and connections."[44]

---

[42] Dictionary.com, "Networking."
[43] Kagan, "Networking."
[44] Public Health, "Networking."

PERSONAL AND PROFESSIONAL NETWORKS

Discovery, entry, and advancement in our authentic health career path requires strong personal and professional networks.

Personal Networks

Most of us have personal networks that can be very beneficial in our life, educational and health career journeys. Some of us have strong networks by virtue of our families, friends, communities, or the schools we have attended or the places we have worked. Personal networks can be an important source of support as you deal with the joys and struggles of completing your education, entering the health professions, and managing your day-to-day work. While health jobs are rewarding, they can also be very challenging and taxing.

Key sources of personal network support include:

◆ Family
◆ Friends
◆ Mentors
◆ Classmates or co-workers
◆ Teachers and college instructors
◆ Career counselors or coaches
◆ Health-related student club members
◆ Professional colleagues you develop a personal relationship with
◆ Alumni from your schools
◆ Religious or spiritual leaders, teachers, and communities

Although parents, family, and friends can be strong sources of personal support, it is common at times that engagement of them in your authentic career pursuit can present challenges or limitations. Many people face the significant challenge of not having parental support for their authentic health career path because it is different from the profession that the parents strongly believe they should pursue.

I have found this to be most common in when people are part of cultures where only certain professions are held in esteem, such as doctors, engineers, lawyers, businesspeople, and, in some cases, nurses. One of the reasons I titled this book *You Don't Have to Be a Doctor* is because I have worked with thousands of talented people pursuing health careers who have really struggled with this dynamic. It can be extremely difficult to go against your parental and cultural preferences even if you know it isn't your authentic path.

Another major challenge that many people I have worked with have struggled with is when your parents support you individually but just don't have the background or experience to understand what you are dealing with or to help you with decisions and connections. These and other challenges and limitations and strategies for overcoming them are detailed in Chapter 10 on belief and courage (starting on page 221). In both cases, developing and utilizing strong personal networks in which others can support and help inform your decisions and provide needed advice along the way is invaluable.

> *It's not just who you know, it's who you know*
> *who knows what you can do and want to do.*
> —Thomas Luten

Professional Networks

Professional networks offer opportunities for support, information exchange, access to jobs, and collaboration to advance your work in the health field. All the sources of personal support listed earlier can also be engaged in your professional network. Additional sources for professional networking include the following:

- Professional, alumni, and student associations
- People in comparable professional roles or fields and/or with similar or complementary interests

- Referrals or introductions from colleagues to people in their networks
- Professors, lecturers, or graduate student instructors
- On-campus or professional school advisors
- People you meet at conferences, seminars, and events
- Current or former boss or co-workers
- Volunteering in your field or another area of interest
- "Random people" you meet on in your travels or daily lives (I met one of my most important advisors on a red-eye flight to Boston)

Professional networking is a way for you to access potential job opportunities, make connections for graduate school, learn about industry trends and best practices, get information, and build relationships to help you succeed in your educational or career pursuits. Professional relationships can also lead to valuable collaborations and resources. For health providers, professional networks may be a valuable source of patient referrals, consultation on patient care, and support for dealing with the rigors of practice.

Many of us are blessed with strong professional networks while others struggle to access and maintain them. No matter who and where you are relative to networking, you can strengthen your personal and professional networks. The key is to set an intention to do so, take consistent action, and follow through. A key first step is often understanding and addressing our perceptions and experiences of networking and overcoming associated barriers.

PERCEPTIONS AND EXPERIENCES OF NETWORKING

Some of us are natural networkers and are confident in our ability and networks. Many of us are not comfortable and/or not confident with networking. Which you are may depend on many factors including your age and experience, personality type, values, and biases. Over the years, I have found that most college students and many early careerists in the health field seem to be uncomfortable with networking or are not confident in their ability to network. Fortunately, like storytelling, you can develop your networking skills and gain confidence with practice and experience. There are many resources available to assist you, and you can pursue many opportunities for practice.

MY NETWORKING JOURNEY

As a college student and in graduate school, I was the world's worst and most uncomfortable networker. Fortunately, I learned from my mentors and internship program that networking was important, and I was able to observe health leaders network for significant benefit. I also became more motivated to continue to grow when I consistently experienced many networking benefits. I didn't realize it at the time, but I had innate networking skills and was a connector. I was too busy being self-conscious and feeling uncomfortable. I would attend networking events and was tongue-tied and shy when I awkwardly engaged people.

I was also concerned about what I perceived to be the "one-way nature" of networking and that I had little to offer the high-level senior leaders and health practitioners I would meet. The interactions initially felt contrived and I felt pressure to "perform." When I was looking for a job or approaching people about graduate school, I felt uncomfortable about active self-promotion, as I had been taught to be humble, to not ask for what I wanted and to be self-deprecating and critical. I also feared rejection from people in authority positions. Even though deep down inside I believed in myself and abilities, I struggled at times with low self-esteem and feelings of unworthiness. I felt like everyone but me was comfortable with and good at networking. I was wrong about that and about my self-worth and networking ability.

> *Being shy means being afraid of negative rejection.*
> —Michael A. Singer

Although networking events intimidated me, I discovered the power of networking through informational interviews (discussed in detail in Chapter 3 on exposure). I was fortunate to learn about and practice informational interviews during my first college internship in health administration. I had the opportunity to do "rotations" throughout the hospital. My rotations involved visiting almost all departments of the hospital over the summer and conducting informational interviews with the leaders and key team members. I also met with senior administrators, nurse leaders, and medical directors. I found that almost everyone was warm and welcoming. I would say a few words about who I was at the beginning of each interview, and then people would spend the rest of the time talking enthusiastically about themselves and their departments. I found that people loved talking about their journeys and imparting their wisdom to a student. I felt the positive connection it created between us and that at the end, most people volunteered to meet again or provide me with additional support. I also discovered that although I was not as good as talking about myself or health issues on the spot, I was very good at asking insightful questions and active listening. These skills became my go-to networking skills to engage and connect with people and are still to this day. The more comfortable I became with asking questions and actively listening, the more positive response I received from the people I spoke with the more I was willing to engage.

I also found people very receptive to referring me to others in their networks. It seemed like, magically, each person I spoke to would provide me with a new gem of information and just the insight I needed at that moment to continue to refine and advance on my career path. They would introduce me to just the right next person or opportunity. The momentum built as did my self-confidence. I was being propelled forward by a flow of people and opportunities that continued to advance me toward my goal of health administration and graduate school.

I also found that networking with professors and advisors proved very fruitful. I would get great advice and "warm" leads to alumni and professional contacts in their networks. The warm leads made me more comfortable in reaching out and engaging with people and made them more receptive to being real with and supporting me.

My networking at events improved when I became a student board member and actively engaged in a professional association called Health Care Executives of Northern California (HCENC). The more I showed up at the monthly events and engaged with members in work to support the association, the more I felt I belonged and was building relationships with people. For the most part, I was the youngest person in almost every event and activity, but that ended up being an advantage as everyone wanted to provide advice and support. I eventually led the annual symposium and become the membership chair; in this position, I met every new and returning member. Within seven years of being an undergraduate intern in HCENC, I became the President and presided over meetings. I knew everyone and had developed a solid network that would benefit me and them for years to come (still to this day). I had the networking bug and now the student who was the world's worst networker teaches networking!

The moral of the story is that no matter where you are relative to your comfort and skills with networking, you can and need to become a strong networker. Fortunately, I found almost everyone I met in the health field very receptive to networking and welcoming and supportive, particularly to students and early careerists. Some of us are natural networkers and self-promoters, but I have found over the years that more students tend to be less comfortable and skilled. Particularly now when many people's primary forms of communication are electronic and calling people on the phone and/or engaging with people face-to-face in person is less common and comfortable. Fortunately, there are and will continue to be increasing networking opportunities online, and you also will benefit from developing the ability to be a strong in-person networker.

SO WHAT DO YOU NEED TO BE AN EFFECTIVE NETWORKER?

Networking often begins with a single point of common ground. The most obvious is a professional affiliation, but some people find effective networking opportunities in a college alumni group, a church or synagogue social group, or a private club.[45,46] Armed with a single point of common ground, you can begin to connect and begin to work toward a productive relationship. To find that common ground, engage the people you meet and go beyond it to develop strong personal and professional networks, I have found effective networking involves a combination of mindset, strategies, skills, and practice. Here's what you need.

MINDSET

Your mindset can influence your networking comfort and effectiveness:

◆ If you don't like the term or connotations of networking, adjust your mindset to be about developing relationships, making connections, or getting assistance to pursue your goals.

◆ Understand that regardless of how you feel about it, networking is an important part of being a person and health professional and how many things get done. Learn that you can be uncomfortable and still actively pursue and get better at networking.

◆ Approach networking with the mindset that most interactions will be for mutual benefit, in the near, mid-, or longer term. For example, you may be pursuing a connection for a job that would be great for you and the company also benefits by hiring a talented, wonderful person. Sometimes students or early careerists feel that an informational interview may be all for their benefit and that they don't have much to offer, but the interviewee

---

[45] Parker, "Tips."
[46] Kagan, "Networking."

usually gets the enjoyment of sharing their life and career journey and meeting a promising young person in their field. They may end up hiring the young person at some point, and wise people know that in the future that person could end up hiring them in some capacity or providing needed information or funding.

◆ Believe in yourself and that you have value to others or be working in that direction (more in Chapter 9).

◆ Be willing and have the courage to go outside your comfort zone, be vulnerable, and put yourself "out there."

> *Sometimes you just need 20 seconds of courage.*
> —Matt Damon in the movie *We Bought a Zoo*

◆ Be willing to risk rejection to advance toward something you value. "You miss a 100% of the shots that you don't take." Wayne Gretzky
"Some will, some won't, who cares." Tony Faulkner
"It only takes one." Jeff Oxendine

◆ Be willing to have your life change in a powerful, positive way. Grace and opportunities happen. Let go of the stories that hold you back or keep you stuck by putting yourself in the flow of people and opportunities (more on page 218).

◆ Develop or utilize a growth versus fixed mindset (more on page 231 in chapter 10). With a growth mindset, you are open to discovering ways in which you can grow and learn, even if things don't go as planned or work out the way you would like.

◆ Set and operate from an intention that you will be of service to others and that networking is a path to do so.

STRATEGIES AND SKILLS

Effective networking involves a set of strategies and skills you can develop and strengthen through resources and practice. Listed below are proven, practical networking strategies. Remote work and education and social distancing requirements may make it more challenging to implement these strategies in person for the foreseeable future. However, many of them can be done remotely and, in some cases, you may have access to people who you might not otherwise have had. Creative new ways of networking will be developed and become common practice.

Strategies

- Informational interviews
- Mentor, professor, or co-worker referrals—when I finished grad school my mentor referred me to several key people in his network, including his mentors, who helped me decide what I wanted to do and opened doors to jobs.
- Professional associations and/or student clubs. Assume leadership roles.
- Conferences and events
- Internships and volunteering
- Informal events in your school or organization—always show up and engage, for example, the Doctor–Administration basketball game, birthday parties, happy hours. By participating, you build relationships and increase your zone of acceptance and get to know people.
- Shadowing
- Contacting alumni
- Class projects
- Access to large numbers of like-minded individuals
- Board participation
- Job or career fairs

I encourage you to check out these additional helpful networking tips from the sources below:

- Networking tips for healthcare professionals by Andrea Clement Santiago: https://www.verywellhealth.com/healthcare-networking-medical-career-1736039
- Six tips for effective networking by Olivia Morrisey on Workit Daily: https://www.workitdaily.com/online-networking-quick-tips
- Resources for students in or recently out of college include: https://www.workitdaily.com/network-after-college-social-media
- It is essential that you become effective at networking through LinkedIn. Heather Krasna, Assistant Dean of Career Services at Columbia Mailman School of Public Health, is an expert on LinkedIn and also offers other valuable career related services through her website at https://heatherkrasna.com/.

Skills

- Don't be afraid to ask.
- Recognize and act on moments of opportunity (even if it means going out of your comfort zone)—for example, asking for an informational interview from a prominent guest speaker in class or offering to meet with students or a person sitting next to you at a conference who does exactly what you want to do.

> *When I was stranded on the top of my house in the flood,*
> *I asked God to help rescue me, a boat, helicopter*
> *and raft appeared but I kept waiting for God,*
> *when I asked again God said, what are you waiting for,*
> *I already sent a boat, helicopter and raft,*
> *please take the next one.*
> —The story of the Drowning Man[47]

---

[47] TruthBook, "Drowning Man."

NETWORKING AT EVENTS

My colleague Catherine Dodd provided me and my students with some of the most practical and powerful advice about effectively networking at events.

Key insights include:

- Research the event. Host and speakers in advance. Understand the event's objectives, topics, and target audiences. Define what you want to learn from the event and your networking.
- Find out the dress code and be sure to dress accordingly.
- Prepare and practice your elevator speech.
- Research the latest news related to the topics and participants. Prepare some key questions and pieces of small talk.
- Use your OAR—make an observation (the keynote speaker was really compelling; the food is really good; this is a great turnout). Ask a question (I see you work at Stanford Medical Center; what is your role and how long have you been there? Are you working on a project related to the topic? I see you have an MBA in addition to your MD degree; why did you pursue that?). Reveal something about yourself (this is my first time at an event of this association, I really appreciated the speaker's comments about the latest trend in community health, I am interested in working in the same organization or profession as you).
- Seek out wall huggers (people who are standing by themselves, not engaged with others). Approach larger groups on the periphery and make eye contact with one person.
- Introduce yourself and thank the host before you leave.
- Ask for business cards and/or professional network information before you go.

Practice

Remember, it's all practice not a performance,
focus on progress not perfection.
—Lydia Oxendine, my wife

When my son was about to enter the seventh-grade dance, my wife provided him with some advice that I wish someone would have told me when I was young, "Remember, it's all practice, it's important to get out there and dance, the odds that you are going to marry one of these girls is a million to one." So practice now so you can become a better dancer when it matters and enjoy it. I encourage you to heed this advice when it comes to developing your networking skills. Start practicing networking early when the stakes are not too high.

MY DAUGHTER'S STORY

My daughter's high school understood that getting career exposure and learning to network are an important life skill. One of her teachers required everyone in the class to conduct and write up an informational interview with a professional in the job and field they wanted to pursue. At the time, my daughter, Elizabeth, was interested in becoming an OB/GYN doctor who treats low-income women. On the way to the interview, my daughter disclosed that she was very nervous. I said that was normal and asked her what she was most nervous about. She said, "What if the doctor doesn't like me?" I assured her this was a natural fear and then asked why she wouldn't like her. I then asked her to reframe her mindset to be "What if she really likes me?" and approach the interview from that perspective (yet be humble and appreciative). She said she would try.

After the interview, Elizabeth bounded happily into my car and told me all the things she had learned and how much the doctor had said she liked her and enjoyed talking with her during the interview. The doctor said that meeting her and having the interview was one of the most fun things she had done all week. She said Elizabeth could call her anytime for advice. Elizbeth learned a valuable lesson about herself and networking. She also learned she didn't want to be a doctor, and no surprise, I told her she didn't have to be one. She then happily explored options and each additional informational interview she does or events she attends still brings nervousness but gets easier, and she is more effective. I encourage you to get lots of practice with informational interviews, networking events, conferences, and professional association meetings. Go easy on yourself and remember it's all practice and your comfort, confidence, and skill will grow. You can also practice with friends, peers, or mentors and get feedback. If you are a student, attending student club events, particularly before you are on the job or internship market provides great opportunities for practice. Take the initiative to organize and run a networking event with alumni and other professionals in your field. I also encourage you to go to office hours with your professors and make time to meet with and take initiative to do informational interviews with professionals, find mentors, and attend conferences. All give you practice and help you advance and build relationships.

> *Build relationships before you need them and keep them alive.*
> —Jeff Oxendine

SYSTEMS AND FOLLOW-THROUGH

One of the most overlooked but most essential parts of networking is having a system for keeping track of your network, following up with people and about opportunities, and maintaining your relationships.

I wish I had a dollar for every business card I brought home that I was very excited about but either didn't follow up within a timely way or do so at all. Busyness, procrastination, and fear of rejection got in the way. I also felt that I didn't have the time. The longer the time between when I met the person and when I followed up with them, the harder it was.

When you say you don't have the time to do something,
it is the same as saying I don't care.
—Maya Angelou

I also felt I didn't have the time because I felt the pressure for the perfect response. Make the time. It will take less long than you think. You will also feel better about yourself, be rewarded for acting toward your dreams and may position yourself for a relationship and/ or opportunity that really matter.

Having an organized system for follow-up and tracking will take your networking to another level.

Key system requirements include:

- A way to remind yourself about what you discussed with the person, key takeaways, characteristics of them, points of common ground and what you are going to follow-up with them about (and when)
- Time in your schedule for following up. Build time in your schedule each week to do it. Schedule the time and take action within a day or two after when you meet them.
- An online or binder- or folder-based filing system through which you can find the people you need when you need them and continue to update records of your interactions with them
- Reminders scheduled to follow up if you haven't heard back
- Templates for follow-up emails, handwritten notes, and LinkedIn requests that you can customize
- Schedules and reminders for following up with important contacts that you want to maintain

MAINTAINING RELATIONSHIPS

One of the most common questions I am asked about networking is "How do I maintain relationships with people I care about when I am no longer in a position to be in regular in-person contact with them?" Examples include professors after you graduate, former bosses and co-workers, a mentor who lives in another geographic area, and colleagues who live in other regions. Although this may seem daunting, there are more options than ever to stay connected and keep key people updated.

Seven practical tips include:

- Sending an email update every three to six months or annually. The email can be customized to the person or a more general update that you can send to others in your network. Don't necessarily require a response. You just want to keep on their radar screen and keep them up to date.
- Connecting through LinkedIn and other networking sites. Posting updates, securing testimonials, and recommending others. Sending occasional messages and asking for quick check-in calls.
- Setting up time for coffee or lunch when you are in town. Even if it is just a 10- to 15-minute hello. Give people ample notice if possible or stop by when you are in town to say hi.
- Sending follow-up gratitude when something someone did for you or worked out! This could include a contact that led to a job or a career direction breakthrough, advice from them that you followed that worked out well, or insights they shared that you applied effectively in their work.
- Informing people of major milestones or accomplishments in your life such as getting into or graduating from health professions school or residency, getting married, or securing a new job aligned with your passion and authentic direction.
- Sending a holiday card or greeting

♦ Sending an email to let them know you were thinking of them and appreciated what they did or do for you.

TERRI'S STORY

Terri was one of my favorite HCC interns. She stood out among her peers in many ways, including her passion, professionalism, and promise as a public health leader. At the end of her internship, she told me she was going to pursue a career in global health that would involve spending significant time abroad. Every six months or so, I would get an email update from Terri. It would be in the form of an email detailing her current role and whereabouts. It would have an entertaining update on some place she recently visited and some of her interesting reflections. I often read them quickly and sometimes sent a brief comment. This went on for about seven years. We hadn't spoken during that time, but I felt I was up to date on Terri and was appreciative of her staying in touch.

One day I received a call from Terri. She was back in the United States and had decided to make a career shift from Global Health to work with underserved populations domestically. She asked for my advice and connections that might be able to assist her. After our call, it dawned on me that Terri might be a great fit for a position I had with HCC. I called her back and within a week we agreed she would come work with me. Her regular emails really made a difference.

NETWORKING FOR PURSUIT OF HEALTH PROFESSIONS TRAINING PROGRAMS

Many people know the value of networking for jobs. Less well known but very beneficial is networking for entry into and funding for health professions training programs. Key tips of health professions school networking include:

- Conduct informational interviews with program directors, faculty, current students, alumni, and employer partners.
- Attend in-person outreach and prospective student events.
- Attend conferences on preparing for and getting admitted to graduate schools.
- Attend admitted students' days in person.
- Visit campuses and attend classes.
- Attend major professional meetings (like APHA) or graduate school fairs where admissions and outreach staff are present for purposes of engaging with students.
- Go out with students for lunch or activities after class.
- Develop relationships with program directors, coordinators, and faculty in your field of study; admissions and financial aid staff; diversity and inclusion team members; and others so that they know you when your application is reviewed and can advocate on your behalf for admissions and funding.

People make admissions and funding decisions. Often committees and processes include faculty, staff, and students. Making a strong impression and having a positive relationship with key players are beneficial in many programs, if not in admissions, then when it comes to assistance with financing your education on acceptance. Do know that some schools will have a firewall and do not engage with applicants, but many more are. For more tips on getting into health professions, please go to Chapter 7.

KAREN'S STORY

Karen was a reluctant networker. She was an introvert who considered herself shy and believed that networking was "fake" or contrived. Though she was uncomfortable, she agreed to try to gather information from and build relationships with faculty members and admissions staff at the Schools of Public Health, where she intended to apply. She met with people when she visited the campuses of her top three schools. She did this before she applied so she could incorporate what she learned into her applications. The insights she gained were invaluable as were the relationships. She felt she that she had made a good impression, and the people she met with encouraged her to reach out with additional questions.

Karen was a solid applicant but not a sure admit. She was glad she got to convey her qualifications in person and convey her sincere interest in the school. When she was notified of her acceptance, she thanked the people she had met. She also reconnected with them in person when she attended each admitted students' day. Costs were high, and she needed financial assistance. She let people know she needed assistance to afford attending and kept in contact with them for updates. The people said that they would advocate for her to secure funding but could not guarantee it. Ultimately, she chose the school that best fit her and was fortunate to secure the funding she needed. Her networking paid off.

Be of Service

One final mindset related to networking that I encourage you to adopt is that through networking you can be of service to others and the things you care about. This mindset can help you overcome some of your networking fears and discomfort. If you sincerely intend to be of service or benefit to the people you connect with, in addition to seeking something from them, it can balance out the concern that networking is a one-way street. It can also strengthen the relationship and make it mutually beneficial.

Knowing that you are networking for a cause you believe in that is greater than yourself can provide motivation and determination and increase your willingness to risk rejection. For example, when I network with colleagues to secure paid internship opportunities for students and grant funding for Health Career Connection (HCC), I am fueled by knowing everything that will successfully benefit students and an organization that I care deeply about. I also strongly believe that hosting HCC interns will be beneficial to the organizations that host them and to the field. Hosting and funding HCC interns are a true win-win in the near and long term, so I network for everyone's benefit.

PUT YOURSELF IN THE FLOW OF PEOPLE AND OPPORTUNITIES

Regardless of whether you are pursuing networking for personal or professional benefit or for employment, getting things done, or graduate school entry, it is essential to do whatever you can to put yourself in the flow of people and opportunities:

- **I** Informational interviews
- **N** Network mapping, development, skills, and practice
- **F** Find and use mentors, faculty, and friends
- **L** Leverage and communicate your strengths
- **O** Open to opportunity with focused and wide lens
- **W** Web-based networking and search strategy

In the "FLOW" of people and opportunities, you can find jobs, mentors, authentic career insights, and build momentum to achieve your life and career goals. If you believe in yourself, you can make more progress on all fronts and create more opportunities.

For more extensive information about networking, visit my online networking in healthcare module on my website.

END OF CHAPTER EXERCISES

Exercise 1: Network Mapping

On a sheet of paper, list the following categories that are relevant for you: family, friends, co-workers, fellow students, teachers/professors, mentors, clergy and spiritual community, professional associations, alumni, employers, and health professions school contacts.

For each category, list people you know who have information or contacts that could potentially be valuable to you in pursuing health career and educational options. Indicate the type of information and people that they could lead you to. You will likely have many more connections that you think, and you wont even know until you reach out who they know and can connect you to.

Prioritize the top five to seven people you will reach out to and set a time frame for engaging with them. Meet or speak with them and then ask for two to three people each whom they can connect you to and ask them to either make an introduction or allow you to reach out and use their name as a referral. Set your time frame for reaching out and action steps you will take.

As part of this exercise, look for gaps in your network, for example, not enough professional association connections, and identify steps you will take to address it—such as joining one or more relevant professional associations.

Exercise 2: Strengthening Your Network

♦   Assess the strength of your network. Identify areas you would like to strengthen and why.

♦   Review the list of networking strategies and select up to three that you will commit to pursuing in the next three to six months

♦   Identify people, events and other action steps you will pursue.

- Follow-up with the people you meet
- Implement your system for tracking the people you meet, prompt follow-up, and follow-up actions. The system should also include how you will maintain relationships and have reminders of when you will reach out to people and how to stay engaged.
- Practice networking by pursuing your strategies. Have compassion for yourself and others.
- Celebrate your networking successes. Reflect on and learn from your experiences.

FRAMEWORK STEP 8

BELIEF AND COURAGE

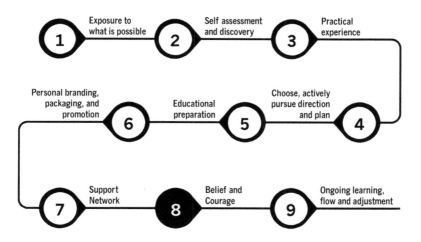

*Being confident and believing in your own self-worth is
necessary for achieving your potential.*
—Sheryl Sandberg, COO, Facebook

*I don't want to sound arrogant, but no matter what, I always
believe in myself, I think that made the biggest difference.*
—Novak Djokovic, on winning Wimbledon
after missing a year due to injury

Learning to believe in yourself will open up
endless possibilities in your life.
—Jack Canfield

In this chapter, the eighth step in the Framework, you will learn practical strategies to strengthen your belief in yourself and the courage to overcome personal, academic, job, and family challenges to choose and live the life and career you want to lead. You will learn lessons and practical tips from the stories of students and health professionals who overcame challenges to live their authentic health careers. You will gain access to a multitude of resources that people in and outside of the health field have utilized to expand their self-awareness and confidence.

You can have a clear direction, an aligned education, solid packaging, and a strong personal and professional network, but if you don't have the necessary belief and courage in yourself it will make it more difficult to make progress and far and as fast as you would like. It will also increase your potential for suffering throughout the journey and not being your best and authentic self. This can undermine your performance and how people who can be helpful see you. Insufficient self-belief and courage can also cause us to avoid or postpone pursuing our life and career dreams or opportunities and relationships that would serve us well.

While many people pursuing health careers believe in themselves, it is common for others to not have enough belief and courage. I have presented the Life and Career Planning Framework to thousands of students and health professionals. I have found that self-belief and courage is one of the Framework elements that people most frequently struggle with and feel they need to strengthen. It is also one of my biggest challenges. For many of us, this is normal and part of our human experience.

Many factors, including ones based in psychology, contribute to challenges with belief and courage including:

- Family history, childhood experiences and conditioning
- Personality type and level of sensitivity
- Common mental conditions/emotional states such as anxiety, depression, substance use, and attention-deficit hyperactivity disorder (ADHD)
- Cultural values and beliefs
- Challenges with academics, the culture of academic institutions, or adverse interactions with students, faculty, and advisors
- Experience with trauma (including intergenerational), racism, oppression, poverty, hopelessness
- Educational performance in health-related classes or prerequisites
- Experience of success and personal growth in education, sports, music, relationships, and so forth
- Fixed versus growth mindset

Many of these factors were beyond our control and are "not our fault." These are common human conditions and life experiences. It is important to realize that although they can create real challenges and suffering in our lives, they are not our fault and there is nothing wrong with us. They may also be temporary, and it is always possible to change your relationship to them in a way that serves you, others and the world better.

While we may not be able to change or control what happened to or is happening to us, over time we can develop the capacity to choose our mindset and reactions and change our relationship to them.

> *Between stimulus and response there is a space.*
> *In that space is our power to choose our response.*
> *In our response lies our growth and our freedom.*
> —Victor Frankel

> *Forces beyond your control can take away everything*
> *you possess except one thing, your freedom to choose*
> *how you will respond to the situation.*
> —Victor Frankel

I have deep compassion for everything you have experienced that has caused pain, discomfort, and suffering and made it more challenging for you to believe in yourself and fully pursue your dreams. I have years of painful experiences allowing my conditioning, self-doubt, and insufficient courage to hold me back from being my authentic self and going for what I really want. Fortunately, we have the opportunity and power at any moment to choose a mindset, practices, and actions through which we can be happy, courageous and fully engaged in our lives and career journeys.

Everyday life presents us with numerous moments and opportunities to choose responses and take actions that will serve us well and advance toward our goals and dreams. We can increase our awareness, emotional intelligence, and self-regulation so that we can better manage our conditioning, triggers, and setbacks and have more freedom to be who we are and fully go for what we want. We can step into our own power and lean into the lives and paths that are our desires and destiny.

> *We hold ourselves back in ways big and small*
> *by lacking self-confidence, not raising our hands and*
> *holding ourselves back when we should be learning in.*
> —Sheryl Sandberg

In my more than 30 years of working with students, friends, and colleagues pursuing their health career dreams and in dealing with struggles along my own journey I have found the many common natural human fears, mind states, and habits:

- Self-doubt and not trusting our desires and inner wisdom
- Lacking long-term direction, plan, or purpose and want answers instantly (don't assume full responsibility for your own future)
- Self-sabotage—"I am not going to apply to that school, they would never accept me anyway and I could never afford it", "I am not a good test taker, so studying for the GRE probably won't matter."
- Wait for right circumstances—"When I get the MCAT score I need, then I will believe in my ability to be a doctor and have the courage to apply"
- Feeling "stuck" and not knowing how to get "unstuck"
- Fear of change/uncertainty
- Fear of rejection
- Fear of being wrong or embarrassed
- Fear of disappointing others
- Fear of missing out
- Fear of failure
- Risk and uncertainty
- Loss—of our self-image, relationships, comfort, habits
- Letting go—the fear of letting go of a health career dream, our image of being a certain professional, or type of person even if it doesn't fit with who we truly are, what we want, and our capabilities and when we prefer something else.

IMPOSTER SYNDROME

One of the most common and painful challenges that students and professionals I have worked with and encounter is imposter syndrome. Imposter syndrome is a psychological term referring to a pattern of behavior through which people doubt their accomplishments and have a persistent, often internalized fear of being exposed as a fraud.[48] Studies show that an estimated 70% of people experience it.[49]

I have found that imposter syndrome is rampant among pre-health students. Particularly at top schools with intense competition among premed students and for students who are bright and capable but, due to where they grew up, do not have the same level of academic preparation, study skills, and role models that more privileged students have. Imposter syndrome is also common for students in health professions schools when people encounter a higher level of rigor and challenges in the curriculum and many other smart students who "appear" to have it more together and be more confident. It is also common among health professionals and executives as they advance to roles with greater responsibility and status. Even some of the most famous and successful people have struggled with it (see this list for examples: https://en.wikipedia.org/wiki/Impostor_syndrome). The challenge is that we often feel we are the only ones and it undermines our belief and courage.

Imposter syndrome is insidious and can not only cause unnecessary suffering but undermine our motivation and cause us to underperform (which reinforces our feelings) and can influence us to make life and career choices from our more limited view of ourselves. Examples include not applying for top health training programs, not going for the specialty or health career path we really want, or dropping out of our authentic health career paths because we think we won't make it. These and other choices made as a result of the imposter syndrome may prevent us from being our authentic selves and health professionals.

So how can you overcome imposter syndrome? I found this blog by Melody Wilding (https://www.themuse.com/advice/5-different-types-of-imposter-syndrome-and-5-ways-to-battle-each-one) useful as

---

[48] Langford and Clance, "Imposter."
[49] Sakulku, "Imposter."

she builds on research by Dr. Valerie Young on different types of imposter syndrome and how you can address them.[50] While there are many strategies for overcoming it, a simple but powerful one I encourage you to consider is suggested by psychologist Audrey Ervin. "Simply observing that thought as opposed to engaging it" can be helpful," Ervin says. "We can help teach people to let go and more critically question those thoughts. I encourage clients to ask 'Does that thought help or hinder me?'"[51] Dr. Valerie Young also has a TED Talk that you can watch and recommends ten steps for overcoming imposter syndrome.[52] A summary of her advice is to stop thinking like an imposter and to not feel like it is going to go away. Notice when it arises and understand that it is normal and not who you are.

TRANCE OF UNWORTHINESS

Another common and somewhat similar phenomenon that people encounter is what my friend and teacher Tara Brach refers to as the "Trance of Unworthiness." She uses the word *trance* to define a situation in which you have certain fixed beliefs about yourself and you are so absorbed by these beliefs that you are unaware of any external stimuli that might refute them. For example, you might feel unworthy in some way (body, mind, emotions or behavior) and you believe this so strongly that you stop looking for any evidence to the contrary. This is what Tara describes you as being in the Trance of Unworthiness.

Without having a name for it I suffered from the Trance of Unworthiness for decades. Being able to name what I was feeling as a trance and learning how common it is and that you can "trans-end" the trance was liberating and life-changing for me. I found Tara's teaching and books, *Radical Acceptance* and *True Refuge and Radical*

---

[50] Young, *Women.*
[51] Abrams, "Imposter."
[52] Young, "10 Steps."

Compassion, to be invaluable. More often now, I can recognize the trance when it arises in me and in others and allow it to be there without being taken over by it or reacting in ways that don't serve me well. As Tara says, our feelings of unworthiness may be "real but not true." Living and making decisions from our highest and best selves, instead of the trance, can empower us to choose and advance our authentic health careers and live with more awareness and freedom.

SELF-DOUBT

Whether or not you experience imposter syndrome or the Trance of Unworthiness, most of us experience some level of self-doubt at some point along our health career journey. According to the Cambridge Dictionary, *doubt* is "a feeling of not knowing what to believe or what to do, or the condition of being uncertain" and "to be uncertain about something or someone, or to have difficulty believing something."[53] Doubt arises naturally in our lives, for some of us multiple times per day, and can be healthy and valuable. Doubt can keep us from making decisions, doing things, or engaging in relationships that are not in our best interest.

Self-doubt can also be healthy to a point, particularly if it helps motivate us to become more clear, certain, or better prepared. However, self-doubt can also be a hindrance to us choosing and going for what we really want. Self-doubt is a condition that humans have struggled with for thousands of years as addressed and chronicled in the Bible, Greek mythology, Shakespeare, and numerous other true and fictional stories.

> *Our doubts are traitors and make us lose the good*
> *we oft might win, by fearing to attempt.*
> —William Shakespeare, *Measure for Measure*

---

[53] Cambridge Dictionary, "Doubt."

We are not alone in self-doubt. The question is whether it will be a traitor that will cause you to not attempt something along the path to your authentic health career.

I can accept failure, everyone fails at something,
but I can't accept not trying.
—Michael Jordan

BRENNA'S STORY

"I am not going to apply, I doubt that I would be competitive for that job," said Brenna, one of my former UC Berkeley MPH students in Health Policy and Management (HPM). An HPM alumni who worked for a major health system had reached out to me with a job posting that aligned perfectly with Brenna's interests, background, and skills. I approached Brenna and encouraged her to apply.

Brenna was graduating in three months and had been looking for a job for a while without even securing many interviews. She was discouraged and was down on herself. Though Brenna was bright and talented and had solid experience, she had a somewhat pessimistic outlook and lacked self-confidence. I had known her since she was a Health Career Connection (HCC) intern as an undergraduate and had noticed that she often was self-critical and approached situations where she had to put herself out there with doubt and pessimism that led to not trying. I understood that habit as I had similar mindset and behavior challenges when the stakes were high, and I didn't feel as comfortable and confident as I would like. While I have found that this is common in many of us, it often doesn't serve us well. This time was no exception.

I encouraged Brenna to reach out to the alum and apply for the position. She said "let me think about it" as she left my office. She didn't end up reaching out or applying. She felt she was not qualified and wouldn't be selected. Fortunately, a couple weeks later,

UC Berkeley held our annual Career Café, networking event with alumni and other health professionals. The alum offering the position attended and let me know that she was still seeking candidates. I asked Brenna if I could introduce her to the alum and say that I recommended her for the position. Brenna was hesitant, stating that she wasn't sure she was qualified, but reluctantly agreed. I walked her over and made the connection. After they discussed the position, the alum asked Brenna to send her a resume and come in for an interview. Within two weeks, Brenna was offered the position at a great starting salary. I got an email from the alum telling me how impressed she was with Brenna and how she stood head and shoulders above the other candidates. She said how proud she was as an alum that we had done a great job preparing Brenna with the technical and leadership skills that made her stand out and made her so well qualified. Not only did Brenna succeed in that job, but she has risen quickly to assume progressively increasing responsibility and positions and has thrived in the organization as well. None of this would have been possible had she not gone beyond her limiting beliefs and pursued the position.

Never self-select yourself out of an opportunity by not applying or giving it your all, believe in yourself and go for what you want with courage, let others turn you down (though you will succeed more times than you think).
—Jeff Oxendine

I wish I had a dollar for every time I didn't pursue an opportunity that I really wanted because I didn't think I was good enough and/or didn't want to risk rejection. Actually, I wish I would have pursued them instead of having the dollar. For someone who also has a fear of missing out, negative self-belief and avoiding discomfort caused me to miss out on many things and life experiences or endure negative consequences for delaying needed actions.

If you hear a voice within you say you cannot paint,
then by all means paint and that voice will be silenced.
—Vincent Van Gogh

There are more quotes, powerful insights, and resources available now than ever to assist us with overcoming whatever is holding us back from manifesting the glory that is within is and having the impact as people and health professionals that we truly are meant to have. Over the years when you experience common fears, self-doubt, imposter syndrome, trance of unworthiness, or any other conditions that undermine your belief and courage, it is helpful to reframe your mindset. A couple of ways I have found to do that are this story and developing a fixed vs. growth mindset.

FIXED VS. GROWTH MINDSET

Some of our challenges with belief and courage may be rooted in our mindset. As you pursue our authentic health careers, we will encounter personal, academic, and professional challenges at many steps along the way. The mindset we bring as we work through and respond to these challenges and how we view our selves as a result can influence our success, perseverance and resulting feelings. In her book *Mindset*, Stanford Professor Carol Dweck and her colleagues have found that people approach challenges from either a fixed or growth mindset.[54]

According to Dweck, in a **fixed mindset**, people believe their qualities are fixed traits and therefore cannot change. These people document and defend their intelligence and talents rather than working to develop and improve them.[55] They also believe that talent alone leads to success, and effort is not required. They may avoid

---

[54] Dweck, *Mindset*.
[55] Develop Good Habits, "Mindset."

challenges, including fully going for their authentic health career or believing that with assistance and perseverance, they can get a better grade in organic chemistry the second time around. They may also avoid making positive changes that would be good for them because they don't think they can do it.

Alternatively, in a **growth mindset,** people have an underlying belief that their learning and intelligence can grow with time and experience. When people believe they can get smarter, they realize that their effort has an effect on their success, so they put in extra time, leading to higher achievement. Difficult challenges are viewed as opportunities to learn and grow with the mindset that they can successfully be worked through. Setbacks and failures don't mean that person isn't worthy and can't achieve what they set out to do. It just means they are not there **yet.** Dweck discusses the power of having a growth mindset and believing you can improve in her powerful TED Talk.[56] She discusses her evidenced-based findings and stories about how students from the most challenging backgrounds can get smarter and accomplish their goals despite the odds by developing a growth mindset and putting in the necessary effort. A key was believing they could improve and having the courage to do what was needed.

Are you pursuing your life and authentic health career from a fixed or growth mindset? Take this interactive quiz to give you an idea: https://www.londonacademyofit.co.uk/blog/interactive-quiz-fixed-vs-growth-mindset.

Having a fixed mindset doesn't mean you won't succeed, nor does having a growth mean you will. However, developing more of a growth mindset and putting in the effort required have been proven to be helpful to many be successful. This blog offers 11 tips to help you learn and grow from more of a growth mindset: https://www.developgoodhabits.com/fixed-mindset-vs-growth-mindset

---

[56] TED, "Dweck."

I encourage you to work on and act from a growth mindset. I have had a mixture of both throughout my education and career. My surface-level mindset is more fixed, and I often act or avoid from that place which has not served me well and caused much suffering. I have been fortunate to counter that with an underlying growth mindset and core self believe that if I put in the effort and persevere, I can succeed. It is easier to do that with things that come easier naturally to me and that are aligned with my passion and interest. If I want something bad enough and have a knowing I can do it, then I will believe it is possible and put the effort in. If not, there is uncertainty I may avoid.

Writing this book and starting my information business were things I avoided fully committing to and putting in all the effort because deep down I was afraid I didn't have the intelligence or ability to do it, didn't know how to proceed and made it a larger challenge than it was, felt only people with certain intelligence could do, and was afraid not doing it would expose my weakness. I didn't do it for years. This is not uncommon. However, I knew my content would help many people and was an important life accomplishment for me to get the book done so I moved forward. With the help of the Author's Academy and support from colleagues I learned necessary skills and had the breakthrough that it would be challenging but that I could do it. It was still challenging but I learned, grew and here it is!

If it is your authentic health career, have the belief, mindset, and courage that you can do it and take action and persevere according. I know you can do it! Developing a growth mindset is one way to strengthen your motivation, belief, and courage. Here are others I have found useful.

HOW CAN YOU STRENGTHEN BELIEF AND COURAGE?

In addition to adopting a growth mindset, there are many ways you can strengthen your belief and courage:

◆ Find and learn from **role models:** more people than you think have come from similar backgrounds and overcome comparable challenges. Be open to people from different backgrounds, races, and sexual orientations who are doing what you want to do or being the kind of people you want to be.

◆ Read **biographies** of successful people: you will be surprised how many of the most successful people had to overcome fear, failure, doubt, and rejection.

◆ Engage and listen to your **mentors:** they can often see you as you truly are and what you are capable of being and help you make good choices.

◆ Utilize your **personal support networks:** friends, family, and peers who know you and have your best interest at heart can help you make great choices and overcome setbacks and challenges along the way. Just be sure they are supporting your authentic direction (not theirs). For more insights into how to deal with family regarding your authentic health career, please see my website Jeffoxendine.com.

◆ **Remember and build on your successes:** each success you have should help you build your belief, courage and confidence; particularly if they are related to your authentic educational and career direction. You can also gain confidence and belief from success in other areas you are good at and enjoy such as sports; music, dance, church, and community. I am still supported by my athletic success and remember how hard work, focus, and teamwork helped me reach my goals.

◆ **Get support from counselors, coaches, or therapists:** some of us, the support of a trained professional can help us become more aware of and address barriers from our personality, experiences, or fears that undermine our belief and courage. We may need to heal and grow in to build our capacity to be who we are, feel good about it, and be able to fully go for what we want. We may need support to get started and throughout our journeys. It is normal and natural and can provide great benefits. A key is finding the right type of person with the right training and approach to meet you where you are and help you grow and take action.

◆ **Spiritual and religious, faith and practices:** for some of us, our spiritual or religious faith and practices can be a vital source of guidance, belief, and courage. Prayer and/or meditation can assist you to help define your path and be sure it aligns with your spiritual goals and calling. They can also support you at key moments of challenge and some of the inevitable dark periods you will encounter. Your faith and practices can help you focus on purposes greater than yourself and assist you to overcome fear and doubt and develop courage. Be honest about what you are really called to do and how you want to serve and have that be a source of guidance, clarity and to help alleviate stress and anxiety. My faith and practices are the foundation for my life. I have followed my purpose and have committed my life to surrendering and service, including writing this book! Faith helps me take risks and have the courage to do what I need to move forward and offsets my subtours. We will often do more for others and God than for ourselves. When you are ready to take a risk, remember my favorite scene in Indiana Jones (where he steps out on the ledge)

◆ **Books and online resources:** I would not be where I am today without the powerful insights and support I received from many books, teachers, and online resources. They always seem to appear at exactly the time I need them. Go to my website (Jeffoxendine.com) to access the list of books and teachers and resources that changed my life and assisted me through my authentic life and career journey. They have also enabled me to assist thousands of others.

MY OWN STORY

I have suffered from anxiety, self-doubt, and the trance of unworthiness for my entire life. I also have an inner tyrant that drives me toward the impossibility of perfection, certainty, trying to control things to fit my plans, and striving for desired comfort. My family background is one in which playing it safe and "being responsible" are the norm, particularly when it comes to financial and security risks. My parents provided me with a stable home and worked hard to provide me with a great life, an education, and many opportunities. They instilled in me a work ethic, honesty, and integrity and ways of dealing with people that have served me very well.

Both of my parents came from humble and poor backgrounds. My father is a Native American who grew up in poverty in the segregated Jim Crow South. He encountered severe racism, discrimination, and oppression and to this day fears for his psychological and physical safety. He forged his mother's signature and joined the Air Force at 17 so he could have the opportunity for a different life. He met my mother, who is the only one in her family to leave her small midwestern town and is still the only one in her entire extended family to graduate from a four-year college, when he was stationed in Fairfield, California. I did not grow up in the South or with my tribe; however, I have suffered from the wounds of internalized oppression and intergenerational trauma.

My mother's side of the family suffers from anxiety and depression. I have struggled with both at various points for my life, particularly when I am not being my true self or pursuing my authentic direction. I also struggle with hurry and worry. Also, from being and showing my authentic self and being comfortable in my own skin. Due to the fear of being wrong, I have been very cautious and deliberate about decisions.

Despite these challenges, I have been truly blessed with many gifts and an abundance of support, experience, and opportunities. I gained confidence from my successes in music and sports growing up and then in academic and health career pursuits in college. I also was empowered by a wonderful relationship in college with a girlfriend who was very focused, confident, and supportive. My summer internship experience was life-changing and really gave me the belief and courage that I could achieve my health career and life goals. I felt special being in the program and my firsthand experience in health administration affirmed that I loved it and was good at it. I also gained mentors, role models and connections to UC Berkeley. I had a clear direction—becoming a hospital CEO—and the belief and courage that I could do it. I returned to school for one last semester and kicked butt. I had a job waiting for me where I did my internship and focused all my efforts on preparing my graduate school application for UC Berkeley.

Getting into Cal's MBA and MPH program a year later fulfilled my dream and made me even more empowered. Imposter syndrome, a lack of solid math skills, and being the youngest in the MBA MPH made my experience challenging, but I muscled through it, knowing that it was a means to achieving my authentic direction and that I could do it. I finished with the most job offers of people I know and realized my goal of becoming a hospital administrator in a prominent hospital that served an underserved community. I succeeded in administration as I knew I would which also built my confidence.

I have since had a wonderful life and career but still encounter self-doubt, anxiety and the trance of unworthiness, particularly when teaching at Harvard and being a non-tenure track faculty member at UC Berkeley (which means you are perceived as second class). Mindfulness, faith, and guidance from God and exercise and a core of self-belief have made all the difference. The best things I have done were the things I was the most afraid of and gulped at first. I doubted that I could do it initially but then acted from core belief with courage and guidance, and all has turned out beyond my wildest dreams; I have grown as a person beyond my limiting self.

> *Your ancestors did not survive everything that nearly*
> *ended them for you to shrink to make someone else*
> *feel comfortable. Their sacrifice is your war cry,*
> *be loud, be everything, make them proud.*
> —Nikita Gill, writer and poet

WHAT IF YOUR FAMILY ISN'T BEHIND YOUR AUTHENTIC HEALTH CAREER?

What if you know and believe in your authentic health career direction but your parents don't?

AADESH'S STORY

I had my first lesson in cultural competency when I told my immigrant Indian parents that I got accepted to medical school but was turning it down to go into public health.

My good friend and colleague Aadesh had thought long and hard about his authentic health career. As a talented Berkeley premed he did all the right things to get into medical school. He had wanted to become a doctor for as long as he could remember, and it was his parents' dream. However, while he performed well in science classes, he didn't really see their relevance to being a doctor or improving health. As a junior, he stumbled on to public health and became passionate about improving population health and social justice, particularly for underserved ethnic minority communities. He could see himself becoming a researcher and a practitioner to make a difference in disease prevention and population health improvement. However, he had gone so far down the path toward medicine and, given his parents' expectations, he couldn't turn back. He went through with the MCAT and grueling med school application process. However, inspired by his true calling, he also applied to public health MPH programs. When he got accepted to both he was at a crossroads. It was clear what he really wanted, but could he really turn down medical school? Disappoint his parents? Shift gears to public health which likely paid so much less? His parents didn't even know what public health was. After much soul-searching, he developed the belief and courage to turn down medical school to pursue an MPH at UC Berkeley. Telling his parents was the hardest part.

He carefully thought about the best way he could position it with them. He did his homework and prepared and practiced his story. As you can imagine his parents were stunned and very disappointed. They couldn't believe he would turn down medical school for a much less prestigious and financially rewarding field.

Ultimately, they loved him and reluctantly supported him. Aadesh went on to be a star in the MPH program and subsequently earned his doctorate in public health. His research is in exactly his passion, addressing disparities among understudied Asian American communities. He also pursued his passion for increasing diversity in the health professions and empowering students through working with me at HCC for a summer job that turned into eight years. He is now a tenured professor and is very visible in the development of talented and promising health professionals, particularly those who value diversity and inclusion. He is doing what he loves to do: research directly aligned with his passion and empowering and mentoring students to excel in their authentic health careers. His role allows him to be at home with and spend ample time with his two children. He is actively engaged in all they do and shares childcare and family responsibilities with his wife. He is living his authentic life and health career and making a difference on so many meaningful fronts. His parents are so proud of him. He is a successful professor, does work they care about, and is a great family man. Every time they go out to dinner with Aadesh, one of his students comes up to the table and tells them how much of a difference he made in their lives. He is also there for them as they are getting older. They are very happy with his choice.

> *I am different from other Pakistani fathers,*
> *I am not saying you can only be a doctor,*
> *you could also be an engineer, lawyer or businessman,*
> *I am giving you so many options.*
> —Father in the movie *Blinded by the Light*

Over the years I have worked with thousands of students, recent graduates and graduate health professions students who have faced challenges when their authentic health career path differed from/ conflicted with their parents' expectations or preferences. Students from many different cultural and demographic backgrounds have struggled with their parents having a specific and limited set of career options that are "acceptable." The most common scenario is when parents, and often extended family and friends, expect the student to become a doctor, though nurse, pharmacist, or lawyer are also common. While there is nothing wrong with parents wanting their children to be doctors, particularly when the students also have that ambition, challenges develop when students end up changing their mind, are unsure, and/or not able to meet the high bar of getting into medical school. Students often feel intense pressure to continue their pursuit of medicine even though it may not be the best fit path for them. I have found this particularly true for many immigrant students. Many don't want to disappoint or disobey their parents after the risk they took in coming to a new country and how much they have sacrificed, often working two or three jobs, so that the student will have food and shelter, a high-quality education, and the opportunity to become a doctor. In many cultures, honoring parents' wishes is a core value and expectation as are taking care of and contributing to the family.

In many cultures, the pressure of expectations can be particularly high for the oldest child, males, only children, or the "smartest or most accomplished." It can also be challenging when siblings are doctors or in other professions held in high esteem by a family. It can also be challenging when your single parent has made huge sacrifices for you and doesn't support your authentic direction.

Having the belief and courage to choose and actively pursue your authentic health career in the face of going against parental and cultural expectations can be very difficult. However, it is ultimately your life, and you are the one who has to complete the prerequisites, get accepted to a health professions school, endure and succeed in the challenging training, do the workday in and day out, and live the lifestyle. So if, after going through all the other steps in the Framework, you decide that your authentic career is different from your parents' expectations or you are unsure and want to pursue other paths, what strategies can you use to deal with family-related challenges in order to still achieve your authentic health career?

STRATEGIES TO HELP WITH FAMILY CONCERNS

> *If I were to summarize in one sentence the single*
> *most important principle I have learned in the field*
> *of interpersonal relations, it would be this:*
> *Seek first to understand, then to be understood.*
> —Steven R. Covey

A key first step to is to seek to understand why your parents take the position they do regarding your education and career direction. Your parent(s) or guardians love you and want you to be happy and successful. While their approach may differ, they ultimately want the best for you unless they are more focused on meeting their own needs (which is also important to know).

You may be able to learn their why's through active listening without trying to influence them to understand your perspective. If you have already encountered some challenges or conflict, it can be tricky to find out their primary motivations but take an open, caring approach to listening and see what you can learn.

You will likely hear things like we want you to: have a solid, stable, well-paying career so you will have prosperity and security, be in a position to have a better life than we can provide or do something I didn't get to do, make us proud, have a job that is important and has status with your extended family and community, contribute to the family, find a partner and have and support a family, do meaningful work that makes a difference; do something you love, and be happy and healthy. As outlined in Chapter 4, this is also a good place to utilize the 5 Why's to get at the core of their motivation and interests (though you may not want to formally go through their 5 Why's directly with them).

Once you know more about their interests and needs, not just their position on your career, you will be in a much better position to have conversations about your authentic path. You can show that you hear, understand, and respect where they are coming from and tailor the reasoning and case you make for your career path to address their interests. For example, if you are interested in becoming a hospital administrator instead of a doctor and your parents are motivated by status and high pay, you can show them that a CEO is an important job and that the average salary of a hospital administrator in California is $800,000 per year. If it is importance, security, and impact they care most about and you are interested in promoting access to care, you can show them that the top issues in the presidential election and on the front page of newspapers are about health coverage and access to quality, affordable care.

Armed with knowledge about your parents' preferences you can also consider these other strategies:

◆   Education and exposure about the career direction(s) you want to pursue. Many parents are not exposed to the wide range of growing, needed health career paths and jobs. Provide articles, insights, studies, or take them to events. You might also provide information about the outlook for the career paths they want you to pursue if they are not favorable, such as 50% of doctors would not pursue medicine today and 49% would not recommend that their children become doctors.[57]

---

[57] Study Finds, "Doctors."

♦ Secure an internship or job (preferably paid) to demonstrate that what you want to pursue has solid options and is valued.

♦ Demonstrate that your authentic path is aligned with who you are and what you are good at and enjoy doing. Provide examples of your joy and success. Have them see you in action and/or with peers doing something that would impress or inspire them.

♦ Provide evidence of future trends showing the need for what you want to do. For example, when I embarked on becoming a hospital administrator, it was the third-fastest growing career. If you wanted to show the current and future need for primary care, behavioral health, or older adult care professionals you could use the California Future Health Workforce Commission Report that I co-wrote: https://futurehealthworkforce.org/our-work/finalreport/.

♦ Provide a role model or mentor from a similar background who is successful in your field.

♦ Show that you can make a living in the field you want to pursue. Most health jobs are well paying; those that are not are still in need.

♦ Show your struggles in the field they want you to pursue, like grades in o chem, and what the bar is for getting into health professions school. Show the cost and competitiveness. Compare to what you want to do.

♦ Show you have a well-thought-out path and plan and have done your homework—use the Framework and share the action plan you will work on in Chapter 12. Show that it leads to a stable place where you will be happy.

Ultimately this could be a negotiation and a process to get their support. Some potential tactics to consider include:

♦ Find the parent who is more open and sympathetic and get them to be your ally.

- ◆ Address each of their objections related to your career path and show how it aligns with their values and interests and needs.
- ◆ Discuss after you have had a major success in your chosen path or painful failure in the one you don't want to pursue.
- ◆ A different messenger, have someone else who they respect and listen to, speak on your behalf—uncle, religious leader, teacher, grandparent, and/or professor.
- ◆ Show how much you really care and are happy with the path you want to pursue and how it is a great fit.

If, ultimately, you don't have the support you want from parents, other family members, or partners, remember it is still your life and your decision. You are the one who has to complete your education requirements and do your work. Have the belief and courage to choose and actively pursue your authentic health career.

The medical school experience is close to torture,
it will be very difficult for someone who doesn't really want
to be a doctor to endure and successfully get through it.
—comment I recently overheard from a physician to a student
who said she is only considering becoming a doctor because her
parents think she should

Courage doesn't mean you don't get afraid,
it means that you don't let fear stop you.
—Bethany Hamilton, Surfer

Be Bold and Mighty forces will come to your aid.
—Johan Wolfgang von Goethe

In some cases, parents support you but can't understand or don't have the background to assist you. This is where you find others to help including mentors, role models, and use of website resources and tools.

FINDING AND UTILIZING MENTORS

Mentors can provide invaluable support to supplement or take the place of family support. Mentors can provide you with powerful personal and professional support. I and most people in the health industry would not be where we are today without the tremendous support and opportunities provided by mentors. Many people in the health industry are caring people who like helping others and giving back to those behind them in the health professions pipeline. Being a mentor is also a very rewarding experience. As a result of these factors, chances are good that you can find and benefit from mentors to help you decide on and advance toward your authentic health career.

Given how busy health professionals, faculty, and others are in their professional and personal lives, it can be challenging to find mentors. Many people also face the challenge of not having access in the course of their lives to the kind of mentors they are seeking, or they don't know how or are not comfortable with approaching potential mentors.

Often, mentors will find you. They will recognize positive qualities in you and your potential. They may reach out to you or may maintain a connection with you after an informational interview or some kind of interaction. In the event you are fortunate to secure such a connection, then please pursue it and enjoy it as fully as you can. Please follow up with mentors and the people they connect you with.

I have found and benefitted from three types of mentors:

1. Personal or professional mentors who have found me or I have sought out and developed a relationship with.
2. Mentors who are assigned or matched as part of a formal mentorship program.
3. Mentors who you admire and follow who don't or barely know you but who serve as inspiring and empowering role models and sources of wisdom and insight (some of my best mentors are in

this category). Examples may include senior health leaders where you work or whom you meet, religious leaders or spiritual teachers, faculty, authors or speakers, and people who lead programs or professional associations.

In addition to working with mentors who find you, here are eight tips for finding and utilizing mentors:

1. Approach work or internship supervisors or faculty who you admire and request a conversation about your career and educational direction, particularly if you feel they like you or they have a reputation for being a mentor (not required). If you feel like you had a positive connection and they have a genuine interest in, you and your direction follow-up with them to request a time to meet again in a month or two. Let them know you appreciated their advice and contacts and how they worked out. If you have a positive interaction again, ask if you can continue to check in with them or if they might consider being your mentor. You may not need to ask if they are willing to continue meeting; at some point, they may ask you about it, or it could turn into a mentor relationship. Ask them for referrals to others in their network who could mentor you.

2. Conduct informational interviews with alumni of your school, people who come to speak at your school, or professionals you have positive interactions with. Follow the same approach as outlined in number 1.

3. Join a health professional association, such as the Student National Medical Association, American College of Healthcare Executives, or the American Public Health Association. Participate in events, conferences, and networking activities. Find people who you want to meet with and follow the approach in number 1.

4. Sign up for a formal, structured mentorship program through your school, alumni association, or a professional association.

Be clear about who you are and what you would like in a mentor and be open to people who are different from your background and path.

5. Utilize online mentorship resources, such as Mi Mentor, and participate in events.

6. Be open to people you meet during the course of your day and travels. I met two of my most influential mentors "by chance" on airplanes.

7. Utilize peers as mentors and be a mentor to others.

8. Follow people who inspire you through in-person events and online resources. There are more and more of both kinds of activities. Approach the people and ask for an informational interview. Follow the approach in number one or be happy with the information and examples they provide. Reading biographies of people you admire who are alive or dead can also be inspiring and instructive.

I highly encourage you to seek out and utilize mentors as much as possible and to mentor others along the way. If you don't have mentors now, be patient, put yourself out there, and cultivate relationships. It will work out and be beneficial to you. Treasure and express appreciation for the mentors you have or have had. Reach out periodically to let them know how much they have meant to you and update on your life and career.

END OF CHAPTER EXERCISES

Exercise 1: Cultivating More Belief and Courage

◆   On a scale of 1 to 10, what is your current level of belief and courage relative to your ability to choose and succeed in your authentic health career?

◆   Do you have more of a fixed or growth mindset?

◆   What are some of your challenges?

◆   What are your sources of courage, resilience, and support?

◆   What are some of your opportunities for growth by putting in the effort required?

◆   How will you cultivate more courage and support?

◆   Who are people or resources where you can get the support you need?

◆   What are three key action steps you will take in the next three months to strengthen your belief and courage? How will you measure your progress and success?

◆   Check out belief and courage resources on Jeffoxendine.com

Exercise 2: Getting Greater Support from Family for Your Authentic Health Career

1.   Do your family, partner, or friends support your authentic career and educational direction?

2. If not, why do you think they take the position they do? If so, why do they, and how do they support you?

3. What strategies can you use to strengthen their support or acceptance?

4. In the next three months, what are three next steps you will commit to taking related to these strategies? Who will assist you?

11

LIFELONG LEARNING, ADJUSTMENT, AND FLOW

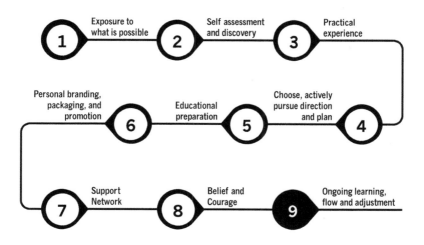

The best laid plans of mice and men often go awry.
—John Steinbeck

It's not the species that is the smartest or strongest that survives,
it's the one that adapts best to change.
—Charles Darwin

Whether you are contemplating a personal or professional change now, dealing with a setback, or fully enjoying a major success, you need to strengthen your ability to make well-informed adjustments in your educational and career path to stay aligned with who you are and what you want and advance toward your authentic career. Our lives and careers and the health industry will change over time, and we will encounter wanted and unwanted developments. COVID-19 and other disasters have shown that our lives and careers can change dramatically and require huge adjustments and adaptations. In this chapter, which is step nine of the Framework, you will strengthen your ability to proactively plan for and respond to developments and make adjustments that will serve you well as you create and achieve the life you want and your authentic health career.

In this chapter we focus on the importance of navigating your authentic career path with the mindset and knowledge that your journey will include lifelong learning and adjustment as the world, the health field, and your life change. Choosing and actively pursuing a clear and authentic health career direction that is well aligned with your values, passions, and goals and with what you are good at and enjoy will increase your motivation and probability of living a fulfilling and successful life and career. You can achieve the power and intrinsic and extrinsic rewards that come from living in the "being stage" as depicted on the Life and Career Alignment Triangle from Chapter 1.

While you may be able to live in the being stage and be happy in a career or job for a long time, we must always remember that the only thing we can be certain of is change. Our passions, goals, and lifestyle preferences will change through our life and professional experiences and as we grow and change as people.

CHANGES IN PERSONAL PREFERENCES

My priorities and the characteristics I wanted in a job and career were very different when I was an early careerist and single in my twenties and early thirties compared to when I was married in my forties and had three young children. I also found after 20 years as a health executive, while I enjoyed and was good at my work, I was more driven by the desire to work with students that I was to work on health administration issues. I also wanted to have the time and flexibility to be a good father. As a result, I made a huge adjustment and took a 70% salary reduction and left my health executive role to become a faculty member at UC Berkeley. It was the right decision for my family and me. In 2018, it was time for another adjustment to focus more on writing this book and increasing the scale of my work to support students. I also wanted to work for myself and have the time to focus on the major statewide health workforce and diversity project that I initiated and got support to do.[58]

CHANGE IN THE HEALTH INDUSTRY AND ORGANIZATIONS

Simultaneous with changes in our personal preferences the health industry will also change, only faster and more dramatically. During my more than 30 years in the health field, it has always be characterized by relentless change. Changes in policies, regulations, payment methodologies, and levels and health coverage drive health industry change. Response to these changes drive change within public- and private-industry stakeholders including providers, payers, community-based health organizations, public health, and vendors. Advances in medicine, technology, pharmaceuticals, biotech, equipment, and health IT also drive changes in the industry, career paths, and jobs. The rate and magnitude of technological change in the health field is predicted to be exponential in the next decade and beyond. Artificial intelligence, robotics, virtual reality, gene therapy, and telehealth and continued advances in health information technology and big data will have a significant impact on healthcare and

---

[58] California Future Health Workforce Commission.

population health and associated health jobs. Check out these sites to learn more about the major trends and how they could impact your authentic health career and future jobs: https://www.visualcapitalist.com/5-ways-technology-healthcare-industry/ and https://medical-futurist.com/ten-ways-technology-changing-healthcare.

Get as much future trend exposure, experience, and knowledge as possible so that you can make well-informed choices about your next steps and long-term plans. You don't want to make costly misaligned career choices and spend thousands of dollars on preparing for a path and jobs that will be much different from you envisioned.

I view technology changes as a huge opportunity for you and for change in the health field. The key is to choose and actively pursue a direction that is on trend and adjust as needed as technology and other changes lead to changes in jobs and opportunities.

Whether we like it or not, these changes will have a dramatic impact on health jobs now and in the future. Many new jobs and professions will be created, many will change, and some will be eliminated. There will be many new opportunities and many challenges.

> *80% of the jobs that will exist in 5–10 years*
> *don't even exist now.*
> —Genil Washington, Director of Talent Acquisition,
> Stanford Health Care

> *Skate to where the puck is going to be,*
> *not where it has been.*
> —Wayne Gretzky

The bottom line is that to live and succeed in your authentic health career, you will need to be good at anticipating changes and adjusting your direction, roles and training to position yourself for success as industry changes evolve. I encourage you to be mindful of and adjust to changes in the macro health environment, your organization, and your local marketplace and community. I designed the Life and Career Planning Framework so that you can continue to use the steps to inform and guide the adjustments you make to be sure they are aligned with who you are and where you want to be and go. Regardless of your life and career stage, you can engage in the elements of the Framework to stay on top of personal, job, and industry changes; learn from your experiences and connections; and adjust your plans as needed to stay in alignment and achieve your results. Armed with clarity of where the world is going and what you want you will increase your ability to choose and live the life and career you want and show up as the person you want to be.

YOU ARE THE CEO OF YOUR LIFE

My good friend Margaret Lapiz, former Vice President and Board Member of The Permanente Medical Group, told me many years ago, "I make my life and career choices from the place of being the CEO of my life. I can create the life and career I want and make sure it is aligned with who I am and what I want." Armed with this mindset, I encourage you to make the choices and adjustments along your path that suit your ultimate definition of success and align with who you are and want you want. Just like the CEO of a company, you need to have an eye toward the future, step into your power, and make difficult choices that not everyone will understand and agree with. From this place of power and freedom, you can make proactive adjustments along the way if needed to align with your priorities. As we have already discussed, sometimes those adjustments cause you to change course from a path you have been on for years that may have served you very well but now may not given your new preferences or life circumstances.

> *The first half of my life was about success;*
> *the second half is about significance.*
> —Dan Wilson, former catcher, Seattle Mariners

This quote guided me to make major life- and career-altering changes that aligned with my new life situation and stage of life. As Richard Rohr, says, in his book *Falling Upward*, "The things that served us well in the first half of our life may not serve us well in the second half." As previously described, I left my prestigious, high-paying health executive job to align my life more with my passions, values, and goals as a father with three children and a life calling to help people discover and realize their full potential. I had many accomplishments as a health executive and much professional and financial success. I also had considerable personal success but wanted to be in a position to have more significance. I felt that being in a better position to have a successful marriage, be a great father and son, and fulfill my life's purpose was the significance I was seeking in the second half of my life.

While many of you are still in the first quarter rather than the second half of your life, the concept of continuously learning and making adjustments in your life and career to be in authentic alignment still applies. Having this mindset and making choices from it early on and throughout your life and career will serve you well. If you truly want to pursue public health instead of medicine and not give up your twenties and early thirties, then do it. If you truly want to become a doctor, regardless of your premed science grades, what your unskillful counselor says, and how medicine will change in the future, do it! You are the CEO so make choices that provide you with the life you want.

LEARNING AND ADJUSTMENTS FROM SETBACKS OR FAILURES

As we pursue and live our authentic lives and health careers from a place of purpose, choice, and power, we will inevitably encounter challenges, setbacks, and failure. Not only is this part of life, but the process of getting into and completing your health professions training, securing jobs, and working effectively in the rapidly changing health environment is also in inherently challenging.

CHALLENGES IN YOUR EDUCATIONAL PATH

The top reason why pre-med students at Stanford and UC Berkeley discontinued their pursuit of medicine is because of negative experiences in chemistry courses.
—Donald Barr, Stanford, and John Matsui, UC Berkeley

Everyone who has pursued becoming a doctor, nurse, or pharmacist knows that getting through organic chemistry courses with a high enough grade to be competitive for health professions school can be a huge challenge. On many campuses, O Chem (Organic Chemistry) is designed to be a "weeder class" for pre-health students or is taught by instructors who teach material in a way and a pace that that is best suits chemistry majors. Organic chemistry became a premed requirement as a result of the 1910 Flexner report, which triggered much-needed reforms to make medical education more rigorous, standard, and science-based. Many doctors today question why it is still a requirement and believe it is not necessary for someone to be an effective practitioner. I have met thousands of students who either had to overcome setbacks and failures in O Chem, including repeating the course, or chose to abandon their health career dreams due to the challenges and how it made them feel about themselves.

My colleagues Donald Barr and John Matsui documented that adverse experiences in chemistry courses are often the turning point that discourage otherwise qualified premedical students, particularly underrepresented minorities, to pursue medicine.[59] Fortunately, there are now more positive and effective ways to teach chemistry that have emerged, including Professor Angelica Stacy's courses and

---

[59] Barr, Matsui et al., "Chemistry."

use of students as teachers at UC Berkeley and her book *Living by Chemistry*.[60] There are also many doctors who failed or did poorly in O Chem but persevered and are wonderful practitioners today. There is hope so if you need to get through O Chem on your way to your authentic health career, please keep going with a growth mindset and get the help you need.

Setbacks or simply not liking O Chem or other premed science courses lead many people to pursue other health careers. They discover that there are many other ways to impact health and rewarding career paths that do not require a hard science education and/or are a better fit for them. Public health is often a path that people shift to from premed so that they can focus on prevention, population health, social justice, or policy and systems change to improve health on a large scale. For many I know, this was their true calling, and they lead very rewarding lives and careers. Challenges with premed were actually a blessing in disguise or led them to their authentic health careers.

So don't let academic setbacks derail you. Either stay the course, get help, and persevere with belief and courage or shift to a path that suits your talents and passions and still leads to fulfillment.

KNOW WHEN IT'S TIME TO CHANGE COURSE, DON'T GET ROPE BURN

Some people who encounter repeated challenges in the health career direction they are pursuing should use this as an opportunity to reassess their direction and change directions. I am not suggesting that people give up when they know their true calling and with concerted effort and a growth mindset can succeed. I am suggesting that some of us need to be honest with ourselves and know when it is time and in our best interests to change course. For example, students who have very low GPAs after repeated efforts to get the help they need and

---

[60] Stacy, *Chemistry*.

improve and are at a point where it will be very difficult for them to get entry into their desired field should reconsider their direction and use the pathway elements to pursue other options. It is very difficult to let go of a dream, particularly when your family and friends expect you to keep going and may be disappointed if you change course. Letting go is one of my biggest challenges, so I know. However, as my teacher Jack Kornfield says, "Fear of change is natural, but we are in a river of change, and if we try to hold on what we end up with is rope burn and suffering."

We also need to be honest with ourselves when it is time to change jobs or career paths. In my case, I resisted changing directions from my health executive role because of fear of giving up my identity, financial security, status, and long-term career path. I was also afraid of uncertainty. I had to fail in some of my responsibilities and get physically ill and depressed before I was in enough pain to change. But it was time. I finally had the courage to change, and the day after I did, an opportunity presented itself that was the perfect fit.

> *Man cannot discover new oceans unless*
> *he has the courage to lose sight of the shore.*
> —French Nobel Laureate André Gide

I can't tell you how liberating and energizing it was to pursue my authentic direction and do the work I loved to do instead of holding on to what was no longer my path. It was priceless and I never looked back.

By the way, the same goes with relationships (though not the subject of this book but very important to our life and happiness). Sometimes you just have the faith to take that important first step to leave what you are doing and embark on your new direction.

> *Faith means taking the first step,*
> *even when you don't see the whole staircase.*
> —Dr. Martin Luther King

REDUCE THE LAG TIME

I have found that a key to life is to reduce the lag time between when you know it is time to change and when you take action. So much time and opportunity can be lost, and suffering can be endured. When you have done the work and self-reflection to get to a clear seeing and knowing that it is time to shit, then acknowledge the fear and uncertainty and take the plunge. It allows you to be in the flow of the universe rather than stay stuck in resistance.

Michael A. Singer, in his book *The Surrender Experiment*, emphasizes the power that can come from surrendering to the flow of life. Opportunities that, at first, may seem to not fit with our preferences and identity can open doors that lead to growth and directions that we never imagined. While the primary focus of this book is for you to proactively choose and pursue your authentic health career, I want to emphasize that there are forces beyond our consciousness and control that shape and awaken our life and career direction and options. The key is to be open to what is presented, be discerning, and know when it is something to pursue, and if it is, act and put yourself in the flow. As described in Chapter 6 about recognizing and following "moments of knowing," my decisions to pursue public health, marry my wife, the internship that changed my life, engage in meditation, and follow a higher power and my church all came about when I least expected it and were different than what I was pursuing. I was called and compelled to pursue them, and once I did a path of opportunities, experiences, and people opened up in flow that led me to discover and live the incredible life I am blessed to enjoy today. Remember that luck is where opportunity and preparation meet. I am confident that you can opportunities will be presented to you in addition to the preparation and action you take. Be sure to recognize and pursue them when they do, guided by your internal compass including your heart, head, and intuition.

What we avoid is often the key to our future.
—Miles, from the television show *God Friended Me*

GOING WITH THE FLOW

Many people in the health people will say that had no idea what they were going to do and could have never imagined the jobs and career paths they pursued. For many, it works out to be an amazing success. Your authentic health career might find you instead of you finding it. If that is the case, fully go for it from your highest and best self and know that you can succeed. If it turns out that the path you pursue isn't working for you or needs to be changed, then adjust with less lag time.

Follow and Surrender to Opportunities that Are Presented

One example of adjusting career paths to go with the flow of what is presented was my shift to medical group management from hospital administration. I had worked hard to be a successful hospital administrator and had an offer from a physician group to become the President of a management company that was managing their business. The first time the physician group approached me, I didn't even listen to their offer. I was firmly on my path of being a hospital administrator. The path I had spent eight years working very hard to pursue. Fortunately, they asked again after the person the group chose didn't work out. I had experienced more frustration in my administrator role, and the hospital was going through painful changes due to our financial situation. I reluctantly decided to hear what they had in mind. I decided that at that early stage of my career and at the age of 28, I could take a risk and try something new. I decided that I could try working with the physician group for two to three years and if I liked it, I would continue. If I didn't like it I could go back to being a hospital administrator and be more effective because I would learn more about how doctors viewed the hospital and how to more effectively work with them. My hospital peers and mentors were dumbfounded. How could I leave my promising hospital administration path they had worked hard to support me to pursue to go work for doctors.

Many said they would never work for doctors. They also said I could never go back to hospital administration. Fortunately, my risk worked out. I got a 60% salary increase and had tripled my income within five years. I also got a much better pension plan and benefits. I learned what is was like to run a small, entrepreneurial business rather than a large institution and that if you consciously run your own business you can choose the lifestyle you want to have. I had much more vacation time. I worked very hard but had much success and became a national expert and statewide leader in a growing, profitable niche area of health. This led me to having unique knowledge and skills and becoming a consultant, which I still am today, and my role teaching at Harvard. It provided me with the money to be in a position to take the 70% salary cut to adjust my path to work at UC Berkeley to pursue my passion because I already had savings, a pension, a house, and cars. It also wasn't my dream work, so I ultimately had enough pain to choose my current true path.

In his book *The Surrender Experiment*, Michael A. Singer explains the importance of surrendering to what is presented and fully following it as a way to go with the flow of life, of getting out of the way of your ego and passions and preferences and going with opportunities that are presented and people you meet along the way. My pursuing the radiology physician group job is a good example. This led me to go with the opportunity that presented in Boston so that I could honor my promise to my wife of trying to live on the East Coast and to myself of deciding once and for all if I wanted to stay in administration or pursue education and nonprofit work. This led me to Berkeley, which I only was chosen for because I had worked at Harvard and had an executive role at Partners. I was proactive and followed the flow. I encourage you to do the same to see where life takes you. Michael A. Singer's story also involves a major health career so for that reason and all the life insights he provides I encourage you to read it. I read it after I had surrendered to many changes but still had breakthroughs to see all the things I was resisting and how by being open I could learn, grow and live more fully and aligned.

UNFORTUNATE DEVELOPMENTS ALONG OUR PATH

Many of us have suffered the unfortunate experience of being in our authentic health career and a role that we truly love, only to have organizational changes or dynamics take it away. Changes such as new leadership, a re-organization, a merger, or increased financial constraints/budget cuts can lead to the end, sometimes abruptly, of our dream job or a good thing. There are also cases in which we don't get the job or promotion we expected or earned. We may also encounter being fired or failure, which leads to the loss of something we valued or a direction we were pursuing.

PAM'S STORY

Pam's goal was to become a hospital CEO. She had worked hard, built the relationships, and had many accomplishments to rise through the ranks within her large health system. Her hard work paid off when she was appointed CEO of a hospital in her region. She thrived in the role and loved it. Her hospital was doing well she had built a solid team. She had an innovative long-term vision for the hospital that the team was inspired to achieve. Though her health system over-all was doing well financially and on its quality and service metrics, system leadership was concerned that emerging marketplace trends and competition posed serious threats for the system going forward. Leadership decided that to position the system for success in the future a major reorganization was needed to "shake up" the status quo, reduce costs, send a message that business as usual would not work in the future and to create greater regional efficiencies.

Unfortunately, Pam's position was eliminated as part of the restructuring. She applied for one of the consolidated leadership roles that would still allow her to lead hospitals but was not selected. She was stunned and saddened. One minute she was living and thriving in her dream job; the next she was without a role. She did end up with a meaningful leadership role within the system, but it was not the same. She ended up deciding that she needed a break and time to figure out her next steps. Pam ended up becoming a consultant working for herself to make some money and stay engaged while she figured out what she wanted to do. She liked consulting and was good it at. She ended up launching her own business that she has now led for many years. She enjoys working for herself and with her many diverse clients. It also allows her to have time and lifestyle flexibility that she would have never had as a CEO and to pursue her personal passions and nonprofit work she values. She has made an incredible difference to many people and organizations and won awards for her accomplishments and contributions. She made a strong adjustment to a significant unwanted organizational change and forged a new career direction that allowed her to achieve her life and professional goals.

> *My journey to where I am today was not the straight line that*
> *I envisioned. I had a daughter early in college and my career*
> *has taken several unexpected turns. However, everything that*
> *I encountered, and all my experiences contributed to the person*
> *I am today and prepared me for my dynamic professional role*
> *aligned with my passions and goals.*
> —Laura Long, Kaiser Permanente

Life, family, or relationship changes can also require us to make career path adjustments. A health challenge, the birth of a child, or the need to relocate for a partner's job may be transition points in which we reassess our priorities and goals and make adjustments to our direction.

WHAT IF YOUR JOB ISN'T WHAT YOU THOUGHT IT WOULD BE?

Clinician burnout is one of the most serious challenges that individuals and our health system are facing. As indicated in previous chapters, more than 50% of doctors are dissatisfied, and 49% would not recommend that their children go into medicine. Physician suicide and is on the rise. Part of it stems from the culture, administrative responsibilities, and systems that don't enable clinicians to take care of patients and practice in the way they went into medicine to do. Not only do they have the professional joy and satisfaction, but they may also not have the lifestyle and personal satisfaction they seek.

If you are faced with a situation in which your job and life isn't what you thought it would be, then you can choose to try to make changes that will make it so and use your power to do so. You can change organizations or roles that may be better aligned with who you are and what you want. You could also change paths and leverage the training, expertise, and drive you have to make a difference in other paths. Particularly in medicine you can make those changes. Do the work of the pathway framework and make the choice and navigate the changes necessary to adjust to have the life and career you really want. Life is too short, and you have worked too hard. You are going to spend more time with your work than family, unless you choose differently. Choose what you want.

> *In both life and football, failure is inevitable. You don't always win. You can, however, learn from that failure, pick yourself up with great enthusiasm, and place yourself in the arena again.*
> —Tom Brady, New England Patriot's six-time Super Bowl–winning quarterback

RECASTING

Whether you encounter the need to make life or career adjustments due to personal, organizational, or environmental challenges, you have the ability to choose how you respond and make adjustments that will serve you well.

In their book *How We Choose to Be Happy*, my good friends Greg Hicks and Rick Foster describe their proven nine-step model for choosing to be happy. One of the nine behaviors of the happiest people is that they practice recasting. They found that happy people universally move through painful and challenging situations through the process of recasting. Recasting is not simply saying, "I just need to get over it and get on with my life." It involves two stages: diving into the negative feelings head-on and experiencing them deeply. They honor their emotional experience and learn from what their minds and bodies are telling them. They don't avoid the pain and difficulties. Once fully engaged with their emotions, they begin to transform their feelings with new actions and insights. They ask, "What lessons can I learn?" "What new meaning can I create for my life?" and "What opportunities for the future can I create from this experience?" From this place you learn and grow from your experience, you believe in and act from a place of strength and that you can handle what occurred and you choose to move forward in an authentic new direction that offers meaning and new opportunity.

Recasting is a powerful process that can be applied to fears, personal loss, trauma, and educational and professional disappointments or failures. To learn more about recasting check out Chapter 5 in *How We Choose to Be Happy*.

What have you experienced that you need to recast in order to move forward and succeed in your authentic health career path? Realizing you don't want to be a doctor, failure of a major project, not getting into the graduate school you wanted, loss of a job, death of a family member? These are all very painful and difficult challenges. I encourage you to have the courage—I know it is not easy—to go through the recasting process as part of your action plan for moving forward that we will develop in the next chapter.

FALLING UPWARD

In his book *Falling Upward*, Richard Rohr discusses that failure and challenges are part of life, but when you fall, you can actually learn and grow in a way that a setback is a temporary situation in which you can actually fall upward along your journey toward your authentic and best self. The key is to have the mindset that this is possible, choose to recast, and then move forward with intention armed with new insights. We can actually fall upward toward our highest and best self and toward our higher power.

7 TIPS FOR MAKING EFFECTIVE ADJUSTMENTS

Regardless of your reason for making an adjustment in your life and career direction, here are seven tips to help you make solid choices:

1. **Be clear about your why and your definition of success:** It can be easy to feel dissatisfaction, pain, and frustration with your job or life circumstances which can be a catalyst for making a change. Use those feelings as fuel to push past any resistance, fear, or inertia related to making a change that is needed. However, as you decide on what's next, be sure you understand the problems or causes of concern with your current situation. This will help you assess if working thorough them and staying the course is the best option; sometimes, we would rather leave than work through uncomfortable situations, step into our power, or advocate for ourselves in ways that would help us grow. This will also help you not change to another situation that has similar problems (for example, I have a friend who always leaves because of his boss and then selects another situation in which the new boss has similar unwanted behaviors). It is also important to become clear about your "why" you want to make a change and why now. Your why will also inform your criteria for and definition of success or your next steps and new direction. Clarity about your why and definition of success will help you make a well-informed choice and help motivate you to take the necessary steps and risks.

2. **Do your internal work:** As you define your why and success, be clear about who you are and want to be going forward (personally and professionally). Consider how things have changed and what you

have learned from your experiences. Do the work of deciding on the factors at the bottom of the Triangle: what are you good at and enjoy doing and what are your passions, values, goals, and life preferences.

It is also important to continuously increase your self-awareness, emotional intelligence, and personal growth. We have many unconscious and conditioned patterns and mind states that we should be mindful of as we make life decisions that are in the best interests of ourselves and our families.

3. Create and explore aligned options: Creating and believing you have options is one of the nine behaviors Foster and Hicks identified. It is exhibited by the happiest people and most successful leaders. While you may be tempted to take the next promising opportunity that appears in order to leave your current situation (and that may be fine), I encourage you to take some time to create and explore, through exposure and experience, one to three new directions before you make the change. I had an intuition that I wanted to teach and work with students but before I made a major career change I taught several classes and put myself in an academic setting to be sure I would enjoy it if it was the center of what I did rather than something fun and rewarding I did on the side. I also did informational interviews with people who like me had been health executives and then chosen to get a doctoral degree at mid-career and shifted to work in an academic setting. Not only did this help me learn more about the direction, but it also led to one of the interviewees recommending me for the job at UC Berkeley that I left being a health executive to do.

4. Position yourself for success in your new direction: Once you identify your new direction then you can position yourself for success by leveraging your networks and building key new relationships, gaining credibility (certifications, education, experience), developing your story of how the new direction aligns with your vision and strengths, and making the case on how your skills and experience are transferrable. For example, if you decide to transition from working in research to project management within a health provider organization you want to tell the story of why you are making the change, how your skills and experience are transferrable, secure a project management certification, and become a regular attendee at your local healthcare executive association to build your network.

5. **Get your significant others or family on board:** If you have a significant other or family member that you want to support and/or be part of the change you want to make, be sure to engage them in your process. Engage them as early in your process as you think would beneficial to you and them. Help them understand your rationale, feelings, and intentions for making the change and your definition of success. Include them in thinking through your options before you decide. Consider their concerns and aspirations and how the change could impact them and your relationship with them. Realize that they may react initially and throughout the process from the perspective of their comfort level with the change and how it will impact them. It may be a process to get them on board, and some may never agree. Others may totally support you and have more confidence in your ability to successfully change than you do. For example, at times when I have struggled with doubts about major career changes and have been hesitant to make decisions, my wife, Lydia, has always believed in me and encouraged me to take risks and go for what I want and know is right. She has provided invaluable support and wisdom, along with making significant sacrifices. Regardless, in the end, remember that it is your life and career and your decision. For more insights and tactics into how to get support of others for your authentic career and changes in your path, see Chapter 10 and my website.

Don't let the noise of others opinions drown out...
somehow your heart and intuition already know what.
—Steve Jobs

If you are changing jobs and care about your relationship with your boss and having their support for the change (before or as a reference after), you may also want to include them in your process. The same goes for a valued mentor or colleague. While it may be uncomfortable and risky to let them know you are considering a change, it is beneficial to include them in your process so that they feel valued and considered and so it isn't a complete shock when you make your move. If you engage them, they may have valuable insights and connections and may be more likely to be a strong reference when you make your change and a supporter beyond. Relationships are everything, and you will find out just how small the world is and you will likely be in your career for a long time so prioritize keeping good relationships with the people you value and how can assist you. Particularly those people who have helped you along the way and have your best interests at heart. After you have made the change, occasionally let them know how well it has worked out for you and how much you appreciate their support.

6. **Figure out the finances:** Often, making major life and career adjustments may involve the need to make new investments, to take risks related to an uncertain path, or even require a reduction in your compensation. For many of us or our families, including me, who has a deep fear of suffering adverse financial consequences, overcoming real or imagined financial barriers to pursue your authentic path can be one of the most difficult challenges to making and taking action on a change or new direction. I delayed many of the changes I knew I needed to make because of imagined financial ruin. Given the importance of finances and the increasing cost of living, it is important that you understand your financial resources, take steps to strengthen your position, and have some options or a plan for how you will meet your financial needs in your new direction. At minimum, it would be helpful to know the level of resources you need to meet your basic needs or maintain an acceptable lifestyle. Often, we could get

by on less than we think, and we are more resourceful than we give ourselves credit. It may not be what we want for an extended time, but many of us have been poor and/or students, which required us to make ends meet with little. One of my best friends, who has taken many risks to pursue his dreams, has done so knowing that in the end, he can make it work because he can live like a student.

> *We'll get a little place in Harlem and we'll figure it out.*
> —From the musical *Hamilton*

The truth is that, more likely than not, if you are following your authentic health career path, then the resources you need will follow. Your path will develop, and opportunities and key people will be presented along the way. Believe in and trust yourself that when you fully engage you can figure it out. I know this from experience. As I previously mentioned, I took a 70% salary cut and moved across the country with my third child on the way and my wife not working to pursue my authentic new direction. It was rough, and we have had to make many sacrifices and dig into savings or investments that we didn't want to, but my wife and I agree that the results have been priceless! I have been blessed to be living my authentic life and health career for more than 18 years and have an amazing family and fulfilled my purpose in many ways.

As you focus on the risk and fear, it is also important to focus on the definition of success and rewards for you and the impact on others. You are often exchanging your money for your life and your life and living authentically and fully it is priceless. We are all going to die, and our lives are shorter than we think. Live and have faith that what you need will be provided.

> *What are you going to do with this one*
> *wild and precious life you have?*
> —Mary Oliver

While having faith is important, combining it with solid mindsets and plans related to finances is also important. There are many powerful resources available to assist you in developing a plan. There are also many powerful resources to assist you in developing a mindset and behaviors that will enable you to develop the resources you need and be successful in your dreams. There is no reason to believe you can't succeed other than your own conditioned fears and beliefs. Be mindful of how your family's beliefs and fears may influence your mindset, plans, and willingness to act. I grew up with a security and scarcity mindset and the programming that "I am lucky to have a job." With all due respect of your family background, circumstances, and beliefs, please remember that you have abilities that can help you transcend your past and present situation and that in each generation, there is an opportunity for upward mobility. I realized this after my father had cautioned me that I would have a hard time getting a job in health administration and that as many as 800 people applied for jobs and that I ended up being the one who got the job.

For medicine and other health careers with expensive education, there are more ways to pay for it than you think. (See these resources: Association of American Medical Colleges (AAMC), Association of Schools and Programs of Public Health (ASPPH)). Don't be the person who doesn't go medical school or other careers you want to pursue because of the cost of education or fear of debt. The average primary care doctor is paid $180,000 to $200,000 and often marries another high-income professional, so paying off loans isn't fun, but is doable and your return on investment (ROI) for living the life and career you want is off the charts!

7. **Develop the Belief and Courage and Support Systems:** As we discussed in Chapter 9, deciding on a clear, authentic health career path and corresponding educational choices is important and you must also have the necessary belief and courage to commit and follow

through on your plan. From my experience, developing enough belief and courage can be a process that takes time. It took me several years to decide on and finally pull the trigger on some of my major moves. Chapter 9 includes many suggestions on how to do this as does my website. Each of us is different. I encourage you to figure out what you need in terms of inspiration, support, and guidance. Talking with mentors and close colleagues can be a very helpful part of the process to get their feedback; ensure that you have thought through all the considerations and that you are acting from your authentic self. It may also be valuable to utilize a certified coach to assist you. I have greatly benefitted from the support of a coach at each of my major life and career transition points.

There are different kinds of coaches. There are life coaches, executive coaches, high-performance coaches, and business coaches. It is important to be clear about what you want in a coach and your objectives and desired outcomes. Many coaches focus on personal and professional goals through a holistic approach; including how you show up for what you do. Some focus just on business. Many use assessments such as Meyers–Briggs, Strength Finder, or Whole Brain. Solid coaches put the onus on you to clearly define what you want in terms of career and lifestyle and what success means, among other aspects. They can help you overcome your own barriers or saboteurs and practice difficult conversations with family, friends, or supervisors. I highly recommend coaching. You can access authentic health career coaching through my website at Jeffoxendine.com

I also found value in attending workshops and conferences as part of charting a new course or preparing for a change. Topics in the fields you want to pursue provide knowledge and skills and information in the areas you want to pursue. They also provide for networking and potential employment opportunities.

There are also personal growth or mindfulness and meditation-related conferences through which you can develop the skills, inspiration, and plans for moving forward.

Practicing mindfulness and meditation have helped me to become clearer about who I am (and who I am not), the thoughts, beliefs, and stories that serve me well and those that don't, and increased my awareness and freedom to choose, pursue and enjoy the life I am supposed to lead. My practice also helps me deal with the challenges, stresses, joys, and sorrows that are part of my journey. It also helps me manage the transitions associated with major life and career changes, I encourage you to develop a practice that works for you or find other ways to increase your awareness, health, and happiness and ability to navigate the vicissitudes of your authentic life and career. It will be rewarding and fulfilling but isn't supposed to be easy.

Learn to surf or duck under the waves
rather than be knocked over by them.
—Tara Brach

ACTION AND ACCOUNTABILITY PLAN

While I am confident these tips will help you move forward, you can significantly increase your probability of success when you develop and implement an action plan for advancing toward and achieving your goals. Action and accountability plans are discussed in the next chapter, and you will have the opportunity to create one. If you are ready to create one now, you can go to my website at Jeffoxendine.com to download an Authentic Health Career Action Plan Template and example.

END OF CHAPTER EXERCISES

Are Adjustments Needed?

Exercise 1: Are you living your authentic health career now or making progress toward it?

1. Please rate your current status (on a scale of 1 to 10, with 10 being the highest). If you are not where you want to be, what is different from where you want to be? What is missing? What are the barriers?

2. Review the Life and Career Alignment Triangle and the stages of knowing where you are relative to your authentic health career (scale of 1 to 10). Are you at the surviving, searching, or being stage (remember, wherever you are is exactly where you are supposed to be)?

3. Where are you relative to where you want to be regarding clarity about your authentic career direction (scale of 1 to 10)? Progress toward your goals? Are you not where you want to be relative to where you want in terms of your authentic health career (scale of 1 to 10)?

4. What is the future market like for the one to three career directions you are considering? Your current job? The education and training you have, are pursuing, or plan to pursue?

5. How will technology advances and other likely changes impact what your life and job will be like? Will you still have a viable role? Will you find the work and lifestyle fulfilling?

6. Will the path you are on lead to the life and impact you want to lead?

7. Given your current situation and projected future state of the market and your profession, is it time for you to consider adjusting or changing your direction now or in the coming year or two?

8. If adjustments or changes are needed, are you in the process of or ready to make the change? Are there current barriers that are preventing you from making the change? Are they real or imagined?

9. What are three things you can do to strengthen your position and readiness for change?

10. Who do you need to get on board? How will you go about it?

11. What can you do to strengthen your financial position and readiness to make a change?

12. When will you take the plunge? What else do you need to know?

Exercise 2: Financial Beliefs and Positioning

1.   What will it cost for you to actively pursue your authentic career at the level and pace you want to pursue it?

2.   What are some options for you to reduce the cost? Secure funding or financial support or loans to be able to pursue your goals?

3.   What will be your level of compensation when you are fully living your authentic health career?

4.   How much money annually will you need to support the lifestyle you want? What level of other assets do you need?

5. Do you need to generate these resources all on your own or can your current or future partner contribute? Other sources? How can you reduce these costs to go for your dreams if needed?

6. What will be your "return on investment" for making the change and/or pursuing your authentic health career? How compelling is it to you (scale of 1 to 10)?

7. Do you have any financially related fears or beliefs that are making it more challenging for you to choose or actively pursue your authentic direction? To make an adjustment or major change in your direction? Are they real or imagined?

8. What can you do to address and mitigate your fears? What is a different story you can tell?

9. What are three things you can do to strengthen your financial position to make the change?

DEVELOPING YOUR ACTION PLAN

TYING IT ALL TOGETHER AND TAKING ACTION NOW TO ADVANCE YOUR AUTHENTIC HEALTH CAREER

The distance between your dreams and reality is called action.
—Unknown

In this chapter you will pull all you have learned in the book to develop a practical action plan for advancing from where you are now toward your authentic health career. Your action plan will serve as a road map to lay our clear next steps, timelines, and how you will gain the support and accountability you need to be successful. You can start working on the action plan and making progress as soon as it is done and feel more in control and empowered to achieve your goals.

Knowing is not enough, we must apply.
Willing is not enough we must do.
—Goethe

A clear vision backed by definite plans gives you a
tremendous feeling of confidence and personal power.
—Brian Tracy

A goal without a plan is just a wish.
—Antoine de Saint-Exupery

Now that you have done all the hard work, using the elements of the Life and Career Planning Framework and Life and Career Alignment Triangle, to choose and strengthen your readiness to actively pursue your authentic direction or to take the next steps to discover it, it is time to create your action plan. An action plan is a practical tool for you to clarify your vision, goals, and definition of success and create clear action steps and timelines to make them happen. Through action plan development, you can pull together and synthesize all the work you have done on the elements of the Life and Career Planning Framework into one actionable document. Your plan will be your road map to your authentic health career and all the benefits!

Having an action plan will significantly increase your likelihood of success and give you a feeling of greater control of your destiny. The process of developing your plan and making required decisions will help you refine and focus your direction and outcomes. An action plan can also empower you to get others on board with your direction and decisions. An action plan with well-thought-out outcomes, steps, and timelines can help people who are important and care about you but may be concerned about your direction see that you have a solid plan. It will likely give them more comfort and confidence, particularly when they see you taking action, having successes along the way, and building momentum.

Though I have a recommended format in the End of Chapter Exercises and on my website, there is no right or wrong way to develop an action plan or format you should use. There are dozens of useful tools available. The key is to choose and use a format that is practical and works for you. You will be more likely to use it if you can easily incorporate into the system you use (if you have one) to organize yourself and get things done. If you don't have one, it is okay, and implementing your action plan can be a catalyst for developing one. If you don't have a system find some way for you to review the plan and track your progress on a regular basis.

Action plans typically include some or all the following core components (go to the links for more detailed definitions and examples):

1. **Authentic Life and Career Vision:** Your aspirational future vision (10 to 20 or 30 years) of the life you want, how you want to be, the impact you want to have, and how your authentic health career will be aligned. If you are guided by a life purpose, incorporate fulfillment of it into your vision.

2. **Core Values:** Consider up to five values that define what is most important to you and will underpin your life and career choices.

3. **Definition of Success:** How will you define and measure success for your life and career. How will you know? Include how you live now and throughout your journey and your ultimate impact. Link to your vision, purpose, and core values.

4. **Priority Goals:** List up to five priority goals (time frame to be determined by your ambitions and needs) to focus your efforts and advance toward and achieve your vision and definition of success. You may want to have longer (five- to ten-year), mid (three- to five-year) and near term (one- to three-year) goals.

5. **Measures, Milestones, and Deliverables:** For each goal, specify how you will measure success. Include specific and quantifiable outcomes (e.g., become a hospital administrator, make $X, spend $Y amount each week working out), and some key milestones (accomplishments) along the way to your goal (graduating from college, getting a job, getting accepted to an MPH program). You may want outcome becoming and process milestones (secure job as a doctor, get accepted to medical school, good enough score on the MCAT, survive O Chem).

6. **Action Steps and Timelines:** Specify the major priority action steps to achieve each goal and the timeline for completion.

7. **Who Is Responsible:** Identify the person responsible for completing each action within the timeline (many of them will be you!). You can also specify others who are involved and who will provide support.

8. **Status:** For each of the actions, indicate the current status relative to the outcome and completion timeline. Choose and use a status indicator that will motivate and support you. Some people like "on schedule," "behind schedule," and "not started." You can also include factors such as "waiting for Jeff to respond or waiting for test results. Application submitted." Many of us use colors to indicate the status such as green being on time, yellow in danger of being behind, and red being behind. Including status helps you focus on the progress you are making and areas you need to devote more attention to stay on track.

9. **Next Action:** Personal productivity guru David Allen changed my life many years ago when I learned his approach to action plan management and getting things done. One of the many lessons I learned was to include the next action related to each action step. Focusing on the next action allows you to be motivated and put your effort into getting the next thing done rather than listing out every action step and getting overwhelmed or paralyzed and not acting at all. Crossing off a next action feels good and builds momentum. It also allows you in limited time to quickly identify something that you can do to move things forward.

These nine elements or a subset of them go into your action plan. I encourage you to make it simple to develop and maintain. Most important is that you will develop and use the action plan and that it is a tool that will motivate and assist you to make progress toward your authentic health career.

You will have the opportunity to develop these at the end of the chapter or you can go directly there and get started now!

MARGARET'S STORY

Margaret was a motivated premed student at UC Davis. The daughter of farmworkers, she was the first in her family to attend college. Margaret was bright and intelligent but struggled with science courses and the intense premed culture. She studied hard and did well enough to be on track toward her goals. However, she was not finding much joy and meaning in her course work and other preparatory experiences. Fortunately, she did internships that exposed her to mental health and public health. She loved the works she did and the communities she worked with. She decided to shift her focus to public health.

I met Margaret when she was in a predecessor program to what is now Health Career Connection (HCC). I spoke about my MBA and MPH education and my work as a hospital administrator. Margaret decided she was going to become a hospital administrator and go to the MBA MPH Program at UC Berkeley. Highly motivated and determined she set ambitious goals and committed to an action plan to meet her goals. The action plan included specific steps and timelines and milestones. It was clear and compelling. She carved out time in her schedule and treated the time as if it was another class. Her plan included studying for the GMAT, completing her statement of purpose (with input from editors and mentors), securing letters of recommendation, meeting with the MBA MPH program director, and following up on his advice. She kept the plan in front of her each day and tracked her progress. Each time she had an accomplishment, she moved it from the plan to the completed section. She was completely motivated by meeting each milestone along the way. Margaret's focus, hard work, and following the action plan paid off. She got accepted, though deferred and got more work experience. She ended up going to the UC Berkeley MBA and MPH and using similar action plan techniques to graduate and get a great job with Kaiser Permanente. Her focused approaches, along with her talents and skills aligned with her authentic path, enabled her to quickly rise through the ranks to become the youngest VP and Board Member ever in The Permanente Medical Group. Margaret has given back to many others through programs she created and funded at Kaiser Permanente and with partners to increase diversity in the health professions and give others like her opportunity. She has taught many others what she learned about focus, motivation and action plans.

BLOCK OUT TIME ON YOUR SCHEDULE

One of the lessons learned that Margaret conveyed from her journey was blocking out time on your schedule to work toward your career and graduate education goals. When she wrote her statement of purpose, she blocked out time on her schedule as if it were another class. She estimated how much time it would take her to do multiple drafts, get feedback, and refine it into the product she needed. She scheduled that time and treated it just like it was a class that she had to prepare for and attend.

I took a similar approach to finally getting this book written after a decade of trying to squeeze it in on top of all other things I was trying to do (and not getting it done because there was always something more pressing). I scheduled an hour or more per day and stuck to it. It made all the difference. I now do this with other life and career priorities including spending time with family and exercise.

I encourage you to devote significant time in your schedule to Life Career 101. You are the instructor and set the objectives, scope, and outcomes. Treat it at least like a one-unit class in which you have a couple hours a week devoted to the task at hand and an hour of prep time for each hour devoted. So, only four hours per week. I know you are busy, but everyone can find four hours out of a week with at least 112 waking hours. Giving up one movie on Netflix and several YouTube videos will do it. Schedule the time if you want to advance. At least one hour of the time should be devoted to reviewing and updating your action plan and reflecting on your progress and accomplishments.

KEEP IN FRONT OF YOU

Scheduling time to review your action plan and goals is a key success factor. It is one way to keep your action plan in front of you. Find ways that work for you to keep the plan and the key outcomes and task at the forefront of your attention for at least some portion of your day or week. This will increase your likelihood of following it and success. Be creative and use things like screen savers, bathroom mirrors, and reminders. Engage with others who can support you and help you stay on track. Avoid the common tendency to avoid changes that are scary or difficult and go with things that are more familiar. Schedule at least one hour a week to review your action plan, progress, and priorities and develop a plan on how to focus and best proceed with the next steps.

> *The weekly review is key, it's the one thing that people don't do.*
> —David Allen

ACCOUNTABILITY PLAN

One reason to keep your plan in front of you and share with others is to increase your level of accountability for following through and achieving the results. While I believe you will be successful in accomplishing your action plan, I encourage you to increase your chances by developing an accountability plan. An accountability plan will include being clear and having a system to hold yourself accountable and engaging others in holding you accountable. *Accountability* means the quality or state of being accountable—*especially* an obligation or willingness to accept responsibility or to account for one's actions.[61]

---

[61] Merriam-Webster, "Accountable."

Another way of thinking about accountability is being responsible to yourself and others for doing what you say you are going to do. In the end, implementation of your action plan and achievement of your goal means the most to you, so at minimum have a personal accountability plan. It is sometimes hard to hold ourselves accountable, so it can also be helpful to engage supportive people you know and trust to help hold you accountable. In writing this book and pursuing other major endeavors, I found it invaluable to have regular meetings with friends and colleagues, during which I made commitments regarding what I was going to get done by the next meeting and had to provide updates.

Your personal accountability plan can include regular times you will review, track progress and make adjustments to your plan. Having a regular system of reminders is also important. It is also important to have milestones for success along the way and celebrating your successes. You should think of creative ways you can reward yourself for great progress and meeting your timelines and deliverables. You can also have some way to keep yourself on track and for making adjustments and learning if you don't meet the timelines.

Having others hold you accountable can be informal or formal. Many people have peer groups that the form who meet regularly to share progress on goals and discuss how to overcome barriers that arise along the way. Some of these groups can be informal among friends while others can be through professional peers or paid "mastermind" groups or academies in which people are working toward a common end of making a change. Sometimes more effective when you are paying for something and have to report.

A mentor can be another way of keeping you on track. Set regular meetings or calls or send updates on things you promised to do.

Many people hire coaches to help them set goals, overcome challenges, and be accountable. As mentioned in the previous chapter, I have benefited tremendously from coaching and from being part of formal and informal groups. I am a very goal-oriented, results-driven, and disciplined person. However, I also have many competing priorities and deadlines. I would not have gotten this book done without being part of peer groups who were also writing books that had regularly scheduled meetings and expectations of progress between weeks. I also had a coach that assisted me to stay on track. These groups also provided valuable support. They also help you realize that you are not alone in being busy and having a hard time following through, your attempts to avoid discomfort or sabotage ourselves and challenges that are encountered along the way. We are all human, and we can find benefit in allowing ourselves to be human and get support and sometimes tough love to push past barriers and get what we want to get done. Groups can also see the gold and promise in you and your plans when you can't and will be there to celebrate your successes.

Accountability works best when it is built into your system of how you get things done. Incorporate your goals and reminders and tasks into a system you already use such as Outlook or Gmail tasks, a daily planner, a whiteboard, or a project management system. Include reminders and times for updates. The easier you make it to stay on top of your commitments and meet your timelines and adjust as needed, the more likely you can follow through.

Find a personal and group accountability plan that works for you and leverage it to meet your goals. You will find it feels really good to do what you say you are going to do and make progress toward the plans and goals that matter most to you. That in itself is very reinforcing, and the progress and results will help keep the momentum going. It will build your confidence and expectancy that you will meet your goals. You will also advance toward your goals, which is the purpose.

FOCUS AND GETTING ACROSS THE GOAL LINE

A senior public health leader I work with always reminds me that many people can get the ball inside the 20-yard line but the teams that win are able to get the ball all the way across the goal line. The same goes for your personal goals and professional initiatives. There will be many distractions and real and imagined barriers to you meeting your goals. Stay focused on your direction, goals, and action plans. Adjust as needed but keep going until you get to the finish line or over the goal line. I have learned that things don't always happen the way and on the timeline I would like, but if I have a strong intention, focus, and action plan, I persevere and allow others to help I will eventually accomplish my goals and have them impact I want to have. I am confident you can do the same. Hopefully this book has inspired and empowered you to discover and achieve your authentic health career. Please utilize my website and other resources to help you throughout your journey. I look forward to you leading the life and career you desire and were meant to lead and to positively impacting the world with your passions and gifts.

Never, Never, Never, Give Up.
—Winston Churchill

END OF CHAPTER EXERCISES

Exercise 1: Developing Your Action Plan

I recommend the following steps to develop your action plan:

1. Clarify your authentic health career direction and definition of success.

2. Draft your goals.

3. Working backward from each goal, list the five major action steps to get there.

4. Identify the timeline you want to meet and milestones along the way.

5. Draft a plan and be sure you can commit. Develop your plan in a practical, actionable format that you will use. If you need a template or an example, go to my website at Jeffoxendine.com to download the Authentic Health Career Action Plan.

6. Build time and action steps into your schedule to devote sufficient time to getting it done.

7. Set and keep regular times to review your progress on your own
and with a buddy, mentor, or group. Celebrate successes and
make adjustments as needed.

Exercise 2: Accountability Plan

What does accountability mean to you?

Why is it important to reaching your goals?

What areas do you need help with to be accountable?

What things work well to help you be accountable?

How will you hold yourself accountable? What challenges do you
anticipate?

When will you review and reflect on your action plan?

What kind of additional support do you need? How you will get support? Who can best provide it?

Who will hold you accountable?

How will you reward yourself for progress along the way and for success?

To develop an action plan to achieve your own life, health career, and educational goals, go to my website at Jeffoxendine.com to download an Authentic Health Career Action Plan Template.

CONCLUSION

CONGRATULATIONS!

You have worked through the Framework, or at least the elements that are most relevant to you, and have your action plan. You are now ready to accelerate progress toward your authentic life and health career. I am confident you will be successful!

As you move forward, please remember that you can refer to the Framework and tools in this book at any point and throughout your journey.

You will want and need to keep getting more **exposure** to the changes, trends, and opportunities in the dynamic health field and understand their implications for your health career.

You will want to regularly assess your values, passions and goals; what you are good at and enjoy; and what you want in a work environment as you go through different life stages.

You will continue to gain and learn from your **experience** and position yourself for education and jobs that will provide you with greater success.

You can consciously make new choices about your **career direction and actively pursue** your authentic paths and **make adjustments** as your life and career priorities change or you encounter new opportunities and challenges.

You can continue to strengthen your **educational preparation** to help you get the specialized knowledge, skills, and credentials you need to achieve your goals.

You can enhance your **personal branding and packaging** so that employers, educational institutions, and colleagues know how well prepared, qualified, and amazing you are.

You must continue to strengthen and utilize your **network** to advance in your career life and get things done—remember it's either network or not work—and enjoy the incredible people you get to improve health with.

You will continue to grow as a person and professional and build the belief and courage that you need to achieve and fully live your goals and purpose.

You must continue to have a road map and action plan to keep you on track for your authentic health career and life goals and have the self-discipline to make it happen.

I look forward to your success!

REFERENCES

CHAPTER 1

1. U.S. Bureau of Labor Statistics, "Healthcare Occupations." https://www.bls.gov/ooh/healthcare/home.htm
2. U.S. Bureau of Labor Statistics, "Employment Projections, 2018–2028." https://www.bls.gov/news.release/pdf/ecopro.pdf
3. Liu, Jenny X., Yevgeniy Goryakin, Akiko Maeda, Tim Bruckner, and Richard Scheffler. "Global Health Workforce Labor Market Projections for 2030." *Human Resources for Health* 15, 11 (2017). https://doi.org/10.1186/s12960-017-0187-2

CHAPTER 2

4. *The New Oxford American Dictionary.* "opportunity cost." New York: Oxford University Press, 2005.
5. Sinetar, Marsha. *To Build the Life You Want, Create the Work You Love: The Spiritual Dimension of Entrepreneuring.* New York: Griffin, 1995.

CHAPTER 3

6. CDC, "Ten Great Public Health Achievements—United States, 1900–1999." https://www.cdc.gov/mmwr/preview/mmwrhtml/00056796.htm

7. Rosenstock, Linda, Gillian B. Silver, Karen Helsing, Connie Evashwick, Ruth Katz, Michael Klag, Gerald Kominski, Donna Richter, and Ciro Sumaya. "On Linkages: Confronting the Public Health Workforce Crisis: Asph Statement on the Public Health Workforce." *Public Health Report.* 2008 May–Jun; 123(3): 395–398.doi: 10.1177/003335490812300322

8. Casalotti, Adriane and Carolyn Mullen, "Stronger Together: ASTHO and NACCHO Team Up for Public Health Advocacy." https://www.astho.org/StatePublicHealth/Stronger-Together-ASTHO-and-NACCHO-Team-Up-for-Public-Health-Advocacy/02-11-20/

9. Castrucci, Brian C. and Monica Valdes Lupi, "Coronavirus Responders Deserve Better." https://www.healthaffairs.org/do/10.1377/hblog20200316.78816/full/

10. HIMSS, "Five Growing Health Information and Technology Jobs." https://www.himss.org/resources/five-growing-health-information-and-technology-jobs

11. U.S. Bureau of Labor and Statistics. "Radiologic and MRI Technologists." https://www.bls.gov/ooh/healthcare/radiologic-technologists.htm

12. Association of American Medical Colleges (AAMC), "New Findings Confirm Predictions on Physician Shortage." https://www.aamc.org/news-insights/press-releases/new-findings-confirm-predictions-physician-shortage

13. Pellitt, Stephanie. "New Federal Analysis of Behavioral Health Care Workforce Released." National Council for Behavioral Health. https://www.thenationalcouncil.org/capitol-connector/2018/12/new-federal-analysis-of-behavioral-health-care-workforce-released/

14. U.S. Bureau of Labor Statistics. "Nurse Anesthetists, Nurse Midwives, and Nurse Practitioners." https://www.bls.gov/ooh/healthcare/nurse-anesthetists-nurse-midwives-and-nurse-practitioners.htm

15. U.S. Bureau of Labor Statistics. "Physician Assistants." https://www.bls.gov/ooh/healthcare/physician-assistants.htm

16. Thomason, Sarah and Annette Bernhardt. "California's Homecare Crisis: Raising Wages is Key to the Solution." UC Berkeley Labor Center. http://laborcenter.berkeley.edu/californias-homecare-crisis/

17. U.S. Bureau of Labor Statistics. "Medical and Health Services Managers." https://www.bls.gov/ooh/management/medical-and-health-services-managers.htm

18. USF Health - Morsani College of Medicine. "Health Data Analyst Job Description and Salary." https://www.usfhealthonline.com/resources/career/health-data-analyst-job-description-and-salary

19. Health Catalyst. "The Changing Role of Healthcare Data Analysts—How Our Most Successful Clients Are Embracing Healthcare Transformation (Executive Report)." https://www.healthcatalyst.com/the-changing-role-of-healthcare-data-analysts/

20. American Association of Colleges of Nursing, "Nursing Fact Sheet." https://www.aacnnursing.org/News-Information/Fact-Sheets/Nursing-Fact-Sheet

CHAPTER 4

21. Association of American Medical Colleges (AAMC). "Statement for the Record Submitted by the Association of American Medical Colleges (AAMC) to the House of Representatives Committee on Small Business: 'The Doctor is Out. Rising Student Loan Debt and the Decline of the Small Medical Practice,'" https://www.aamc.org/system/files/c/1/498034-aamcstatementtothehousesmallbusinesscommitteeregardingmedicaled.pdf

22. Physicians Foundation, "2018 Survey of America's Physicians." https://physiciansfoundation.org/wp-content/uploads/2018/09/physicians-survey-results-final-2018.pdf

23. Loffredo, Saundra. "Do Your Career and Work Values Align?" Inside Higher Ed. https://www.insidehighered.com/advice/2017/11/13/ importance-aligning-your-career-your-core-values-essay

24. Collins, Jim and Jerry I. Porras. "Building Your Company's Vision." Harvard Business Review. https://hbr.org/1996/09/ building-your-companys-vision

25. California Institute for Behavioral Health Solutions (CIBHS). "Behavioral Health Careers Presentation." October 2017.

26. SAMHSA-HRSA Center for Integrated Health Solutions. "Core Competencies for Integrated Behavioral Health and Primary Care." https://www.integration.samhsa.gov/workforce/ integration_competencies_final.pdf

27. Public Health Foundation (PHF), Council on Linkages Between Academia and Public Health Practice. "Core Competencies for Public Health Professionals." http://www.phf.org/programs/ corecompetencies/Pages/Core_Competencies_Domains.aspx

28. Nurse Practitioner Schools. "What are the NP Core Competencies?" https://www.nursepractitionerschools.com/faq/what-are-the-np-core-competencies

29. American Association of Physician Assistants (AAPA). "Competencies for the Physician Assistant Profession." https://www. aapa.org/wp-content/uploads/2017/02/PA-Competencies-updated.pdf

CHAPTER 5

30. Association of American Medical Colleges (AAMC). "Age of Applicants to U.S. Medical Schools at Anticipated Matriculation by Sex and Race/Ethnicity, 2014–2015 through 2017-2018." https://www.aamc.org/system/files/d/1/321468-factstablea6.pdf

31. Mental Health Daily. "At What Age Is the Brain Fully Developed?" https://mentalhealthdaily.com/2015/02/18/at-what-age-is-the-brain-fully-developed/

CHAPTER 8

32. Castrillon, Caroline. "Why Personal Branding Is More Important Than Ever." Forbes. https://www.forbes.com/sites/carolinecastrillon/2019/02/12/why-personal-branding-is-more-important-than-ever/#7a13a8852408

33. Ibid.

34. Hogshead, Sally. "Fascinate Test." https://www.howtofascinate.com/store/fascination-advantage-assessment

35. Hogshead, Sally. "How to Fascinate." https://www.howtofascinate.com/

36. Doyle, Alison. "How to Write a Cover Letter." the balance careers. https://www.thebalancecareers.com/cover-letters-4161919

37. Doyle, Alison. "A Step-by-Step Guide to the Job Application Process." the balance careers. https://thebalancecareers.com/job-application-process-2061600

38. Doyle, Alison. "How to Write an Effective Resume." the balance careers. https://www.thebalancecareers.com/job-resumes-4161923

39. O'Donnell, Riia. "Eye tracking study shows recruiters look at resumes for 7 seconds." HRDIVE. https://www.hrdive.com/news/eye-tracking-study-shows-recruiters-look-at-resumes-for-7-seconds/541582/

40. UC Davis. "The 30 Second Elevator Speech." http://sfp.ucdavis.edu/files/163926.pdf

41. Career Builder. "More Than Half of Employers Have Found Content on Social Media That Caused Them NOT to Hire a Candidate, According to Recent CareerBuilder Survey" https://www.prnewswire.com/news-releases/more-than-half-of-employers-have-found-content-on-social-media-that-caused-them-not-to-hire-a-candidate-according-to-recent-careerbuilder-survey-300694437.html

CHAPTER 9

42. Dictionary.com "Networking." https://www.dictionary.com/browse/networking?s=t

43. Kagan, Julia. "Networking." https://www.investopedia.com/terms/n/networking.asp

44. Public Health. "Professional Networking in Public Health." https://www.publichealth.org/resources/professional-networking/

45. Parker, Tim. "10 Tips for Strategic Networking." https://www.investopedia.com/articles/personal-finance/091615/10-tips-strategic-networking.asp

46. Kagan, Julia. "Networking." https://www.investopedia.com/terms/n/networking.asp

47. TruthBook. *The Drowning Man.* https://truthbook.com/stories/funny-god/the-drowning-man

CHAPTER 10

48. Langford, Joe and Pauline Rose Clance. (Fall 1993). "The impostor phenomenon: recent research findings regarding dynamics, personality and family patterns and their implications for treatment." *Psychotherapy: Theory, Research, Practice, Training.* 30 (3): 495–501. *doi:10.1037/0033-3204.30.3.495.*

49. Sakulku, Jaruwan. "The Impostor Phenomenon." *The Journal of Behavioral Science*, 6(1), 75-97. https://doi.org/10.14456/ijbs.2011.6

50. Young, Valerie. *The Secret Thoughts of Successful Women: Why Capable People Suffer from the Impostor Syndrome and How to Thrive in Spite of It.* New York: Crown, 2011.

51. Abrams, Abigail. "Yes, Impostor Syndrome Is Real. Here's How to Deal With It." *Time.* https://time.com/5312483/how-to-deal-with-impostor-syndrome

52. Young, Valerie. "10 Steps to Overcome Imposter Syndrome." https://impostorsyndrome.com/10-steps-overcome-impostor/

53. Cambridge Dictionary. "Doubt." https://dictionary.cambridge.org/us/dictionary/english/doubt

54. Dweck, Carol S. *Mindset: The New Psychology of Success.* New York: Ballantine Books, 2008

55. Develop Good Habits. "Fixed Mindset vs. Growth Mindset: What REALLY Matters for Success."https://www.developgoodhabits.com/fixed-mindset-vs-growth-mindset/

56. TED. "Carol Dweck: The Power of Believing That You Can Improve." https://www.ted.com/talks/carol_dweck_the_power_of_believing_that_you_can_improve?language=en

57. Study Finds. "Survey: Half of Doctors Consider Leaving Medicine—Because of Insurance Company Headaches." https://www.studyfinds.org/survey-half-doctors-consider-leaving-medicine-insurance-company-headaches/

CHAPTER 11

58. California Future Health Workforce Commission. https://futurehealthworkforce.org/

59. Barr, Donald A., John Matsui, Stanley F. Wanat, and Maria Elena Gonzales. "Chemistry courses as the turning point for premedical students." Adv Health Sci Educ Theory Pract. 2010 Mar; 15(1): 45–54. doi: 10.1007/s10459-009-9165-3

60. Stacy, Angelica M. *Living by Chemistry.* New York: W.H. Freeman, 2012.

CHAPTER 12

61. Merriam-Webster. "Accountable." https://www.merriam-webster.com/dictionary/accountable

ACKNOWLEDGMENTS

It took me many years from the time I knew I wanted to write this book to finally get it done. It was quite a journey with many starts, stops, distractions, and detours. Like many important accomplishments in life, it was quite a challenge, but an incredible learning experience and well worth it. I could not have done it without the support and inspiration of many people along the way.

I finally put a stake in the ground and started seriously pursuing the book the day after the celebration of life of a cherished friend and mentor, Francisco X. "Wimpy" Garcia. He lived a great life and always inspired me to live life to the fullest. His granddaughter, Christina Knueven, was an aspiring writer. I had reconnected with her at the celebration. The morning after, I had a moment of knowing that I should ask her to help me get started writing my book. Christina assisted me with editing and writing some initial drafts of the first chapters and developing a book proposal. This was key to getting me started and building momentum. I am grateful for her collaboration, expertise, and support.

During the long periods that followed, when I focused on other priorities and had doubts about whether I should and could write this book, I received invaluable inspiration and support from many others, including my wife, Lydia, and my amazing children—Jake, Elizabeth, and Ben—my parents Carl and Jeanne Oxendine, my friends Kevin Barnett, Rob Chrisman, Joe Cortes, Tony Faulkner, Fran Garcia, Pam Hallagan, Sandy Hessler, Marshall Kauffman, Kathy Kwan, Dave Monaghan, and Fred Rosenzweig. My coach Eileen Blumenthal, friends and successful authors Greg Hicks and Rick Foster, and my teacher and friend, bestselling author Tara Brach also provided me with invaluable guidance, example, and support exactly when I needed it. Luz C. Gonzalez provided valuable support, accountability and online business advice.

I would not have gotten the book done if I had not participated in the Publish Your Purpose Author's Academy. With the guidance and practical tools provided by Jenn Grace and PYP and with support from my peers, I was able to finally believe that completing the book was possible and established a road map and accountability to get it done.

The inspiration from the incredible students, alumni, and colleagues from Health Career Connection and UC Berkeley are what truly inspired me to keep going every time I had questioned whether I should really complete the book. They also inspire me with their commitment to discovering, achieving, and enjoying their authentic health careers and the difference they are making and will continue to make in improving health for all of us.

ABOUT THE AUTHOR

Jeffrey Oxendine has been an educator, health executive, and consultant, for over 30 years.

Jeff's passion is inspiring and empowering students and health professionals to discover and achieve their authentic health career dreams, lead happy and fulling lives, and optimize their impact on the health of individuals and communities. As an expert, leader, and champion for health workforce and diversity, he is also committed to advancing strategies, programs, and policies to build the next generation of health leaders and professionals.

Jeff is living his passion and authentic health career as an author, speaker, consultant and coach, and as Founder and CEO of Health Career Connection (HCC), a national nonprofit that empowers undergraduate students to pursue health careers (www.healthcareers. org). He also works with undergraduate students at UC Berkeley to pursue careers in healthcare and public health and serves at Director of Health Workforce and Diversity at the Center for Health Innovations and Organizational Research.

Jeff also works closely with health employers, health professions schools, foundations, professional associations, advocates and government agencies to determine future health workforce needs and to develop strategies to ensure a robust, well-trained and diverse health workforce. He is a health workforce consultant and Co-Director of the California Health Professions Consortium, a statewide coalition of over 150 organizations working to strengthen health workforce and diversity and the health professions pipeline.

Jeff recently served as Co-Director of the California Future Health Workforce Commission. He co-led design, planning, and support of the Commission's work to develop an actionable statewide health workforce strategy for California. He is now engaged in efforts to advance Commission recommendations (https://futurehealthworkforce.org/).

At UC Berkeley School of Public Health, Jeff was the Co-Faculty Director of the Undergraduate Public Health Major. He also served as Associate Dean of Public Health Practice for 12 years and as a faculty member in Health Policy and Management for 16 years. Jeff founded and directed the Center for Public Health Leadership and Practice, which provides students with comprehensive career, professional, and leadership development services.

Prior to his roles at Berkeley, Jeff was a senior executive for 20 years in leading Bay Area and Boston hospitals and medical groups. He was a Lecturer in Health Management for five years at Harvard School of Public Health.

Jeff has received numerous rewards for his work, including the James Irvine Foundation Leadership Award, The Distinguished Teaching and Mentorship Award and Zak Sabry Mentorship Awards from UC Berkeley School of Public Health, and the Champion of Health Professions Diversity Award from the California Wellness Foundation. He was recently named one of UC Berkeley School of Public Health's 75 Most Influential Alumni from its 75-year history.

Please visit Jeffoxendine.com for additional information, resources, and services to help you throughout your journey.